CW01433278

08

Travels of a
Welsh Preacher
in the U.S.A.

Peregrinations of William Davies Evans
during the later nineteenth century

Margaret Morgan Jones

ISBN: 978-1-84524-108-7

Cover design: Sian Parri

Printed and Published in Wales by
Llygad Gwalch, Ysgubor Plas, Llwyndyrys,
Pwllheli, Gwynedd LL53 6NG
☎ 01758 750432   📠 01758 750438
✆ gai@llygadgwalch.com
Web site: www.carreg-gwalch.co.uk

Contents

Acknowledgements

I am indebted to members of my family and close friends on both sides of the Atlantic for the encouragement, support and advice they have given me throughout the time I spent translating my great-uncle's account of his travels in the United States of America, some century and a half ago.

My special thanks go to Professor Nancy Lawler, Professor Ivor Wilks, Reverend Richard Evans, Mr Lyn Ebenezer and Mr Alan Rogers for their help and guidance at all times. I also wish to convey my sincere gratitude to Myrddin ap Dafydd and the staff at *Gwasg Carreg Gwalch* for their co-operation.

My cousin, Margaret Griffiths, and I visited relatives in the United States during November 2004. We were given a very warm welcome by everyone we met and taken to see many of the landmarks mentioned by William Davies Evans in his book. Those of his descendants whom I have been able to locate have shown enthusiastic approval for publication of the English version.

Margaret Morgan Jones

Explanation regarding the Map

The map used as a background to the cover was a gift from the owners of the famous *Chicago, Milwaukee and St Paul* railroad – the largest railroad in the world. I obtained it by means of A.V.H. Esq., a kind gentleman who has our nation at heart. Governor Smith, one of the most reputable men in America, said that the owners of this railroad were the most honourable people in America. The map is remarkably accurate and precise and the author, no doubt the readers too, are very grateful to the company for such a valuable gift.

It is a degree of misunderstanding by the person appointed to adapt the map for inclusion in this book that has accounted for the red numbers to be slightly unsatisfactory. Although, they are fairly reliable, I hope that I shall be able to mark the Welsh settlements more clearly in the map that I shall provide for my next book: *HANES TALEITHIAU UNEDIG AMERICA A'R CYMRY YNDDYNT* (THE HISTORY OF THE UNITED STATES OF AMERICA AND THE WELSH LIVING IN THEM).

The settlements symbolized by the following numbers are very large and include several churches:- 3,6,21,23,44,53,54,85,91,101,108,129,130. (Many important cities are located in 21 and 23). The country's railroads are indicated by fine, black lines.

Introduction

Dear Reader

I am addressing you in the same way as my great-uncle, William Davies Evans, did in his book 'Dros Gyfanfor a Chyfandir', an account of places and events in the United States as he experienced them in the mid to late nineteenth century. His American descendants, having lost their Welsh, had often expressed their great interest in learning what William Davies Evans had written in the *heniaith*, 'the old language'. I was thus inspired to undertake a translation of his book and I have tried to accomplish this task on the basis of what he wrote. This assignment has taken me a few years to complete owing to other commitments. I can say, however, that I have much enjoyed the process from beginning to end. I greatly hope, reader, that you will find the book a pleasure.

My great-uncle, William Davies Evans, was married to my grandfather's sister, Jane Jones of Penwernhir, a farm near Pontrhydfendigaid, Ceredigion, where she and I were both born and brought up. William Davies Evans hailed from Berth Neuadd, Talsarn, in the Aeron valley, Ceredigion. I, myself, have spent most of my adult life in the nearby market and university town of Lampeter.

William Davies Evans had crossed the ocean more than once before he and his family decided to emigrate to the United States. Their last home in Cardiganshire – the county's name during that era – was at Wellington House in the village of Pontrhydfendigaid.

The system of translation involved certain sensitivities relating to nationality, race and religion. Many mid-nineteenth century terms have greatly changed in meaning and this raises issues of what has now become known as 'political correctness'. This applies particularly to certain racial descriptions. I have, generally speaking, retained the mid-nineteenth forms, urging the reader to remember that these may not have had the same connotations as they now have and certainly William Davies Evans did not inflict any discrimination against any of the people of varied ethnicities with whom he came into contact. Place names presented less of a problem but have also, in some cases, undergone spelling changes. A few have been renamed and no longer appear on modern maps, others may have vanished. The reader should, however, have little problem in following the traveller's route with the aid of a modern map.

Reader, enjoy the peregrinations of a Ceredigion Welsh-speaking Methodist minister making his way through a young country, and in doing so, deciding to uproot his family and move to America.

Margaret Morgan Jones

The Chicago, Milwaukee and St Paul Railroad

One can journey 4,500 miles on this railroad, through Illinois, Wisconsin, Iowa, Minnesota and Dakota. Its route is through every important city, town and neighbourhood in the massive north west, that is, without traversing over the same track twice. This is the only through-line that runs from Chicago, Milwaukee, St Paul and Minneapolis and by means of its connecting branches, one can travel along the beautiful Mississippi valley, between Minneapolis and St Louis. The carriages of these trains and the facilities are the best in the world. This is the route for people who wish to SETTLE IN DAKOTA where there are thousands of acres handed over for no payment except the government's tax. In these regions, there is plenty of clean water and the dry, fresh climate is similar to that experienced in Wisconsin, Iowa and Minnesota. People do not encounter many difficulties in such territories.

There are good pastures in Iowa also and these prairies can be purchased quite reasonably with fair payment terms. It would be difficult to find a more picturesque and flourishing area than that found in north-west Iowa. Of great benefit to the Welsh is the fact that a Welshman, William E. Powell (Gwilym Eryri) has been appointed as 'land supervisor' in the north-west. He is Welsh, through and through, and well respected by all Welsh people in the north-west. Immigrants can have full confidence in his honesty and judgement. There are two very honourable Welsh land supervisors in Dakota too and it is possible to receive information and guidance from the British supervisor, Charles E. Norton Esq., 1 Inner Temple, 24 Dale Street, Liverpool.

Preface

Dear Readers,

It happened that I am amongst the early travellers of the new road towards the Golden Gate and the Queen of the Far West after it was opened in the summer of 1881. This entire road is noted for its climate of glorious summers, beautiful and varied scenery, natural and historic wonders as well as other important advantages, successes and shining prospects that cannot be equalled except in America. This, including the immense distance of my detailed travels in various other areas of the country, has made me consider it a valid reason to publish my experiences in book form. I believe by doing so, I shall have the privilege of conveying such information for the first time within the circulation of Welsh literature. Whilst the English language, as well as every other flourishing language, is rich in its history and adventures of its travellers, I do not think that the Welsh language is as enriched with recollections of anyone's travels; therefore this book of mine should be acceptable. Indeed, it was the incitement of hundreds of readers of my letters in *Baner ac Amserau Cymru* (Banner and Times of Wales) that made me consider publishing this book and since, in this issue alone, are found the most remarkable experiences of my travels as well as what I saw and experienced during the 'Great Conflict' and inasmuch as I have lived for twenty years in America, I anticipate that the book will not be uninteresting, even for those of you who have read my letters in the paper. The purpose of my travels was to meet up with fellow countrymen, who are spread across the country, in order to gather material for another book I had in mind, entitled: *HANES TALEITHIAU UNEDIG AMERICA A'R CYMRY YNDDYNT* (THE HISTORY OF THE UNITED STATES OF AMERICA AND THE WELSH LIVING IN THEM) and I propose to publish this book shortly. In view of this, I felt that it was only necessary, in this book, to mention briefly the Welsh organisations. Regarding the noteworthy Welsh in the West, no-one is mentioned. No doubt, there are defects in this book, although I have aimed at correctness. Since, I have not weighed or measured all that is described, I could only rely on the popular testimony given to me. I have compiled this book by using accustomed words in an easy to read format and I have condensed and reserved as much material as I can afford towards my next book, which really was my prime objective. I am grateful to the Welsh Churches of America – of all denominations and to many individuals for kindness and support on my travels. May the blessing of God be upon them and you, my fond reader, inasmuch as you will find enjoyment whilst reading my book.

Yours sincerely,
THE AUTHOR

1

The Author and his family
left to right: Jane, Alfred, Hugh, William and David

The Start of the Journey

It was best to ignore any apprehensions about the long journey ahead whilst saying farewell to loved ones at home. I dealt with that moment with as little ceremony as possible. Hundreds of times, since I came to Aberystwyth in 1872, have I journeyed on the train from the town's station without meeting anyone going to the country I had travelled in when I was young. However, on the morning of 19th November 1880, after saying farewell to some friends and parting with my wife, Jane, I found myself face to face with four men on their way to America – a first time experience for two of them. They were shy and quiet with a solemn expression on their faces, as if thinking of 'Paradise Lost'. The other two were returning to their homes with broad smiles on their faces, like 'Yankees' and talking like people facing 'Paradise Regained'. After lengthy conversations about people, exchanging opinions and comparing Wales with the country of our destination, as was customary with Americans when in Wales, we went on to discuss which ship to board. They wanted me to join them on their ship – a much better ship in their view. My desire was for them to sail on my ship and since we could not agree, either way, we parted in Oswestry. We wished one another *bon voyage* and hoped to meet after landing in the 'far-away beautiful land'.

I was met and taken care of in Llynlleifiad by Mr J.D. Pierce (*Clwydlanc*) – a man by the testimony of many and by my own findings too, I felt I could confidently recommend to emigrants as a person who would make sure that justice prevailed and who would extend a warm welcome to people in his home.

On Board the *Abyssinia*

The following day, whilst looking up from the tender at the vessel that would be home to me over the ocean, who did I see on board, making welcoming gestures at me, but the men I parted with in Oswestry. I was overjoyed when I saw them, not because fate had given me an advantage over them, but because I would have company on board. I took up my place amongst the middle class (intermediates) – a clean and comfortable section as far as rooms were concerned and the quarter I always recommended to sea-voyagers in general, unless they had vast fortunes; if that was the case they were able to sail in the resplendent saloon. If they were very poor, they had to dwell in the wretched steerage. There was only one man of the upper class on this voyage and since the era of sea-voyages had passed, we were in all, only a few over a hundred in number. Towards one o'clock the anchors were raised and our vessel started sailing down the river. It was a beautiful afternoon. Nature was trying to instil happy thoughts in us as we embarked on the voyage. The sky was clear, the breezes were like balm, the sea was calm and maybe it was an act of mercy on Mother Nature's part that mist developed on the shores to spare some with heavy hearts the agony of a last glance at the country of their birth.

The Abyssinia

After sailing for twenty hours, we anchored off Queenstown and a crowd of children from the Emerald Isle joined us. The Irish are people with intense feelings and parting from loved ones was a most difficult and emotional task. I could not help noticing with interest and a certain degree of sympathy, a boy and girl, after returning to the tender and leaving another girl (a sister maybe) on board our vessel, making very moving goodbye signs towards one another. Both sides tried to bury their grief and appear falsely happy. When tears would not hold back, they quickly went into hiding beyond the funnel; there they would weep until eventually they would reappear again to wave farewell with their handkerchiefs, until the distance between them faded into oblivion. How many salty tears has the brackish sea ever engulfed! Next to the grave and war, no doubt it has had its share of these transparent assets.

Illness and Storms
No sooner had our vessel started sailing forward than our newly arrived companions were ill. Yes, at once, without any dawdling, warning or ado, they started vomiting and caused much mess on board. They were throwing up, uncontrollably, food that they had previously enjoyed. When one girl was bending over to vomit, the wind blew her hat off; her hat had been held by ribbons which had got entangled in her hair and thus the hat became an improvisatory bowl for the vomit. She was a long time disentangling the ribbons; all the while the hat and its contents were neatly held under her nose making it a laughable scene for some inconsiderate bystanders. We, the ones who had sailed for twenty hours,

were well composed. What had happened to cause these people to be so sick, so soon?

However, early in the afternoon, we also were struck down and by evening we were all very solemn and serious. It was a very rough night. The storm lasted several days and we were suffering all that time – more so than I had ever been previously. That was the experience of fellow-voyagers who had crossed the ocean dozens of times too. Strong crosswinds prevailed for most of the voyage. The deep waters formed into images of white hillocks. The wind with its strong wings lashed out at the sea whilst laughing and whistling mockingly. It used every imaginable force to harass the waters. The sea in its temper would snarl, wriggle, complain and spit against the wind and would throw rapid blows at it. Such was the controversy amongst the elements that one wondered whether our small vessel could withstand such a tempest. It appeared a mere speck jumping on the turbulent ocean. It was thrown from side to side and often it would land head first until a gush of sea-water would lash into it. Ahead it sailed however, unconcerned as to which one was superior – the waves or the wind. It did not stall once and not once did it stray from its corridor but we could hear its haf-haf-hafe-haf; haf-hafe-haf non-stop, night and day, whilst it continued to make steady headway through the choppy seas. It was, as if it was telling us in its own tongue, that it wanted to deliver its precious load safely in New York. No doubt Mary was worshipped far more than if the weather had been kind. According to the testimony of some, one Irish lad believed that prayers directed at Mary were not enough because he was found making a heroic attempt to place a prop under the inner side of the ship. His explanation was: 'Don't ye see this st'amer almost a fallin and, sure, I thought this pole would hilp to prop her up.'

Isn't it Better to Pray?

I often remember another very tempestuous night on my first crossing in the spring of 1852. We were around nine hundred emigrants on board *John Stuart*, a large sailing ship. On that particular night we were all locked in, so that we would not be a hindrance to the sailors whose noisy activities were clashing with the uproar of the lashing waves and the wind's racket. We could hear the sailors shouting, running, pulling ropes and heavy chains – all this whilst the large vessel was behaving like a drunkard, shaking from side to side with boxes, barrels and crockery sliding and tossing, clitter clatter against each other. We could hear the cries of our neighbours, weeping and directing their prayers at Mary, St

Peter, St Patrick and every other saint they could think of. Yes indeed, all this made the night a very disturbing one.

We had on board a Welshman named Dafydd (David) R. He, when the weather was fine, would call on the name of his father – (The Devil)! This night, however, he was a devout man and wished to be extremely righteous. He approached an old religious deacon by the name (if I am correct) of Dafydd (David) Jones. He wanted Dafydd Jones to invite all the Welsh people, at the strike of midnight, to a prayer meeting. Because, he said, 'we shall all be in eternity within a few minutes. Come and pray with us Dafydd dear'. Dafydd Jones was a reticent person and he answered: 'I have prayed before coming to this place. You pray now; it is high time you started. Get down to it.' Therefore Dafydd R. was left on his own and he made a pact with the New Testament.

By the morning, the storm had abated and at daybreak, Bell, the happy, smiling little sailor, opened the door as was the custom and called out to us to prepare for breakfast. 'Is there any danger now, Bell?' Dafydd R. asked loudly. 'No, it is all over,' answered Bell. 'D-l boys,' Dafydd R. said, 'the storm has passed us by.' The need for religion also passed by! Since I was very young at the time, I only remember parts of what happened on that occasion but what I have written is a good account of events on board the ship.

To return to the *Abyssinia*, we had wild animals on board. There were young elephants, zebras, stags, monkies, birds and other creatures. Some of them died and the elephants were very disturbed by their captivity because whenever we were in their vicinity, we could hear them bleating harshly in their discomfort. One of these animals dislodged the boards of its cell enabling it to break free. An Irishman, who happened to be standing nearby, reckoned the animal was making for him and whilst he was frantically attempting to escape, he found a safe place in the nearest available niche. While the animal was being shaken about by the ship, it fell on its side, right opposite this hideaway and thus trapped Pat. This made him panic and he jumped over the animal. He had been very frightened but the incident made him boast: 'I'm a sprightly ould mon, sure enough, for I jumped over an owliphant in my owld age.'

In the ocean, we saw shoals of fish called porpoises. They leaped up from the waters and by doing so they dashed forward alongside the ship, similar to the way we used to see dogs running after a train. Others were coming from afar as if coming to meet us. What was their intention, I wonder? Was it to chase the ship out of their boundaries or was it in the hope of obtaining something from it; or were they surprised to see such a big creature swimming for such a long time with its head out of the water or was it something else that excited them? These porpoises are tawny, flat creatures with narrow heads and tails. They are between three and seven feet long. I remember seeing water being thrown up, as if by geysers, by the breath of a whale on my previous voyage in 1852. Birds were also seen daily, even in the middle of the ocean and during the most atrocious storms. Where was their resting place? It was said that they slept, even laid their eggs, hatched and reared their young on the crest of the rough waves. I cannot be sure of this but on the ninth day of our voyage (the only calm day we had far from land) favourable signs appeared because we saw fledglings, unable to fly properly, trying to get away from the ship, similar to how we used to see young birds scrambling in front of us on the meadows at harvest-time. How did they come to such a place – hundreds of miles from the nearest land?

End of the Voyage

It was Friday evening, second of December, and the pilot came to see us. By morning, all the elements were perfectly serene. About nine o'clock Long Island appeared to the south of us and whilst sustaining the beautiful scenery of Jersey on our left, we sailed slowly upwards. At three o'clock in the afternoon, we all landed alive and well. Although we had experienced a rough voyage which had lasted fourteen days, we were able to end it just as good as when we started by enjoying very pleasant weather. Hopefully, this is how life's voyage will end. In spite of storms and perils, landing will be a pleasure if conditions are favourable, with goodness and justice shining like the sun upon us and the beauty of the blessed land appearing.

I fewn i'r porthladd tawel, clyd,
O sŵn y storm a'i chlyw,
Y caf fynediad llon rhyw ddydd,
Fy Nhad sydd wrth y llyw.

(Inside the quiet cosy harbour,
Away from the sound of the storm,
I shall be joyfully admitted one day,
My Father is at the helm).

New York

This is the largest city in America and fourth largest in the world. As far as status is concerned, it ranks even higher. It has a population of over a million and between Brooklyn, Jersey City and other suburban areas, it is

New York and Jersey City

as populated as the whole of Wales. New York was initially built on Manhattan Island, which is eight miles long and two miles wide – tapering each end. Its most recent and important roads have been constructed according to the American system, that is, they run parallel to each other; others cross them at right angles. The ones that run north and south are called 'avenues' and they are numbered First Avenue, Second Avenue and so on. The ones that run east and west are called 'streets' and they are named accordingly. Since the houses also have numbers, it is a hundred times easier to find the sixth house on the tenth road in New York than it would be to find the address of Simon, the tanner, in the sixth verse of the tenth chapter of The Acts. Some roads have kept their praiseworthy names; one of them is 'Broadway'. This is the largest commercial road, the most splendid and the wealthiest in the world. Two and a half miles of it are as straight as an arrow. The entire country follows the fashion of Broadway, New York.

Transport in New York and other American cities is similar to that found in British cities. However, the elevated railroads are sure to draw the attention of strangers almost at once. The railways in London run underground and passengers have to travel through the smoke and the smell in total darkness. The railroads of New York run on trestleworks, twenty feet above the ground and the road-users put up with their noise and ugliness. In spite of everything, I prefer the London system; the vehicles of New York are of a better standard though. Every fifth block,

8

high-rise railroad stations, reached by an array of steps, are situated and a long train passes through every five minutes. Ten cents is the fare whether the journey be long or short. It is not possible (within the covers of a book such as this) to attempt to describe the diversities of New York – its buildings, parks, nationalities, institutions and numerous wonderful attractions. Like other large cities, it has its evil and pitiful aspects alongside its many virtues and blissfulness.

Henry Ward Beecher

Yes, like that, without a 'Reverend' before or a 'D.D.' after his name – is how he is addressed and known and that is the way he wishes to be recognized. It was Sunday morning, the only whole day I stayed in this place on this occasion. I went over to Brooklyn to see and listen to this famous man in his Plymouth Church – a very large building. In spite of the wet weather, a large congregation had turned out. On the big platform (not a pulpit) stood Mr Beecher, a well-groomed elderly man, shapely and strong in stature, slightly shorter maybe than average. He had a full face, smooth and attractive with a penetrating and determined look and his grey hair fell loosely onto his shoulders. He was dressed plainly but very smart without any attempt to appear clerical. He is known as a very eloquent and natural orator. He had a very appealing and penetrating voice and his movements coincided with everything he had to say – sharp, methodical and splendid statements, full of imagination like a clear river flowing on clean gravel between green banks. His text was Galatians 6,15 and 16. He preached one of his most marvellous sermons. A great deal of confabulation and articles materialized throughout the country afterwards.

The Train

It is only in America that the train is seen in its prime glory and it is an all-important means of access and development regarding the country's resources; therefore it will be the main residence of the author over the months that his long journey will take. Consequently, it is befitting to attempt to describe it here. Some say, on what grounds I do not know, that the railroads in America bear no comparison to those in European countries. However, it is acknowledged that the American trains and ancillary provision linked to them greatly excel the European ones in general.

First, of course, comes the steamengine, one which is high, mighty and full of pride. With its glossy cast-iron and shining brass trimmings, its huge lamp, branch-like horns, wide-top chimney, melodious bell, glazed rooms and other decorative sections, it conveys a majestic appearance. The carriages correspond equally to it in stature and beauty. Next to it is the baggage car. Affixed to all boxes and portmanteaux there is a small brass plaque displaying a number, as well as a card attached by a strap, identifying their destination station. Every baggage owner is free from all responsibility concerning belongings whilst travelling. The baggage is handed over to the owners at the terminating station when they produce an identical tag to the one attached to the baggage, with all numbers corresponding. My heavy portmanteau's lock broke soon after I received it and it was in this condition it travelled thousands of miles. It passed through many different hands and stations. Often there would be hundreds of miles between it and myself and sometimes a week passed without knowing its whereabouts. In spite of this I never had any bother and I never lost as much as a thread. If something had gone lost, the transport company would have to pay compensation amounting to approximately a hundred dollars. Next to this car comes the express carriage; this one transports light goods and money to various places. It is also a mail-car, one that is a complete Post Office. Many a letter was written and posted in this carriage whilst it journeyed along. The smokers' carriage follows. Since there is a pathway through each compartment and a door and a platform at each end, the worshippers of the god of smoke are able to congregate here from every part of the train.

The other passenger carriages follow, the ones furnished in the warm, cosy colours of mahogany and walnut. They contain silver finger-plates and knobs, scarlet or green velvet benches, colourful glass ventilators, glowing vases, shining mirrors, hygienic closets, clean tumblers, warm stoves or steampipes amongst other beautiful and homely facilities. Seldom is seen anything but decency and gentlemanliness amongst the passengers, who are looked after by three persons who wear hats depicting their roles. Firstly, the guard, who is known as the conductor. He is the boss and he often passes through the carriages to collect tickets when the train is moving. Secondly is the brakesman. When the train starts moving out of the station, he is heard calling 'Newark is the next station', for example, and when this station is reached he calls out again 'Newark, Newark'. Very often another member of staff at the other end calls out the same name. Thirdly is the newsboy; he comes along often with a basketful of newspapers or books, even fruit or toys to sell. The standard travelling fare is three cents per mile, less on some railroads, more on others. Sometimes the carriages are hitched up to a luxurious compartment – a first class one. Here, instead of easy benches, there are easy chairs or reclining chairs which can be adapted to either sitting, lounging or sleeping positions. Some of these trains, when one considers the size of their excellent windows, are like mansions made of glass. They are purposely made in this manner to enable passengers to have a good view of the natural wonders of the landscape. Hitched to some trains there is a dining-car; tables are arranged in the most orderly way and laid with very tasty and nourishing delicacies; a better eating place would be hard to find. The price of a meal is seventy-five cents. Normally, young Negro boys are the waiters. They have black shining faces with woolly black hair, contrasting with their clean, white aprons. This procedure remains in the country as a sign of grandeur, in the same way as the aristocrats of the South, in days gone by, would be waited upon by black slaves. Lastly, come the sleeper-cars with their cosy rooms and clean and comfortable beds – unequalled in any stately home. There is an extra charge of a dollar and a half per night for this amenity.

Parlour Carriage on the Pennsylvania Railroad

It is not always customary for all of the carriages named to be hitched up. There is a cheaper train for the use of passengers emigrating to the West and this is normally very comfortable. It has cooking, eating, sleeping, bathing and other facilities. The steamengines of some railroads are lit by electricity whilst the carriages are usually lit by gas. The airbrake, which enables the engineer to stop the fastest of trains simultaneously, is now coming into common use. It is only on some railroads that one finds dining-cars but trains do stop at appropriate stations long enough for passengers to have refreshments at the dining-halls at the minimum price of half a dollar or at the lunch counters for ten cents or more. No alcohol is served in one per cent of the country's refreshment rooms.

The steamengine, on the railroads of Pennsylvania, does not stop to replenish with water; it just speeds ahead drawing excessively from the water-tank or from the long trough which is found between the rails.

Emigrants' Carriage – The Atchison, Topeka and Santa Fe Railroad

Upstream with the Hudson

Boarding the train in New York, I headed north along the eastern bank of the Hudson River. This river, although a fairly short one, is very wide at this point and is recognised as an important means of transport. Bleak hills emerge each end of it and woody islands reveal themselves in its waters every so often; on its banks there are lofty wooden buildings containing the country's produce – all ready to be transported. I was amazed to find so few ships and steamboats this time. Soon, however, I was given an explanation. Clearly, the further north we travelled, the quicker it got colder. By the time we reached Poughkeepsie (population 22,000), a city ideally situated 200 feet above the river and sixty-five miles from New York, there was snow on every hill and dale. This place is quite famous when one considers its various industries and its historical connections. Here, in 1788, the 'Constitution of the United States Government' was ratified. In Albany, the capital of the state of New York, sixty-seven miles further, the river was frozen over. Albany (population 90,000) is the oldest city in the country apart from Jamestown, Virginia. Between the river, canals, railroads, its natural position and political connections, it is one of the continent's main passageways. Amongst its many civic buildings, its Statehouse is one of the most splendid in the world, covering three and a half acres of land and extends to 384 feet in height. In Troy (population 57,000) twenty miles further, no wheeled vehicles can be seen on the roads, only sliding carts flitting by. The horses have straps attached to the harness, all cluttered with ornamental bells so that people can hear the 'horse and cart' approaching and thus avoid collisions, also of course, to be fashionable. The ground was so hard and slippery that I found walking without wellingtons extremely difficult. The climate was very mild in New York when I departed in the morning but I was experiencing extreme wintry conditions within one day.

The Quarries of Vermont
There are many Welsh people working in these quarries, but I was only able to stop in their midst in three places – in Middle Granville (N.Y.), Poultney and Fair Haven. In the first of these places, I was shown various types of slates, as well as the techniques of mining, chipping, marbling and polishing them; also the method of their transformation into blocks, mantelpieces and other artistic objects. The second place had the appearance of a clean and flourishing village. Taking into account the breadth of its unbending roads, the splendour of its buildings and the planning behind its shadowy trees, I imagine that dwelling there in the summer is like living in paradise. I do not know why the third place is called Haven but the adjective 'Fair' is a good description. The way Poultney is described is appropriate to this town also, with the addition that it is larger and has more spectacular buildings. I saw in this town two mansions made entirely of white marble, comparable to the most beautiful of tombstones. The resident owner of the better one is a gentleman who comes from a humble background and started working as a cobbler. In the town I saw piles of these marble slabs which supposedly weighed ten tons each. From this product they constructed their sidewalks, stairs, large slabs and poles for various purposes. It appears also that the moral values of the town's inhabitants are in accord with the colour, beauty and quality of their marble, because when I was there it was not possible, except at the drugstore, to buy anything containing alcohol in spite of the fact that the population numbered between two to three thousand. No wonder, therefore, that the town is beautiful and the people happy and content. These quarries are situated a

little over two hundred miles north of the city of New York.

The Institutions of Oneida
To go to these institutions, almost one hundred and fifty miles west of the quarries, I had to go through Saratoga Springs (population 10,000) – the most famous place in the states for medicinal springs and fashionable guest-houses. It is considered that the visitors, most of whom are from the upper class, total about 35,000 every summer. I also went through Shenectady (population 14,000) where in the middle of the night in the winter of 1689, the French and the Indians murdered all of the town's inhabitants. Some fled in their nightwear, only to perish on the road in wintry conditions; others managed to reach Albany, a distance of twenty miles. The town was burnt and everything of value was stolen. Farther on, there is an ascent up the fertile valley of the Mohawk River, a tributary of the Hudson. On this river, as well as on its canals, many boats are visible.

By the time I reached Utica (population 40,000) I was in the capital of the county of Oneida, the centre for all circulations relating to the Welsh institutions and Athens of the Welsh people in America. Here *Y Drych* (The Mirror) is published – our nation's main newspaper in the country; also *Y Cyfaill* (The Friend) – the monthly magazine of the Baptists. The city is important as far as commerce and industry are concerned. The beautiful town of Rome (population 13,000) is situated twelve miles further north. Remsen, eighteen miles north of Utica, is a village renowned for its Welsh connections. It is here the *Cenhadwr Americanaidd* (The American Missionary) – the monthly magazine of the Congregationalists is published. Prospect, Holland Patent and at the county's southern corner, Waterville, are all villages serving as centres for organizations relating to the Welsh people. The country folk are usually dairy people. In the southern region of Oneida, as well as in the county of Otsego, hops are cultivated and gathered.

The Valleys of Lackawanna and Wyoming
To go to the famous coalmining regions in these valleys, almost two hundred miles south of Oneida, I went through Binghampton (population 18,000) and in Scranton (population 46,000) in the state of Pennsylvania, I was at the most central location regarding coalmining and commerce in these districts. In Hyde Park, Bellevue, Taylorville, Providence and other places surrounding Scranton, there are masses of Welsh people who make up the Church congregations and it is in these parts, one finds the largest gatherings of Welsh people in the country,

that is, in functions predominantly organised by and for them. These social activities were, and still are, famous for their literary meetings and *Eisteddfodau* (Festivals). After travelling through Olyphant, Jermyn and other villages, as far as Carbondale (population 8,000) in the north-east, where in the year 1822, coalmining in this area began, I backtracked in order to go through Scranton, Moosic, Pittston (population 11,000), Plainsville, Wilkesbarre (population 23,000), Warrior Run, Kingston, Plymouth, Nanticoke and Wanamie. All these places, as well as the intervening towns and villages from Carbondale southwards, are covered by a network of coalpits, whilst industrious miners, like countless ants, pick at the beautiful ground until it appears like a piece of cloth ruined by moths. Anthracite is the coal mined here. Amongst the various buildings in this area, the most impressive are the high-peaked wooden ones, known as 'coal-breakers'. The coal-load is elevated along the incline to the top of the building; it then descends through different rooms and machines and is broken by the prongs of massive rollers before being dropped through screens to the rail waggons. Machinery, operated by steam power, are used to cut the coal into appropriate sizes. The coal is weighed, placed into six separate containers and sold according to the amount required – size 1, size 2 and so on.

Meeting the Negroes

Whilst staying at Wilkesbarre, I went with a friend to a revival meeting of the Negroes. It was late when we went into their over-heated Chapel and the congregation was in high spirits. We sat near the pulpit in order, if possible, to see and hear everything. We were surrounded by people of different colour, from beautiful fair Elizabeth to Topsy, whose skin is as black as the crow. I believe that all the ministers here are black like 'My Uncle Tom' and they are easily identified by their attire, appearance and occupation. They dress very clerically and the white handkerchiefs round their necks contrast brilliantly with the deep, black colour of their solemn faces and their reverent cloaks. In these formalities, they are more careful than anyone in America in preserving the dignity of the ministry. They are also great orators and in the esteem of two 'Jones' men, they are the most able orators in the world. By comparison, it seems, Henry Ward Beecher is no orator at all! Although the congregation is very moved, the ministers behave prudently. Some of them would walk about trying to persuade this one, or that one, to come forward to the mourners' bench; others would stand by the mourners trying to direct and lift them from their sorrow. It was appropriate for these people and everyone else, as a matter of fact, to cry or prayweep loudly, immaterial of what else was taking place at the time. Praying and singing alternatively was the order of the service, if indeed there was an order! Some would take it upon themselves to lead the prayers audibly and heartily, others would follow in their own words in lower tones. Because of these proceedings, the enunciation of the Negroes and the fact that some were weeping and some shouting 'Glory! Hallelujah! I am saved!' 'Praise the Lord' and so on, it was impossible for us to understand what was attested by the main prayer. In spite of this, we were pleased when an elderly, short, stout, tawny-coloured man knelt down. He appeared similar to a warm-hearted, old-fashioned Welshman. Maybe he had Welsh blood in his veins. Many of these people have adopted Welsh surnames such as Jones, Davies and Williams from their former slaveholders. In some cases the slaveholders were their real fathers. Putting all this aside, there was something amazing about this man. The other unruly voices abated as if listening to a melodious nightingale singing its song. His voice was so engulfing and emotional, so warm! His feelings were so zealous and solemn; his topics so wise, methodical and substantial; so effectively did he portray the span of time and the world and its trappings on par with the profound enormousness of eternity. Sins and futile pleasures were considered by him as ghastly and absurd against the crystal clear intense light of the awesome judgement! So unquestioningly, thankfully and lovingly he rested on the one and only approach to salvation, that it was a treat to listen to him. His voice, at times, still echoes in my ears.

Songs were conducted by way of someone, somewhere, somehow – without an announcement, starting to sing a hymn to a familiar tune; then everyone else would join in. Even the calmest of singers would move about latching to the rhythm so that they appeared like trees being shaken by a gale. They also kept up the tempo with their feet, so much that the floor sounded like a drum and occasionally they would intermingle to shake hands, as if going to a far-away land whilst still singing: 'O say! shall I meet you on the happy, happy shore!' They would utter the same words over and over, repeating and trebling again and again, always singing the chorus after one or two lines; they sang enthusiastically and spiritually combining it all with physical movement: 'If you get there before I do, tell 'em that I'm a comin' too, comin'too, commin'too, tell 'em that I'm a comin' too.' Some would lose all self-control, jumping as high as the pews and shouting with all their might and when we thought they were about to stop, off they would go again reiterating the words: 'If you get there before I do,' and so on, with renewed energy.

But let us see what is happening on the mourners' bench. There, a son and daughter are on their knees in a strenuous effort to be reborn. It seems that the son is showing signs of cowardliness and a desire to give in but the spiritual doctors, whilst whispering encouraging words in his ears, give him hope to continue. At one time, I saw the ministers, after watching the lad intently, making congratulatory signs at each other, as if to say, our work is being truly rewarded. As for the girl, she was suffering immensely. She would scream in despair, fling her arms and spin them in the air and her entire body seemed to be grieviously tortured. At last the singers encircled both youngsters and decided to delight the two with their spirituals; it was unending singing until they were all hot and steaming with perspiration. It was at this point that we left them when it was almost midnight. Pity for the children of Ham[1]. They are coming forward from the wilderness and we are pleased to see them. They are now treading the lands that our forefathers back in Wales once trod.

Fe lama'r gwyllt farbariad gwael, fe lona'r Ethiop du,
Wrth glywed am yr anfeidrol Iawn a gaed ar Galfari.

(The wicked wild barbarian leaps, the black Ethiopian rejoices,
To hear about the infinite expiation experienced on Calvary).

Further Journeys in the Vicinity

From Plymouth I went sixty miles west to Danville (population 8,000) where there are iron and steel foundries employing many people from our nation. From here I was ordered to go a hundred miles east to Slatington, through a strange district and a town called Mauch Chunk (population 6,000), situated in a very narrow and deep valley where there is hardly room for the river, the railroad and the row of houses. Here railcars are pulled up an incline to the summit of Mount Pisgah, a thousand feet above the river. From this point, they are released to freewheel for eight miles to Summit Hill. These parts are called the Switzerland of America and many tourists come here in the summer to see the beautiful scenery. Slatington (population 5,000) is a town in the middle of slate quarries on the banks of the Lehigh River, slightly to the south of Mauch Chunk. The Welsh who are brought up here, because they mingle with another nationality, are as learned in German as they are in Welsh and English. Taking a southerly direction from here through Allenton (population 19,000), I arrived in Philadelphia. I shall have a chance to describe this city when I return, therefore I shall refrain from mentioning anything at present. I did stay here for one week before aiming west for more than a hundred miles through Lancaster (population 30,000) to West Bangor. After arriving in Peach Bottom, I waded across the Susquehanna River for about two miles and although the waters were deep, I crossed without getting my feet wet. Another three miles and I was amongst the Welsh quarrymen of West Bangor. After returning through the stony river, I travelled by train along its banks in a north-west direction, passing Columbia (population 7,000) and Chiques Rock whereon beautiful scenery transpires; also after passing under other picturesque rocks alongside the river, I reached Harrisburgh[2], the state's capital (population 31,000). This railroad has a fabulous long bridge crossing the Susquehanna – a very attractive river; alas it has too much of a declivity for sailing. Strewn over the river are delightful islands accommodating farms which have excellent buildings erected on their yards. These islands were the ones purchased first of all by William Penn from the Indians, as well as the land adjacent to the riverbanks. When I last travelled this way, ten years ago, it was summertime and the countryside appeared more paradisial. Then, there was the greenery of the beautiful, sloping hills which emerged beyond each riverbank. The vegetation and everything relating to the islands blended as if sending loving greetings from one island to another. The sun's rays shone on the wide, lively waters. Beautiful buildings, cornfields and orchards speckled the valley and the surrounding districts. The spires of the distant city, the magnificent bridge resting on a long row of arches and the fast train radiated the presence of civilisation, restoration of order and paradise. With nature and the skill of mankind in conjunction with each other, I imagined hearing the sound of a melodious song which Heaven taught the Earth: 'Glory to God in the highest, and on earth peace, goodwill toward men' – (Luke 2,14).

From Harrisburgh, I went north-east for more than a hundred miles, crossing the road I had travelled on earlier at a spot between Danville and Slatington, almost reaching Mauch Chunk. Thick snow covered the mountains and the weather was bitterly cold. I called in Pittsville (population 14,000) – a lively town with several furnaces and iron-foundries situated amongst rich coalfields. The town is surrounded by wild, nevertheless beautiful, countryside above the spot where the Schuylkil River rushes through a long ravine. I also called in Minersville, St Clair and Shenandoah (population 11,000). In all these places, as well as other towns in the area, many Welshmen work in the coalmines. After going in this direction as far as Jeddo and Upper Lehigh, I went west on a sixty mile route through Hazleton (population 8,000) to Danville.

When I was visiting one town on my travels, I went from the chapel to the house of one of the officials, only to discover that an accident had happened. The man's young daughter had fallen against a red-hot stove and had burnt her hands. She was in such pain that it was pitiful to hear the little one crying. 'Will you be so kind as to fetch Mrs _ (a German) here?' asked the father to his colleague.

'Certainly,' was the answer and away he went.

'Do you, Evans, believe in powwowing?' was the question to me. Pow'wow is a North American Indian name for a medicine man or sorcerer.

'I have never come across it and I do not know what it is,' I answered.

'Well, you can witness it presently, if you wish,' was the reply. 'Pain is alleviated and wounds and diseases healed by making signs and saying specific words.'

Before long a man arrived (the lady was not at home); he held the little girl's hands and rubbed them a few times in his own hands while at the same time he was whispering something in such a low voice that none of us could understand what he was saying. The little girl immediately dropped off to sleep. She never felt any pain afterwards and eventually her hands healed completely. I believe that the genius this man was gifted with did not allow him to be paid for his work but accepting a gift was justified. I asked him if he would pass on his expertise to me. He answered that man could not pass it on to man, nor woman to woman; the power could only be transferred to a person of a different gender. However, he was allowed to tell us that after an accident, anyone could slow or stop blood seeping from a wound until assistance arrived by uttering three times: 'in your blood live on', over the wounded person.

The Western Region of Pennsylvania

From Danville I started my westward journey of one hundred and eighty miles towards Ebensburgh[3]. I was now heading towards a very rough mountainous terrain – a very rough mountainous terrain – a location where more than a hundred years ago, two huntsmen, Jack Anderson and his companion, were murdered by the Indians. It was a retaliation since many Indians had been killed by them previously. The place was called 'Jack's' or 'Jack Anderson's Narrows' because of this occurrence. All the railroads in Pennsylvania have double tracks to avert the risk of collisions. This particular route with all its connections is one of the best, safest and most convenient for immigrants and all kinds of travellers. It would be impossible to find better connections to different western places than the ones found here. Under the management of its owners, the main rail system runs as far as Chicago and St. Louis. In Altoona (population

20,000) we started to climb the Allegheny Mountains. Ascending as far as Cresson, the highest point on the line, the train meandered on craggy slopes – giving us access to some wonderful views. The famous 'Horseshoe Bend' is on this part of the railroad. It is a 'hairpin turning' causing long trains to appear as if their front compartments were travelling in an opposite direction to the rear ones. The sharp bend creates such an illusion that many a traveller has been tricked into believing that some of the carriages belonged to another train going the other way.

I descended from the train in Cresson, in order to travel eight miles north to Ebensburgh, a very fashionable place judged by the many tourists arriving there in the summer season. This is the place where the oldest Welsh settlement in the country is found with many inhabitants speaking the Welsh language – the old language. Apart from one other, it is the highest peak in the Allegheny Mountains. It is situated 6,500 feet above sea level. These mountains consist of a range of linking chains about nine hundred miles long from south-west to north-east and from fifty to two hundred miles wide. According to the Reverend B.F. Bowen, author of 'America Discovered by the Welsh', the name Allegheny has a Welsh origin, namely from the two words *gallu* (be able) and *geni* (be born), meaning a very adept or famous parentage. The author believed that the word had been passed down from inhabitants of long ago. He thought that the Alligewi Indians descended from the Welsh people who had gone over to America with Madog ab Owain Gwynedd more than seven hundred years earlier. Further mention of the Welsh Indians is recorded in this book.

From Ebensburgh I went downhill on the west side of the mountains; I was facing the massive countryside between them and the Rockies. This area comprises a range of hills and largest plateaux in the world. On the descent, eighteen miles south-west of Ebensburgh, Johnstown (population 22,000) is situated. It is a lively city situated on the banks of the Conemaugh River. The inhabitants are busily occupied in the coalmines as well as the iron foundries. Here, it is claimed, is the largest steel smeltery in the country. Boarding the train again, I travelled almost eighty miles west through Greensburgh, Irwin and Braddocks (in all of these places there are many coalminers and foundry workers from Wales). I arrived in Pittsburgh, the most famous city for iron, steel, tin, glass and the like in the entire country. The city's chief engineer, in his official report a few years ago, reckoned that if all of the city's industries were lined up, they would measure thirty-six and a half miles. Today, it is considered, they would measure forty miles. It is a very smoky city but in its smoke lies its wealth. Pittsburgh proper (population 157,000) is separated from Allegany City (population 79,000) by the Allegheny River and from Birmingham or South Side (population 9,000) by the Monongahela River. These two rivers merge beneath the city to become the Ohio River. The cities are surrounded by steep, rocky mountains which reach a height of 500 feet above the Ohio. However, they are being masked by new buildings and hanging platforms which are being erected at an amazing speed. The platforms are elevators to transport people upwards and downwards. In Pittsburgh, the Welsh newpaper *Y Wasg* (The Press) is published.

Being a Stranger

At the end of another sixty mile journey towards the north-west, I arrived in Sharon (population 6,000), a place situated on the boundary line between Pennsylvania and Ohio. I had suspected, more than once, that my appearance was not very respectable or pleasant and in this locality my suspicion was confirmed because the persons who came to meet me at the station failed to recognise anyone who represented a minister on the platform, therefore they went away without the man they were supposed to meet! I myself, wandered around the town to seek any Welsh people or a chapel. Whilst doing so, I knocked on a random door. The occupants were of a strange nationality and visibly frightened. Whether they thought that I was an avenger, a detective or had an unpleasant confrontation in mind, I do not know. Although I tried to appear happy and made an effort to soften my voice, all I heard was: 'no, I don't know' with indications of intense desire for me to go away. As soon as I turned my back I heard the door being slammed and the key turning in the lock. In spite of locks and a secure home environment, I would not be surprised that in their dreams they saw me approaching with weapons ready to slaughter them all. At last I found the right house, the right chapel and also discovered that Sharon's Welsh people were good citizens.

I proceeded to the surrounding places in Ohio – Brookfield, Coalburgh, Hubbard and Crabcreek. I travelled on foot in these regions. As I approached Hubbard I became quite hungry. Since I would not come across an eating place for a while afterwards, I went to the first dwelling that appeared to me to be a restaurant. Alas, it was no such place; all I could see were alcoholic drinks and merry drinkers. I approached the barman – an Irishman and told him of my misjudgment. Without another thought, he took me aside and placed a sumptuous meal in front of me and to my surprise he refused to take any payment: 'because ye have a riverend appearance and a ginuine timperance mon.' I

21

was reassured by this man's kindness, convincing myself that this man had discovered some virtue in me, more so than the people of Sharon. Do understand that I did not have an appointment in Hubbard and none of the Welsh people knew of my coming.

Whilst mentioning events of this kind, I am reminded of a day in Pennsylvania when a friend accompanied me (it doesn't matter where) to research the history of the Welsh there. We happened to be in the home of a church minister once when they were preparing a meal and another time in the house of a deacon when he and his family were about to dine. We were not invited to partake with either of these families and therefore we walked through the village in the afternoon to look for a place where we could buy food. After we had failed to find any such place, I spotted a sign advertising a kind of café. I told my friend, 'there's a place over there; we are bound to have something to satisfy us there.' I knew that many houses had restaurant signs outside their premises without any alcoholic drinks being sold there. However, my friend had only recently arrived from Wales and was an abstainer. He replied resolutely: 'I will not enter that house on any account in case someone sees us and maybe dishonour us.' I myself, respecting his feelings and purity, did not mention the subject again. Suddenly, we came across a small shop and the contents of the window gave us hope of getting something to eat there. We asked if we could buy tea. 'You may,' said the man, with a thick German accent. We were then led to the dining-room and whilst the water was coming to the boil, he brought bread and butter and other aliment to the table. As soon as we saw and smelt the food, our appetites diminished. Suddenly, our stomachs seemed full and the desire for any food left us! Our next problem was how not to eat what had been provided for us. We made our excuses and hastily went towards the station, at the same time brushing the dust from our feet as a testimony of our antagonism towards the minister and the deacon.

North-East Ohio

This district is largely a coalmining area – Brookfield, Coalcreek, Hubbard and Crabcreek. When I was in Crabcreek, I was only two miles away from Youngstown (population 16,000), a lively and growing town. The population derives its livelihood from different types of foundries. Commerce, in general though, is flourishing with large coalfields in the entire area. I was a ministerial pastor to a small flock in this town a few years ago; also in Weathersfield and Church Hill. It gave me great pleasure to see that the 'Cause' had advanced in Youngstown and that it was holding its own in the other two places too. After visiting all of them and travelling through Girard, Mineral Ridge and Niles – all close together, I started my journey of around twenty miles west to Palmyra, a village rooted in an old Welsh settlement. Whilst visiting Morddal's drugstore, I discovered him lying on his back on the counter – composing an elegy. He had only written two lines:

Dystawed holl derfysglyd leisiau'r cread
Tra y datganwyf ddyfnder dwys fy nheimlad.

(Let all the turbulent voices of the creation be silenced,
Whilst I declare the intense depth of my feeling).

when the Creator's servant, namely the author of this book, appeared on the scene to disturb him with tales about the difficulties the Welsh had encountered and endured in that part of the universe. From here, I proceeded to Parisville, five miles further north and from there to Tallmadge and Thomastown, thirty miles west, where coal is mined. After boarding the train in Akron (population 17,000), I went thirty-three miles north and discovered Cleveland (population 161,000) on the banks of Lake Erie. Next to Cincinnati, this is the largest and most important city in the state. It is beautiful in appearance and rich in commerce and varying industries. Along its borders – Newburgh, Lake Shore and West Side, there are many Welsh people residing.

Nearby, General James A. Garfield lived. According to his own admission, he had Welsh blood in his veins. I remember vividly his sister-in-law, a Miss Phillips of Parisville – an amiable and beautiful young lady and a very famous singer. The General was also very fond of her. It was a time of great joy in these regions when I was here last because there were large-scale preparations taking place to escort Garfield to Washington the following week when he would be taking over the presidential chair. This President is looked upon as an example of a notable man who succeeded to the position he came to hold by his own exertions alone. He is now recognized in the country's history as a champion of the truth and by his admirable example, he directs sound encouragement to ambitious young people when they are facing difficulties.

Delaware and Columbus

From Cleveland, I had over a hundred miles to travel south towards Delaware and Radnor, a town and village eight miles apart. Agriculture is the industry here where there are many Welsh settlers. I was a student in Delaware (population 7,000) in the years 1868-9, at Ohio Wesleyan

James A. Garfield

University. A Welsh lad came to this college at that time. He had only just arrived in the country from Wales and had a distinct Welsh accent. However, he was not affected by shyness which often inhibits young men when amongst strangers. After he graduated in Ohio and after spending another two years in a theological college, two years at the academy in Hulle, Prussia and some time in France and Brittany, he called with me in Pontrhydfendigaid before his departure to America in the year 1878. He had a string of letters after his name by now – B.A., B.D., Ph.D. He was appointed tutor in the Academy at Delaware and after Professor La Croix died, he took over his work. He was in charge of the teaching of Hebrew, German and French at the Academy; he is also fluent in five other languages. He is known as a very dry preacher but an astonishing scholar. He overcame many obstacles as he progressed in his career. I found him on this occasion, although married to an amiable American lady, as Welsh and as humble as ever.

From here, I went to the district of Westerville to visit my brother and his family and afterwards to Columbus, the state's capital (population 52,000). This beautiful city was home to me at one time. In the Methodist Church here, at the beginning of 1868, I had the privilege of commencing public duties. One finds the large Statehouse here, where Ohio's legislature meets; also the state's prison and excellent purpose-built buildings for the deaf, the mute, the blind and the insane. The military arms station and an agricultural academy are examples of very fine buildings and establishments found in this city.

John B. Gough

I should have stated that it was on my last visit to Delaware that I had the pleasure of listening to the world famous J.B. Gough lecturing to the students on his 'Platform Experience'. He is a hirsute gentleman, advancing in years. Regarding stature, a little taller than average I would say, without being fat or thin, neither rough nor handsome, cheerful nor cheerless; indeed he did not portray an air of being distinguished at all. In spite of this, his physique had such flexibility that he could jump like a child and make grimaces which coincided with his vivid remarks – all this with a very natural ease. As an actor, he could have been a very famous star. The reason, he said, that he had not pursued this vocation was the fact that it implied deceit, disguise, paint and falsehood; he also disliked the poor rags he would have to wear. (He was very much drawn to this kind of livelihood in his youth though). He found the hypocrisy of the vocation such, that he was ashamed to be associated with it. The reason he did not enter the ministry was the fact that he did not possess the most vital qualities required for that calling. He could not guide a congregation in prayer. Whenever he was called to do so, he shook like a feather and would often be susceptical to breaking down. He had a very unpleasant experience when Dr Parker of London asked him to conduct the benediction in the 'City Temple'. Gough has an amazing way of delivering a sermon and his influence captivates his congregation. He can throw a congregation into the doldrums and the next moment pick it up again so that it leaps triumphantly to a high pinnacle. He is able to combine seriousness and amusement making the two qualities contiguous. He also has the gift of pairing tears and laughter in such a way that one can only compare them to a multi-coloured rainbow set against a black cloud. As an important advocate for the Cause of Temperance, Gough was totally dedicated.

Nostalgic Memories

Of all the thousands of miles I have travelled, the plain between Columbus and Newark, as far as sacred memories are concerned, was the most touching for me. In Columbus station, eighteen years ago, I saw my father for the last time and I listened to the last advice he gave me. On this railroad, a few months later, his body was carried to be laid to rest with his eldest son in the cemetery near Newark whilst I and my brother were in the army, in the distant South, not knowing anything about his death. On the same route, afterwards, we accompanied our dear mother's coffin to her funeral. My memory was flooded with recollections of scores of notable sights during this hour-long journey. On the left was Willoughby School, where thirty years earlier, I had my first experience of sitting behind a desk. Again, on the right, the old house, the orchard, the trees and the fields – our first place of abode in this country. In Newark and its surroundings I saw changes – old buildings gone and others taken their place; memories of former acquaintances came flooding back too.

Mae rhai mewn beddau'n huno, a'r lleill ar led y byd,
Nid oes un gloch a ddichon eu galw heddiw 'nghyd.

(Some are sleeping in their graves, others spread across the world,
There is no bell that can bring them all together again).

I went to see our previous farm and farmhouse; strangers were there now; the animals were strangers; even the birds, the furniture, the meadows, the roads and the familiar paths looked different. I remembered everything with great reverence and loved everything about my old home deeply. I was a stranger here now though and there was no interaction. I visited the cemetery; there the skilled stonecutter had tried his best to enhance the resting place of the dead. There were straight paths with evergreen hedges and shrubs dividing the family plots, where decorated tombstones of fine stoneware had been erected. However, the atmosphere here was one of solitude and mournful silence. Whilst sitting by our family's tombstone, I meditated and became so engrossed in nostalgic memories that I could visualise myself as a boy growing up under the care and guidance of my parents. When I was a young lad I tried my hand at composing some poetry. The flair engulfed me again and these verses materialized:

The Author sitting by the Family Tombstone, meditating

Er dyfod dros y moroedd maith
I'r llanerch gysegredig hon,
Nid oes a etyb gri fy mron
Ond daear laith

Dan y twmpathau gwyrddlas hyn
Mae fy anwyliaid wedi eu cloi,
A'u henwau yma wedi eu rhoi
Ar farmor gwyn

Gynt galwent fi, gofalent fwy
Am danaf nag am gyfoeth trwch;
'Nawr, er bod yn ymyl eu llwch,
Nis gwyddant hwy

O drymed ydyw cwsg y bedd!
Llawenydd llawn – gofidiau'r byd,
Ei gri, ei gerdd, a'i dwrf i gyd,
Ni thyr eu hedd!

Pe'n effro heddiw, O fy nhad!
Pe medrech holi annwyl fam,
Pa holi serchog wnelech am
Hen Gymru fad!

Y mannau seiniech ynddynt gerdd,
A'r llwybrau rodiech ar bob darn
O'r wlad o amgylch Talysarn,
A'r fynwent werdd.

O'ch hen gyfoedion gwelais rai
A'u pennau eto uwchlaw'r bedd;
Yn barchus, gyda gwelw wedd,
Gwnant eich coffhau.

Yr hen amserau bywiog gynt
Yn welw rithiau welaf draw
A lwyr ddiflanant maes o law;
Cysgodau y'nt.

Diflana pob atgofion yn
Meddyliau pawb o luaws hil,
Y rhai a ddaeth trwy droeon fil
I'r beddau hyn.

Os un o'r rhain ar ddamwain ddaw
Rhyw gyfnod pell, â heibio'n chwim
I'r fangre hon, heb feddwl dim
O'r llwch gerllaw.

Awelon mwyn ac adar man,
Parhewch er hyn trwy oesau fyrdd,
Rhwng cangau'r coed uwch egin gwyrdd,
Eich galar-gân.

Fy nhad a'm mam, fy mrawd a'm chwaer,
Rhaid i mi eto grwydro'n mhell,
A'ch gadael chwi mewn distaw gell,
Yn nghôl y ddae'r.

A'i yma ai yn Nghymru draw,
Ai arall fan y'm cleddir i,
Gobeithiaf eto gwrdd â chwi
Ar ddeheu-law.

Y ddeheu-law! O gysur gwir!
Mae bywyd eto yn Iesu mwyn;
Anllygredigaeth wedi ei ddwyn
I oleu clir!

(Although I travelled across the great ocean
To this sacred place,
There is nothing that will answer my wistful cry
Except damp land.

Underneath these green hillocks
My loved ones are locked;
And their names have been inscribed
On white marble.

They used to call my name; more so, their
Care for me was far greater than any desire for vast wealth;
Now, although I'm near their graves,
They know not that I'm here.

Oh, how deep is the slumber of the grave!
Complete rejoicing – the world's perplexities,
It's cry, it's music and all its uproar
Do not disturb their tranquility!

If you were awake today, Oh my father!
If you could ask, my dear mother,
What caring questions would you ask
About good old Wales!

The places which delivered the sound of music,
And the paths where you trod over the turfs
In the countryside around Talysarn,
And the green graveyard.

Your old acquaintances – I met a few of them,
Some, who are still this side of the grave;
Very respectable, with ashen features,
However, they remembered you.

The lively times of old are
But diminishing far-away images in my mind;
They will completely disappear very soon,
They are but shadows.

All remembrances will disappear
From the memories of many of various lineage,
The ones that came time and again
To see these graves.

If an associate, by accident, will come one day
In the very distant future, he will swiftly pass
This spot, without thinking anything
About the people interred here.

Sweet breezes and beautiful birds
Perched on the trees' boughs, above the green shoots,
Do keep up – until the end of time,
Your elegy.

My father and mother, my brother and sister,
I must again travel afar,
And leave you in a quiet chamber,
In the bosom of the earth.

Whether it be in far-away Wales,
Or elsewhere I shall be buried,
I truly hope that we shall meet up again
On His righthand.

The righthand! O righteous consolation!
There is yet life through gentle Jesus;
Incorruption has been displayed
In a clear light!).

There is on the west side of Newark the remains of a very strange native existence; maybe the most extraordinary in the country. Whatever they were, they are now called old fortresses. They cover several miles of land and the best one is still in good condition. It consists of a strong dyke, made of earth and perfectly round. Indeed, the best engineers of this era could not improve on it. Encircling the interior of the dyke, there is a deep hollow which could have been a canal. In the centre of this area of land the ground rises into a kind of artistic mound in the shape of a bird. Maybe, this fortress was a walled city and possibly a mansion or a parliament or a temple was erected on this 'bird'. Going by the large trees which grow out of the structure, they probably were constructed around seven hundred years ago. There are in this region many cairns as well. They are called 'Indian Mounds' and human bones, weapons and treasures have been found underneath some of them. Who were these men who constructed these strange artefacts as well as the astonishing vestiges seen in the valleys of the Ohio and the Mississippi? There is no-one left who can tell us anymore. When I was a lad, I used to collect sharp arrowheads made of flint in these parts, but maybe these were relics left by an Indian tribe who lived in this area at a later date.

In the autumn of 1854, when we lived about twelve miles from this place, we were surprised by an invasion of wild pigeons. They flew over our house in an intertwining cloud every afternoon over a period of three years. We could hardly see the sky when they passed overhead. One only had to shoot at random before some would fall to the ground. They were making their way to a forest in marshland about three miles from us in order to get some sleep. It was amazing how they were killed off at night though. Every evening we used to hear shots being fired. The noise was similar to that coming from a battleground. Huntsmen from the countryside and neighbouring villages would bring their guns, lanterns and sacks. Alternating between random shootings towards the branches of the trees, the men with their lanterns and sacks would collect their catch. The markets became so inundated with this meat that the people tired of it, like 'Israel of yore with the quails' – (Psalm 105,40). This was the most remarkable year I have ever experienced concerning birdlife.

Towards the Ohio

After visiting Granville and Bryniau Cymru, places near Newark (population 10,000), I went south on a journey of about one hundred and fifty miles towards the Ohio River. En route I called in Shawnee and New Straitsville. I found lodgings in the home of friendly, humble, yet interesting local people. The elderly lady, Mrs Esther Williams, welcomed me with her warm smile and infectious laughter. She had the gift of making a stranger feel at home instantly.

'Sit down boy,' she said; 'tell us about your past.' 'Where have you been? Have you been to Sugar Creek yet?'

'No, I intend calling there on my return journey.'

'I was there when the Religious Cause started, you see – when Howell Powell started preaching there. It was I who compiled the first school books because we were unable to get other books, so I wrote A B C on white paper and pasted them on shingles; the children learnt them perfectly and they used to call them Esther's Books.'

After coming to the river, I found myself amongst a long narrow line of villages – all named differently as Syracuse, Minersville, Pomeroy and Middleport – comprising a distance of around seven miles. Behind them there are steep, high hills providing a good supply of water which is used in the processing of salt and bromine. Coal is also mined in this area. In front of these villages, one finds the murky, still waters of the wide river which is used to transport valuable goods to market-places by boats. With this insight, I was aware that the inhabitants were coalminers, saltminers, coopers and shopkeepers. From these villages, I went about eighteen miles further, down to the town of Gallipolis. About forty years earlier, the Welsh used to disembark from the river at this spot in order to go twenty miles north to the settlement.

Ohio is an Indian name, meaning so some say, amazement or wonderment. The Indians, when they came to the vicinity of the river when it was flooded and seeing the massive lumps of ice and tree stumps floating down its meandering waters, would raise their hands – flabbergasted, before shouting 'O! Hi! O!' and this is how it was named. This river, in the times of slavery, was the most important boundary between the free and slave states. Many a poor refugee waited anxiously on the banks of this river and after crossing it, felt as if he had crossed the Red Sea out of Egypt – (Joshua 24,6).

In Gallipolis, I took the steamboat to go to Ironton. Since I have previously given a description of the train, it is fitting that I do the same for the steamboat. Outwardly, it appears more like a floating mansion than it does to any of the steamboats on the sea. It has only one saloon which reaches from one end of the upperdeck to the other. Spaced out in this resplendent saloon are many telescope tables which are used by some for writing, reading, playing and so forth. However, it is not permissible for anyone to play for money nor to speak or behave improperly. The smokers have to leave as well. These tables are divided up and arranged into a number of smaller tables during mealtimes. The tables are laid with very rich and sweet delicacies in a splendid order – all in gold-rimmed or silver-plated bright dishes. It is surprising how speedily the waiters set the tables and remove the dishes afterwards. They accomplish it all so spontaneously. There is no company of soldiers who can master this automatic technique better. Each side of the long room there are sleeping cabins – sleeping four; two bunk beds each side of every cabin. It is a pleasure to be in these boats when the weather is favourable, seeing various scenery – hills, valleys, rivers, forests, meadows, farm-buildings and orchards spread out on the shores; passing islands and meeting large steamboats and other entities on the river. Since my river voyage was only forty miles long this time, I came to my destination much too soon.

Ironton is a lively town (population 9,000) and the Welsh play a prominent part in its continued existence and development. The main source of employment is in the iron foundries. I went thirty miles south from Irontown to Portsmouth (population 12,000) where the Scioto River flows into the Ohio. The next stage of my journey is in the Welsh settlement of JACKSON AND GALIA. This settlement is one of the largest and most respected in the country. The dwellers are mostly people from Cardiganshire; some call the place America's Cardiganshire and Moriah here must be their Llangeitho. The workers extract ironore from the ground and melt it in blasting furnaces. The main villages are Oak Hill and Centerville and a little to the north of the settlement, Jackson is situated and is the main town of Jackson county. Because I was there when the ground was muddy, when the ice had melted on cracked roads and an unusual fall of drifting snow had afterwards covered everything, travelling was quite an arduous task. However, I was given a strong horse to ride; yes, I was given Dock, the old, friendly black horse, belonging to the Honourable T.Ll. Hughes. It had carried me quite contentedly for seven months the last time I was in this settlement. He was young then, nevertheless solid and reliable now. I was so pleased to meet up with him again and to find that he was strong and still young in spirit. He was given enough oats until the end of his days and afterwards he was allowed to rest in peace.

Whilst passing an old empty stocks building which was once a small chapel called Berea, I remembered one of the most humorous experiences of my preaching career. I was preaching there in front of the Reverend D. Harries (Chicago now) when a strange bird perched itself on a branch near the window, calling out piercingly and loudly for about five minutes 'Whip-poor-will, Whip-poor-Will, Whip-poor-Will', disturbing me a great deal. When we went outside Harries asked me, mockingly, how had the bird known my name!

Cincinnati

In Jackson, I boarded the train to travel about one hundred and fifty miles west through Chillicothe (population 11,000) to Cincinnati (population 256,000). This is the largest city in the state of Ohio and is also situated on the banks of the Ohio River. This city was first named Losantville, when translated means 'the town opposite the mouth' because it stands opposite the estuary of the Licking River on the Kentucky side. Apart from the one in Chicago, the largest abattoir for pigs in the world is found here. It is also renowned for its commerce and various industries. Between the river and the numerous railroads, the city connects itself directly with all the major places of importance in the country and on one side it is surrounded by rugged hills which are climbed by sprightly youths.

I was met at the station by a friend, who after escorting me on a streetcar, informed me that we would be going through the Garden of

Eden that afternoon. However, before reaching this sacred spot, our vehicle stopped at the foot of a steep hill. Shortly, we felt we were moving again. What kind of movement was this? The horses' hooves were not moving and the car's wheels were not turning either. I could not see that we were passing the railings or anything else, yet I felt that we were going somehow, somewhere. On investigating, I discovered that the car, the horses and everybody were housed in and the house was on wheels being elevated on a platform to the top of the hill. As we ascended, the entire city came into view beneath us. It brought back to mind the scene I had experienced one evening from the top of one of these hills about eighteen years ago. Then, I could only see thousands of gas lightings shining in the darkness far and beyond. Whilst sitting alone on a high hillock, I had tried to imagine the countless scenes and happenings occurring in the city at that very moment – some raving in playhouses, others weeping in homes of mourning and in shelters for the poor, some happy and affluent – silks, gems and gold adorning their parlours; others, almost naked, hungry and seeking refuge for the night; some praying in their rooms and enjoying a secret relationship with their God; others creeping about, waiting for an opportunity to burgle; some being born into the world and starting to experience, in earnest, life's routine; others in their rooms taking their last breath and facing the spiritual world. What a vast mixture of wonders happening in this city was flooding my imagination, all under the mantle of darkness. If only I could borrow the eyes of an angel! Suddenly, I was frightened by the movement of something by my side. I woke up from my reveries and I hurried downwards to be part of the drama myself. It is a solemn fact that a perfect image of all the events of that night and of every other night and day everywhere has been impressed indelibly on the eternal curtains of the spiritual world and that it will appear again in the fervent light of the Day of Judgement! After reaching the top of the hill and going through Eden Park, I found myself in one of the many buildings of Lane Theological College, on Walnut Hill.

A Journey in the Territory of War

I did not visit Tennessee on my last journey, but since it was from Cincinnati I went there in the summer of 1864 and since the events of that journey were varied, I shall write about them here. I had been called to serve as a draughtsman in the army; my brother had already enlisted. I left home in Columbus and after reaching Cincinnati, I boarded the steamboat for an eighty mile trip downriver as far as Louisville (population 124,000). This is the largest city in Kentucky and the most famous of all the American cities for its tobacco market. It stands above the Ohio waterfalls, where there is a drop of twenty-two and a half feet within a two-mile radius. Because of these waterfalls, many goods which are transported via the river, have to be transferred to boats above or beneath the waterfalls. The city has straight, beautiful roads with many shaded by attractive trees. I was unable to proceed further without showing my licence because the railroads and everything else were occupied by the army. I was able to go as far as Nashville in a military vehicle without any mishaps – a journey of about two hundred miles southwards. Nashville (population 44,000) is the capital as well as being the largest city and the most affluent in Tennessee. However, at that time, it had an untidy appearance, as was the case in most of the southern cities during the Great Rebellion. The market-place was a strange sight; it appeared that the whole country had descended on it to find food – there were white, black and yellow people; men, women and children; soldiers and civilians; slaves who had only just been released and white people who had lost homes and possessions as a result of the war. Many people were selling bread, butter, cakes, pasties, potatoes and boiled meat, cups of coffee, cider, soup and all kinds of ingredients from their baskets or aprons; others were buying whilst crowds were seen at every corner and on every stone – some sitting, some standing and others walking about and eating at the same time. They trampled through the mud which was reinforcing and adding decoration to their torn clothing and the multi-coloured patches stitched on them – a strange sight indeed. It was with great difficulty that I found a train to take me further. There was no timetable or routine regarding the trains for ordinary travellers. I went to an hotel to get some sleep the first night. Did I say sleep! No, I found myself in an awful fight with the mosquitoes. Although I shielded myself with the bedsheet (the heat was such that I could not bear more bedclothes, even if they were available), I was bitten so much that by the morning one of my eyes had completely closed and I could only open the other slightly. I spent the second night in the station with the soldiers, therefore I escaped the stinging savages. The third night, I heard that a passenger train was being prepared for a midnight start. Instead of waiting for that one, I was lucky enough to meet a kind soldier who persuaded the commanding officer to allow me to ride in the military train for about one hundred miles.

I was very fortunate to have been able to travel on that train because the one that followed was held up by the enemy – the soldiers were put in captivity, the other passengers were robbed and the road was vandalised so much that it took two weeks before anyone could use it again. The damaging traces of the war were very visible long before we reached Nashville but after passing the city, the war's carnage was seen everywhere. One could not see a hedge, a shrub, a fence or a field of any kind. Since the land had been cleared of many of its large forests, the region had been subjected almost to the same bedraggled barrenland it was before the country was ever occupied. Here and there, were seen some large white buildings – in ruin now; the slaves' cottages were also situated nearby; some were vacant whilst others were occupied by the few remaining inhabitants. I had left Ohio when the hills and the vales were laden with the ripe produce of the soil – crops in abundance with fruit weighing heavily on branches making them lean over. In these southern parts, however, one cannot perceive anything except bareness and rough conditions – in other words 'Death Valley'. Alas! wars bring havoc and destruction and oh, how welcoming are the promises of an end to the conflict. Entire towns and villages were occupied by the army and very often fortresses were built in order to keep vigilance over the road.

This was by no means a journey without risks. It was known that not only were there spies and the enemy's regular army soldiers about but also armed bandits and other thieves lurked in bushes and all around. In spite of strict surveillance, they would often break up the road, wreck the train, kill, injure, capture or abandon people who had been robbed. They would, especially on these adventures, attempt to target civilians because they believed that they were merchants or speculators and therefore their capture would be to their advantage. There was a degree of moonlight that evening and several times I looked out towards a row of sticks or other objects thinking they were robbers or enemy soldiers and I was almost anticipating fire to flash from their guns towards the train as was the case very often. Luckily, the night passed without anything unpleasant happening to us although passengers in the train that followed had a terrible experience. Nevertheless, our train stopped two or three times so that the soldiers could investigate anything that they thought was suspicious.

Whilst staying for quite a while in one place, I had the opportunity to listen to the driver of our train describing some of his experiences. On one occasion, he had seen a large contingent of enemy soldiers hurrying forward near the place where we were – some to break up the road, others to place themselves in convenient places to shoot at the train. After steam-whistling a warning of danger and increasing the steam to its highest point, he had let the engine run free and to quote his own words: 'right over the devils, if that was the way the engine chose to go.' Thus, he delivered his train through safely and the bullets fired by some soldiers who were on the train, flattened many of the enemy troops in such a way that they would never think of such vices ever again.

A Dangerous Trade

After dawn broke, it was not anxiety but mirth that possessed me because of the mischievous antics of the soldiers. They were wicked without any conscience whatsoever. Negroes would come to the stations to sell provisions such as pasties, water-melons and cider but the seller would not dare let go of the food or drink before payment was handed over. If he succeeded in securing a fair exchange, he would be very lucky, because very often, the contents of his entire stall would be snatched from him without any payment. Here comes a Negro with a white apron full of pasties. He holds a pastie in his right hand offering to sell it to a soldier. The soldier then pretends that he wants to see the other pasties in order to have a choice. The Negro understands the plot but the soldier, by then, has grabbed a corner of the apron and 'with a tug of war' between the two of them, the pasties, one by one, drop to the ground and are picked up and possessed by the unscrupulous soldiers and the poor Negro has to turn away with a heavy heart while his clean apron is torn into a ragged cloth. Farther on, in another station, spread on the ground was a large display of: cakes, pasties, fruit, water-melons and two or three jugfuls of cider containing three gallons each, all belonging to a couple. They were black merchants and they could return home with their pockets full of money if only there was justice. As it happened an argument arose between the woman and one of the soldiers about a glass of cider. The soldier maintained that the glass was not full and by trying to get a free refill, he grasped the jug while the woman held tight, resulting in the cider spilling over to the ground. The other soldiers, pretending to be spectators to the scene, stole the water-melons, the cakes and the contents of another jug. This was the pattern all along the road. Didn't these soldiers have a conscience? What is that? Wasn't there a law or rule within the army to protect these poor people? Dear me there was – but how could it be enforced? Where was the officer who was supposed to control the behaviour of the soldiers? Before he could be found, the train had departed.

We gazed constantly at the new bridge, half a mile in length, which crossed the Tennessee River because a few months previously the old bridge had been wrecked by the enemy causing a long train, full of soldiers, to plunge into the river. We even looked more intensively at Point Lookout when it appeared – a place well-known for its historical connections as well as its romantic setting. By early afternoon I was in

Chattanooga (population 13,000), a military town then, situated on the banks of the Tennessee River where fierce bloody battles had been fought. It was stated that nowhere in the country was there a town with such mighty fortresses as Chattanooga. Apart from the dextrous fortresses, the surrounding rocky mountains and the narrow ravines make this town a very difficult one to capture and invade anyway.

Lookout Mountain

I believe that this mountain in some respects is quite unique. It bears resemblance to the highest mountain in Cumberland. Three miles south of Chattanooga and rising two thousand feet above it, is the peculiar nose called Point Lookout. The small black spot seen at its peak, high in the sky above, was the house I was supposed to go to before dark and it was meant to be a home for me for several months. It was three miles away but if I took that route I would have to fly like a bird. The usual route of seven miles would be much easier to climb if it had been made longer. Between the pain I felt in my eyes and failing sight because of a burning sensation from cinders blown from the steamengine as well as the intense hot weather, the weight of my heavy overcoat and the length and steepness of the ascent, I do not know how I would have accomplished the climb if I had not met one of the kindest boys out at the base of the mountain – if a boy indeed. I cannot imagine an angel with more concern than this young soldier. I had not met him before and I never saw him afterwards, although I wish I had many a time. He carried my overcoat and walked along with me. We took a breather every so often until we reached the summit. He drew my attention to the dangers, tribulations and temptations of the place and expressed such heavenly remarks with such simplicity and naturalness, in a way that I had not come across in a youngster before. I was convinced that he was gifted with supernatural glow and warmth. Why did he take such interest in a complete stranger? He perspired whilst carrying my load and wept for me. Why was there such compassion towards me? He must have been a live branch of His love and mercy appearing from Heaven towards a world full of sinners. Whatever became of him; wherever he is now, may he be blessed for ever. His companionship shortened and eased my journey enormously. Because of his help the hill did not appear so steep and we reached the top safely.

In spite of the sides of this mountain being very steep and high, its ridge is crowned for many miles by a jagged rock about 100 feet high, more or less. In places it has vertical straight peaks whilst in other parts it is wide and extends outwards. Climbing this area is an impossibility except by ladders or through random narrow gaps. Scattered along are many boulders which could be used to crush an aggressive enemy and in the whole region there are confluences, streams and lakes; hence it is well irrigated and enough crops can be grown for subsistence if ever there was such need. A handful of brave men on this mountain's summit, with proper surveillance, could stop any military force invading the area. The highest rock is called Eagle Cliff but Point Lookout, the most noticeable nose on the romantic brow of the mountain above the town of Chattanooga and the Tennessee River, is the most remarkable. The drop to the ground from this point was so horrendous that I had to go on hands and knees to creep within a few yards of the edge. This was the procedure taken by thousands of visitors who came here as well. Once, a reckless young man with the idea of showing off his prowess, tried to stand on the rock with only part of his heel on it before swinging the other leg. He lost his balance and it is believed that he was dead before he touched the ground. Another one, more stupid still, was so curious to see the drop that he tried to drive his horse-drawn car to the edge. The animal was very scared and was reluctant to go forward for quite a while. However, it was egged on and cruelly whipped that in the end it made a horrendous jump and over the edge they plunged – horse, car and man, all disintegrating into pieces by the enormous fall.

A Home above the Clouds

It was on top of this rock our log cabin was built and it was here, over a period of four months, I rested at night on hard boards under the glassless skylight of our almost roofless studio. I watched the moon, the stars and the clouds drifting overhead before closing my eyes; the chanting of the breezes and often the roaring turbulent wind would hustle me to sleep. Yes, the gales were so strong at times that the stones we threw towards them hurled back over our heads as if they were light feathers. Our family, in this place, consisted of six members, namely: Robert Linn, his brother James, my brother Lewis and myself, together with two young Negroes who had been slaves. One of them, John, had white, red and black ancestors. His job was to carry water and wash our clothes. The other one, Bob, was a Negro through and through with skin as black as a cave at midnight. His duty was to prepare meals for us. Our food consisted of brown bread, treacle, coffee and other easy to prepare rations. When we woke up, what caught our eyes first of all were bright blue lizards climbing the walls and when we picked up our sleeping-boards in the morning, large numbers of scorpions with distinctive stings appeared. If someone fell victim to one of these stings it could be fatal.

Fair play to them though, they did resolve not to harm us except in self-defence. Poor John was unlucky to be stung on his hand by one of them. Without any delay he bandaged his wrist so tight that no blood could flow through and he hastened to the doctor in Summerville, a place two miles further back on the mountain. The doctor treated him and praised him for his wise action. John was a sensible and handsome lad. If Bob had been the victim, I do not think he would have acted so quick and he would probably have died as a consequence. This lifestyle was a very weird one, yet I was never healthier nor fitter than at this time.

The view from Lookout Mountain was magnificent. It rises above all the surrounding mountains and on a clear day, visibility is such that one can see terrain within a radius of one hundred miles and distinguish places in seven different states. The encircling ground was undulating and rugged, nevertheless interesting. Opposite, nearby, was the battlefield of the Mission Ridge Combat. The town of Chattanooga was beneath and the soldiers' white tents were spread out across the valley. These tents appeared quite minute and the roads between them seemed like thin threads. The Tennessee River looked like a small stream and the steamboats like small ducks carrying smoky horns on their backs. As far as the railroad's steamengine was concerned, we almost believed it was a small dog running across the mountain's periphery. Although these objects appeared in miniature, they were very clear and voices and noises reached us with amazing clarity. However, visibility on a clear day was unimpressive compared to the scene when it was overcast. Fog and dense clouds would cover the country almost every morning and sometimes the mountain peaks would appear above them and the upper linings of the clouds seemed to be floating in a clear sky with the dazzling sun shining through. You reader, have seen the edges of the clouds when the sun is about to appear. Well above the clouds one finds a sight comparable to an ocean of melted silver with the sun's rays penetrating through as if it was playing, running and dancing above it all. When the clouds are tossed about by strong winds, the panorama is undescribable. These sights are very impressive and almost rate as high as Niagara Falls or some other unique scenery, I am sure. Occasionally, following this splendid show, lightning and roaring thunder would cause heavy rain to fall on the valley below.

Ca'em edrych ar stormydd ac ofnau, taranau a mellt dros y tir,
A ninnau'n ddihangol o'u cyrraedd, ar dalgraig a'n awyr yn glir.

(Reverend D. Charles)

(Storms and consternation, lightning and thunder can be observed over the land),
We, however, are safe from their grasp, on a high rock under a clear sky).

This mountain and the route to its summit is the most perfect resemblance to the journey of a Christian I have ever experienced. The lower region is full of clouds and darkness, storms and dangers, whereas the upper region is full of glorious brightness and a vision of wonders and gladness. 'And the ransomed of the Lord shall return, and come to Zion with songs and everlasting joy upon their heads: they shall obtain joy and gladness and sorrow and sighing shall flee away' – (Isaiah 35,10).

What about the night, Full of wonders! It appeared that the moon and the stars shone more in this location than I had seen them at any time. We often sat on the rock after dark, looking at the lights and listening to the trumpets, the drums and the rejoicing voices of the soldiers from the town and camp below. We also watched the light of the 'Signal Corps' on the distant mountains. The troops, in full view of others, would transmit the army's official orders over a line covering hundreds of miles in a very short time. The orders were deciphered by the way the light moved. The sparseness of the trees amongst huge rocks as well as the terrestrial surroundings and the circumstances added to the eerie nature of our plight. There was no dwelling to be seen anywhere. Disguised conspirators and bandits tramped over the region contributing to our interesting and somewhat romantic circumstances.

Snakes

I do not believe that this mountain is a haven to many snakes, yet I was frightened by a snake once on my way to Chattanooga. Instead of walking on the road normally used, I descended the rock by a ladder and slid down the slope in the straightest way possible until I landed at the bottom. There I was engulfed by bushes and thick, tangled reeds – twice my height! It took me several hours before I could wangle my way out of this jungle. Feeling tired by the excessive heat, I sat down for about quarter of an hour with my back resting on a piece of rock. When I looked sideways, what did I see on the stone by my head but a black snake about two feet long. I do not have to say that I jumped like a child and with the thick stick I was holding I killed it right there on the stone, in case it would make a move towards me as is customary with the black ones found in the South. I was told that the ones there were fond of a chase. These serpents are not poisonous; their method of attack is crawling stealthily, winding themselves around their victims and squeezing them to death.

Whilst I am narrating about these species, I remember feeling tired after running across a field near Newark where I once lived. I decided to lie down on the ground but as soon as I touched the grass I felt a movement and suddenly I saw a large, mottled snake slithering beside me. I was scared and I think the snake was too; both of us were quite happy to part company. Another time whilst spreading dung and moving from one mound to another without being very watchful, what caught my eye as I was about to put the pitchfork into one mound but a copperhead snake lying on it. It was one of the largest of its kind. The copperheads are extremely vicious and poisonous. There it was coiled up like twisted rope on this heap of dung. From the centre of the convolution a red head emerged, shining like deep coloured copper with its eyes staring at me and I believed it was about to reach my face. Without further ado, I pierced my pitchfork into it and fortunately one of the prongs penetrated through its body. Having got the better of it on the ground, I then killed it off. If every prong had landed between its folds, my career would have ended instantly. The copperheads and the ones with the rattling tails are the most dangerous of all the species. Many black snakes were to be found on our farm near Newark. They would climb the trees and crawl in front of us in the fields and we were not disturbed at all by their presence. They were to be found in knots in the rivers and in the canals – amongst the tortoises. Myself and other young friends, both white and black, would bathe in the river in their midst.

Once, in 1871, whilst preaching in a small chapel about fifteen miles from Portsmouth, Ohio, the service was interrupted by a lady who sat on my left. She was trying to communicate with her husband who sat on the other side of the chapel. He, however, failed to understand her twice so she repeated the third time: 'there's a snake under your seat trying to sting you.' There it was – a large snake with its head reaching towards the man's leg. He thrashed it instantly and after the kill and the disposal of the remains outside, the service resumed. Nobody should be afraid of snakes, they are decreasing rapidly. I know of no-one who has had significant harm by them. I remember people in Wales reciting amazing stories about snakes. Apparently, when I was a small boy in Talysarn, I picked up a live, mottled one instead of an eel and took it home. My mother was petrified and instead of feasting on my first catch, I witnessed the serpent being thrown out as fast as lightning.

Happenings on Lookout Mountain

The main historical occurrence on this mountain was that of the Army of the Union. This took place after Chattanooga and the valley below had been seized. The rebels believed that the mountain would give them foolproof protection but they were mistaken. One afternoon we saw the large cannons of the Union Army being pulled up to the summit of the opposite mountain. This mountain's peak emerged high above the clouds very often. Early the following morning, the Army assembled on this mountain and started to aim its fire towards the enemy's camp on Point Lookout. The enemy also, with all its might, fired back from the Point and for hours balls of fire were crossing simultaneously above the clouds. In the meantime General Hooker with all the strength of the Union Army marched quickly but very quietly, under cover of the clouds, to trace a gap about eight miles further back in order to reach the summit of Lookout Mountain and when the enemy soldiers on the Point rejoiced, thinking that the Unionists from the other mountain could hardly be a threat, an act of destruction and death descended upon them – Hooker and his men created mayhem, causing some to fall headlong over the coarse rocks, others fled in other directions whilst some were captured as prisoners.

I remember the evening when an attack on Chattanooga and the mountains by the rebel General Hood was anticipated. General Sherman had moved almost all of the Union's soldiers from these parts to regions in Atlanta, one hundred and fifty miles further and was starting on his big historic campaign, namely, proceeding beyond all the Southerners in order to meet General Grant. In the meantime, Hood with his powerful army was approaching Chattanooga. We heard his cannons destroying Ringold, twenty miles away. We also saw the smoke rising to the sky and we expected him to reach us the following day and needless to say fear was evident on everyone's face. Robert Linn, our instructor, had taken the warning to the North. Lewis, my brother, had been in Chattanooga for a week and James Linn, myself and the two Negroes were in charge of the house and the work on the mountain. James Linn said to me, about four o'clock in the afternoon, that he wanted to take the warning to Summerville, a village on the mountain two miles away. The nearest house to us was in this village. Linn promised to return before nightfall but there was no sign of him I went outside to look for the two Negroes but they had also disappeared and I found myself all alone. Now, if an attack was imminent, this rock would be the first target of the cannons as it had been many a time before. Our cottage would be blown to pieces immediately in case spies or secret agents were lurking inside. Fear of this prospect was the reason why James Linn and the two Negroes absconded. If some of the mischievous soldiers or the spies in the area had known of my lonely plight and the wares I was in charge of, they could easily have given me a licence to go over the rock! I spent the night listening to carriage after carriage bringing soldiers and arms down from Nashville. The commotion whilst greetings were being exchanged, the beating of drums and the squealing taking place, made the rocks echo. When dawn broke the whole valley was covered with white tents. Sixty thousand soldiers had arrived overnight. Hood, realising the heat was on, kept away whilst James Linn and the two Negroes returned.

My list of wonders on Lookout Mountain would not be complete without mentioning Mr Forster and his daughters. Mr Forster was a rustic mountain-man who dared not side with the Union because of fear for his life. The most daring thing he did was commemorate the fourth of July – the National Festival Day of the American Union – when the mountain was occupied by the rebels and their tents surrounded his house. He and his daughters celebrated that day by having a gun salute and waving the Union Flag. He also narrated the 'Declaration of Independence'. This contempt was more than the enemy could endure. The old man was captured, found guilty and sentenced to death. However, when the time came for him to be executed, the commanding officer, taking into account his age and astounded by his bravery and steadfastness, ordered his release. The old man was of a strong constitution with a determined look on his face. He reminded me of the Reverend Edward Mathews. He was known as 'the old man of the mountain'. Army officers and sometimes their wives would visit him and his daughters. By now, I understand that people from all areas visit the place regularly because of its historical relevance as well as its natural phenomenon.

The Return from the South
We camped in Chattanooga for several months after descending from the mountain. Half of the town consisted of tents then and our tent was wide and outstanding inasmuch as I had a big, comfortable bed. We were thus admired and deemed to be of the same rank as princes. Because of this status, we were more at risk from night robbers. Hardly a night passed without news of a shopkeeper or other salesperson's merchandise being robbed and occasionally a report of a murder was attached to the bulletin. An intruder entered our tent once but when he realised that we were all awake and ready to give him a 'warm welcome', he retreated. Our door was just a canvas flap and closed by tapes.

Since General Sherman refused permission for us and other civilians to continue with him on his long southerly route, my brother and I decided to go home. We had no hindrance as far as Nashville but in this city we had to bribe a soldier in order to board the military train. What an unruly lot of soldiers we had joined. The soldiers of Kentucky, who belonged to the Union Army, were known to have the most atrocious characters. At midnight pandemonium broke out throughout the carriage. An inhuman brute, after hours of indignation, started an awful feud inciting almost all of the soldiers to pull out their rifles and knives in a most threatening manner. My brother and myself were the only aliens in civilian clothes in their midst and there was no escape from the devils. We conversed in Welsh with each other because we thought that the cause of the turmoil was their plan to oppress and rob us since we were sure that we were looked upon as speculators. We had been questioned by several of them regarding the sphere of our occupations and about our success in the South. Nevertheless, before a bloody scene started (because blows were being thrown by now), officers from other carriages rushed in and after a scuffle, the most violent soldiers were overpowered and kept in custody. Calm was restored at last and we went home safely but there was no joy awaiting us. Alas, it was anguish and despair.

Disgwyl pethau gwych i ddyfod, croes i hynny maent yn d'od;
Meddwl 'fory daw gorfoledd, 'fory'r tristwch mwya' erioed.

(When glorious events are anticipated, opposite occurs;
Thinking tomorrow brings rejoicing, tomorrow brings the most awful sadness).

We discovered that our mother was a widow. Our father's funeral had taken place two weeks earlier. Letters had gone astray and my brother and I were hearing the news for the first time. The loss of my father determined, once and for all, my decision not to return to the South for the second time. Our arrival home did not happen a day too soon either because, as soon as we had passed through, the road was blocked by the rebel, General Hood, making it impossible to travel that way afterwards for weeks on end. Since every contact with the North had been broken, the people left in Chattanooga and on the mountain suffered severely from the cold and from famine.

Western Ohio
Now, it is high time to move on to describe my latest journey. I left Cincinnati, travelling through Hamilton (population 13,000) to Dayton

(population 39,000) thirty miles north. This is a beautiful and flourishing town; it has wide roads and excellent buildings. I was here for several months during the spring of 1864 and was actually in the town when Valandingham escaped from exile to Dayton, his home town. This man was a very able lawyer and politician as well as a kind and useful friend to the rebels of the South. President Lincoln was therefore obliged to ban him from staying within the circuit of the Union. After a term in exile in Canada, he had ventured to return home. A large gathering of his supporters assembled outside his house to congratulate him and he reciprocated with a defiant speech. A rumour spread that soldiers had been summoned from Columbus to catch him and therefore it was an anxious time in the town. After I had gone to sleep that night, I was awakened by the noise of carriages, galloping horses and men running and shouting. I was told by a friend to dress quickly, that a battle was about to begin. Through the window I saw flashes of fire rising in the air. Why were there no sounds of shotguns though! Tut, it was just the noise of firefighters trying to dampen down a house-fire as well as the chatter of spectators at the scene. We never witnessed a battle and Valandingham was not disturbed.

From this point, I aimed my direction eighty miles north to the counties of Allen and Putnam. In the Welsh settlement, Gomer, in the county of Allen, I saw the most fabulous farmhouses that I ever noticed anywhere. It is a custom with some householders to transform their dwellings into mansions. I tried to imagine the different thoughts that would preoccupy two gentlemen, a nobleman and a countryman from Wales, as they would approach one of these dwellings. Sight of the beautiful mansion and its shining black carriage would make the nobleman feel happy and his facial expression would show delight. He would hope to enjoy the intellectual companionship of the high and mighty. The countryman would be more apprehensive, afraid that he would not be worthy of the family's decorum. However, after entering the residence, one discovers an entirely different atmosphere. The occupiers are humble people and their habits are simple and unassuming. The nobleman would probably feel let down and the countryman would be at ease.

From here I travelled through Delphos to the Welsh settlement in the county of Van Wert, about twenty miles further west. There were important changes to be seen in the appearance of the countryside since I was here last, some twelve years ago. Trees had been cleared, splendid buildings had replaced log cabins and the village of Venedocia had been built.

Shakers

Residing five miles from Dayton was an establishment of Shakers. They called themselves 'The United Society of Shakers'. They dress plainly and somewhat shabbily and claim to possess miraculous talents and a visual fellowship with the angels. They allege that the second coming of Christ has already taken place in the most glorious person of their prophet, Ann Lee – Mother Ann, as she is known and that their denominational conviction is in association with the latest resurrection and since they are children of the resurrection, they do not seek a spouse. If any married person wishes to join them, the marriage has to end because everyone has to have a sibling relationship within one family, so to speak. They have to support each other from one pool of money, take care of the same things – seasonally and spiritually and always co-operate towards the same advantages. They do not involve themselves in wars or political issues and they do not influence anyone to join their Cause but accept whoever wishes to do so, that is, if judged to be worthy. They are recognised as being chaste, clean, honest, diligent and kind people. They used to visit me regularly when I lived in Dayton and they presented me with a lovely bunch of flowers once – an indication of great friendship. I had permission to attend one of their religious services, something I had wanted to do for a long time, especially as I had read the following in a book: 'in dancing during their public worship, they resemble the jumpers of Wales, and mingle their joy with cries and singing.' I never saw 'the jumpers of Wales' and I never heard of any activities relating to them when in Wales. They started their service by walking round the room holding hands and murmuring songs. Gradually, they escalated their steps and the singing got louder. They went on to dance a specific dance and whilst doing so, they turned on their heels in a very skilful way. By increasing the tempo, the slow dance became faster, the walking turned into sprinting and the singing became wilder, more irregular and louder still. Later their movements whirled into jumping and a customary hurrah. Running around, they would make facial gestures and movements with their arms as if they were driving the devil from the room. Others would close their eyes turning their faces upwards. Some were very solemn, others would smile in amazement as if they were experiencing a heavenly vision. The service ended by a man delivering a word of advice.

Feet-Washers

Since I am mentioning strange religious people, I shall now write an account about another experience with a different kind of worshippers in southern Ohio several years ago. Some call these people 'Feet-Washers', whilst others call them other names. They believe that it is the duty of people to consecrate one-seventh of their time to praise their Creator – immaterial what day of the week it is. It is on Sunday they usually conduct their services though and they are held more often in winter when country folk have more time to attend. They make up for the lack of attendance in summer by doubling meetings in winter. Their place of worship was a schoolhouse. It was seven o'clock when I went to the service and the building was full of people. After about an hour the preacher arrived – a tall, bearded man, rough in appearance and about thirty-five years old. He wore a Jim Crow hat and one of his trouser legs was tucked into a high wellington boot whilst the other one was half-in, half-out. He walked onto the spot which served as a pulpit area and after sitting there for about ten minutes, he took off his hat, because it was very warm I expect. He then started the service and read one of the lengthiest chapters in the New Testament; he prayed for a complete hour and a half and if you believe that the English rumbustious, passionate singsongs are not in the same category as similar singsongs in Welsh, I'm sure you would be convinced otherwise if you listened to this brother and the Negroes, as well as others that I have heard. Whilst embracing the eternal gospel, this man was able to lift off to a high pitch three times during his sermon and fly triumphantly, like an eagle, to heaven. He carried me with him the first time, in spite of my prejudice. The second time, I held my seat and listened to him like an adjudicator. The third time, I felt I was descending a level for each one he was ascending and as for the fourth time, I decided I was not going to be affected. His text was John 13,17: 'If ye know these things, happy are ye if ye do them.' His message emphasized how important it was for the saints to continue the ordinance of washing each other's feet. At the end of the sermon, an interval of fifteen minutes was allowed for the congregation to go outside for some fresh air while the youngsters played in the woods nearby. Then the second half of the service began. The preacher, by now, had tied a girdle around his waist and had a towel fastened to it. Holding a bowl of water, he began to wash the feet of the disciples who were lining up barefooted for this ritual at the front of the schoolhouse. After this liturgy, the disciples put their socks and boots back on and the preacher removed the bowl, the towel and the girdle. Then everyone participated in the Lord's Supper; each one was given a small portion of bread and a small cupful of wine. After they sang a hymn, the preacher announced: 'arise, we now leave'. By then it was the middle of the night.

Chicago

From the Van Wert Welsh settlement in Ohio, I travelled through Fort Wayne (population 27,000) and almost two hundred miles farther to Chicago – a city situated on the south-west corner of Lake Michigan. Like Venice, Chicago was built on a wet swamp. However, it is a city quite different to Venice; a special foundation was constructed enabling it to be built on a dry plane. The inhabitants of Venice have to use gondolas to transport them from house to house but in Chicago vehicles are used on the wonderful roads; some of these roads have a base of over ten feet in depth. Although this city is in its infancy concerning stature, importance and maturity, it is considered one of the major cities in the world. In the year 1830, it was merely a small dilapidated village. In 1837, the population was 4,170 with two places of worship. In 1882, the population is 504,000 with hundreds of Chapels and other public centres. In 1871, the most important part of the city was burnt down with the most ferocious fire that America has ever experienced. Within thirty-six hours, 12,000 buildings were destroyed and only by demolishing many other buildings was the fierce element brought under control. One hundred and fifty thousand people were made homeless and the overall loss amounted to forty million pounds. However, as a consequence of this disaster, the city was cleansed and it was rebuilt in a very short time in an impressive design. Chicago is the third most populated city on the continent and there is a wider variety of boats arriving in its harbour than is seen in Boston, New York, Philadelphia and New Orleans all put together. One cannot find in the entire world as many abattoirs and storehouses as the ones found in this city. There are more meat, grain and timber processed here than in any other place on earth. Its grain storehouses, the ones called elevators, can hold around seventeen million bushels. Dismissing the suburban areas, the city itself is situated on forty square miles of land with forty-three miles of navigable river flowing through it. There are thirty-six bridges crossing the river and they rotate on pivots to enable steamboats, sailing ships and other vessels to pass through. There are two tunnels beneath the river, each a thousand feet long, for the passage of carts, trolley-cars and other vehicles. The city has seven hundred miles of roadways and twenty-four railroads converge upon it whilst one hundred and fifty-six passenger trains arrive and depart daily. The magnificent parks, the buildings and other wonderments are too numerous to name, let alone describe. Amongst many other nationalities, many Welsh people live in Chicago.

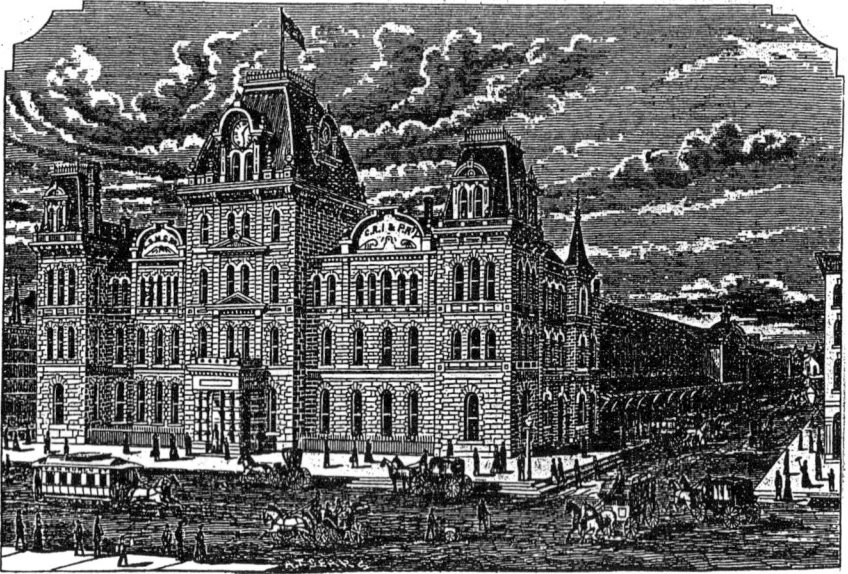

Chicago, Rock Island and Pacific Depot, Chicago Illinois

Milwaukee

From Chicago, I took a route of more than sixty miles north to Racine, in Wisconsin (population 17,000). Here is situated the best harbour of all the ones on Lake Michigan. Twenty-three miles farther and I was in Milwaukee (population 116,000). This place is called 'the creamy city' because of its cream coloured brickwork. This is the largest city in Wisconsin and it is both beautiful and impressive. It possesses wide, straight roads, magnificent buildings and beautiful parks. All features, in fact, bear a clean, healthy and welcoming aspect. As a market-place for wheat, it equals any other city in the Union. It is situated on Lake Michigan, just over a hundred miles north of its most southerly point. This lake, so it seems, is larger than Llyn Tegid (Lake Tegid) but its brother, Lake Superior, is larger still! It was in the main office of the largest railroad in the world – *The Chicago, Milwaukee and St Paul*, that I met W.E. Powell Esquire – Gwilym Eryri. He was an immigration steward and the highest ranking land supervisor in the country. Connecting with this man was always beneficial to immigrants as he was a kind compatriot.

The railroad's office is a superb building and it was here that I experienced my first ride in an elevator from the basement to the top

W.E. Powell Esq.
Gwilym Eryri

floor and back again. For a moment, the contrivance was stationary, then it started and stopped before us; a door of latticed steel was unlocked and we were allowed to enter. We sat on a comfortable bench, our feet touching a beautiful floor-covering and our handsome faces were reflected in shining mirrors in front of us! We were elevated as quiet and untroubled as a feather. The first stop was on floor number one; some people left and others entered. Thus we proceeded from floor to floor until we reached the top. From this upper platform we had to climb some steps and we found ourselves standing on the temple's pinnacle, a place where we could view, what appeared to be, all the realms of the world in their splendour in the space of one minute. We were enticed by the scenery and engulfed by a desire to worship – not the devil – (Luke 4, 1-13) but nature and the visible craftsmanship surrounding us. These scenic views did not bewitch us for long though, since like other good angels, they uplifted us and we could imagine them saying: 'praise ye the Lord. Blessed be the name of the Lord' – (Psalm 113,1-2). 'Thine hands have made me' – (Job 10,8). How marvellous are all components of your work! How impressive is your greatness. Your wisdom and your virtuousness are so brilliant that they infiltrate into all entity. Such ability you also placed in man's hand. Behold, all the great wilderness has been transformed to a piece of lavishness and blissful habitation. Instead of dark forests, cruel barbarians, rapacious beasts, horrible crawlies and swampy wetlands, we have attractive buildings and fragrant orchards – all creating an appearance of a flourishing existence in the entire region. The rural cornfields and urban commerce congratulate each other lovingly; the hills and the valleys emerge in song and all the trees clap hands.

The steamengines, which come from the far west, whistle at large steamboats, signalling them to collect the produce they have on board, namely, corn and fruit from the countryside. These commodities are then transported over the lakes and the oceans so that Wales, Europe and the whole world can benefit from them. Science and skill are at work untying knots, opening locks and digging out nature's treasures whilst fallen man, through God's grace, is given strength to regain his domain in the world. Indeed, all of God's arrangements appear so splendid:

> Pob natur doed a'u nerthoedd oll yn awr
> I ddatgan clod Duw, eu Creawdwr mawr.
> Yr awyr glir, a'r cyfan dan y rhod,
> Y môr a'r tir, rhoddent eu rhyglyddawl glod.

> (All nature, come now with all your might
> To proclaim praise to God, your great Creator,
> The clear sky, and everything in the Universe,
> The ocean and the land, give forth your worthy praise).

The time came for us to descend. When the elevator returned, we entered it and dropped from floor to floor until we reached the ground.

Hundreds of immigrants from the old European countries are to be seen daily in the stations of Milwaukee and Chicago. They have come to acquire the rich land of this region. Indeed, America is a large country, a rich country and a blessed one. Thank Heaven it exists – it is a place of refuge for nations which have been under oppression and despite the fact that many people have settled here and are still arriving, there is still room. The better regions are being populated quite rapidly though.

The County of Waukesha

About twenty miles west of Milwaukee one finds the oldest agricultural Welsh settlement in Wisconsin, namely, Waukesha. You, reader, have probably thought of Wisconsin as a state comprising mostly of agricultural land, inhabited by many Welsh people. It is also a region full of beautiful and natural resources. Since I intend publishing a book entitled: *HANES TALEITHIAU UNEDIG AMERICA A'R CYMRY YNDDYNT* (THE HISTORY OF THE UNITED STATES OF AMERICA AND THE WELSH LIVING IN THEM), I am not going to describe in this volume anything except the most spectacular events that I myself have encountered. The town of Waukesha is famous for its medicinal wells. There was thick snow – deeper and later than usual – covering the whole area when I was here. The winter extended from the beginning of December until mid April. Outside, it would be very cold; inside the houses and the train it was very warm. In spite of this different extremity in temperature, I was fortunate not to develop any colds and no harm came my way at all. This is symbolic because when I am in Wales, I am forever catching colds. I therefore conclude that the cold, dry, constant and long winters of America are much healthier than the damp and changeable ones experienced in Wales. The terrain is flat, almost like a table, from the lakeside in Chicago to Milwaukee. The region of Waukesha tends to be hilly and craggy except for its farthest point which is more level – similar to the surroundings of Bark River. The countryside is strangely enhanced, not only by crystal-clear lakes but also by trees such as groves and poplars, all planted in rows and thereby sheltering the dwellings and their outbuildings. These outbuildings consist of large, well-constructed barns and high windmills made in the west for the purpose of drawing water from the ground. They are neat and pleasant spectacles on the land that they cover. Wisconsin is a very desirable state.

Ixonia, Watertown and Madison

A little to the north-west of Waukesha is situated Ixonia Center, a village and station in an agricultural area. It was here that I had the pleasure of reuniting with three of the four Welshmen I had met when I set out from Aberystwyth. They came through wind and rain to see me. That's how it should be because the storm helped us to remember the rough voyage on board the *Abyssinia*. I was so glad to see them again and to find that they were responsible members of the community.

About eight miles further in the same direction, Watertown is situated (population 8,000). The town is inhabited by many Germans and a few Welsh people. Amongst the Welsh is Bardd Gwyn (a bard); he and his family were engulfed with despair at the time. They had been standing on the riverbank to watch their son pass through the 'Jordan' to the 'Other Side'. Before his illness, the deceased had been a very able journalist in the town. It was here also I saw the amusing woman-preacher, Mrs Rachel Evans (Rachel from Anglesey). Although a staunch Baptist, she said she was quite comfortable with the few Welsh Methodists in the area! I heard her preach many times in Ohio in the year 1871 and without a doubt, if she was a man, I am sure no-one would doubt her suitability for the calling. I can recollect that one of us who had arrived recently from Wales saying that he believed that the Apostle Paul himself could not deliver a sermon as well as Rachel from Anglesey. I met her again in Watertown – full of enthusiasm in her proclamation of the Word. Family commitments were now preventing her from being as active as she had been previously.

After going south-west for about thirty-five miles, I reached Madison (population 11,000), the capital of the state. It is situated on a spectacular, hilly strip of land between two crystal-clear lakes. In the beautiful Statehouse found here, I came across one of the best libraries relating to history that I have ever had the privilege of visiting.

Iowa County

From Madison, I contemplated going to Picatonica, in the county of Iowa (not the state of Iowa). The distance as the crow flies would be forty miles south-west but I was tricked by my map which showed a railroad, whereas the reality was, that a railroad was in the planning process. Because of this confusion, I had to do a round tour of about two hundred miles through Milton Junction, Jamesville (population 10,000), Hanover Monroe (population 5,000), back to Hanover Rockford in Illinois (population 14,000), Freeport (population 10,000), Warren, Darlington and Mineral Point – a place where at nine o'clock, the second evening, I found Mr Robert W. Hughes. He was pleased to see me as he said he had been to the station many a time thinking I would turn up but had been disappointed. I was made to understand that it was in the large Chapel, eight miles farther on I was expected the following evening. We went there almost on time but when we arrived we were told that it was in the stone-built Chapel, almost five miles further yet, I was expected. I was in a predicament really, since it was believed that there would be no congregation at this Chapel because I had failed to keep two or three previous appointments there and possibly the members would now feel that the preacher had not turned up again. Because of this assumption as well as the distance and the time of day, I discounted the thought of holding a service there at all. My aim now was reaching the minister's home by bedtime. However, after arriving there, I had no alternative but to conduct a service in that particular Chapel. To the Chapel we therefore went, travelling three miles over a hilly, potholed road – in a buggy of course. By now it was pitch dark and when we arrived we found very patient people outside the Chapel. When they saw us, the door was opened and we all entered. Before we could start the service, quite a time was spent trying to find material to light the building since it was not customary to hold evening services there. It was my turn to wait for them now but since they were so complacent about the situation, it would be very rude of me if I started complaining. At last the service started and in order to be brief only one verse was sung. They prolonged it though, doubling and trebling, all singing in high spirits and to a certain extent very expressive. They had no say in the length of the reading, the prayer or the sermon, therefore I abridged them to save time. The congregation, however, made up for the time I had gained by melodious singing whilst people were constantly entering in twos and threes until the end of the service. Except for this slight disturbance, the congregation listened attentively, thoughtfully and courteously. After the service ended, I expected everyone would be eager to return home. Not so indeed, the minister rose to his feet to make a speech. He thanked me for my service to them at their Chapel and reminded everyone of his association with me in Ohio. He also invited me to address them again on Wales and the purpose of my travels through the states. Myself, by now, believing that they intended spending the rest of the evening there, resigned to speak and a more intense fervour was experienced during this episode than in the first part of the service. Even after it all ended, nobody was in a hurry to go home. They approached me one by one to enquire about people and events back in the 'Old Country' and to reveal their recollections. They told me not to tell people in Wales that I had been to a Chapel made of stone. They said they were about to demolish it and build a larger and better one of wood. However, one person said that he believed that people in Wales would think that one made of stone was grander. These people were quiet, contented and kind and it is possible, in spite of everything, that each one had a few minutes of sleep before sunrise!

I returned the following day to Mineral Point. The day after that (Sunday) Mr R.W. Hughes took me in his buggy to Dodgeville, eight miles farther north. According to my programme, I was supposed to be there by ten o'clock. Again, when I arrived, I was made to understand that it was in Salem, four miles further, that they had arranged for me to be at that hour. The minister harnessed the wonderful mare and we set off in the buggy. What a mare! I am sure that the cattle dealers of Tregaron and Ffair Rhos would be amazed at this mare's performance. Whether it was over the countryside or through the air we travelled, whether it was one rambling terrain or whether there were forests and fields, whether I was awake or dreaming, the first recollection I have is the fact that we had stopped by Salem and somebody was asking me to descend and enter the Chapel.

I preached in the afternoon and evening in Dodgeville, to a congregation consisting of three denominations, Baptist, Independent and the Calvinistic Order. I am stating this fact in order to indicate that congregating together is a custom, not only in Dodgeville, but in several other places in America. Whenever a visiting preacher arrives, whether famous or not, the Welsh from all denominations unite to listen to him. The following day, the amazing mare took me south on an eighteen mile journey to the agricultural area of Blue Mounds, where it is said, one finds the highest peak between the Alleghenies and the Rockies.

Welsh and Portage Prairies

After a journey of more than a hundred miles north-east through Milton Junction and Watertown, I descended first of all in Columbus, a large village in the middle of agricultural land, where many Welsh people live. From this place, I went northwards and found the old very densely populated Welsh settlements of Welsh and Portage Prairies. I am sure these places had a great deal of valuable material to offer any author who was interested in writing a book about the Welsh Americans. I cannot say that anything worth recording happened to me during my visit though. In Welsh Prairie, one finds the villages of Cambria and Randolph and at one end of Portage Prairie lies Fox Lake as well as other lakes – all situated in beautiful countryside.

Whilst travelling in this region, I noticed in the press articles under the heading 'Flashes from the Spiritual World' by such famous people as Dewi Emlyn and Eos Glan Twrch. I recorded, without hesitation, the following anecdote as I was told it by a dependable woman, a person highly commended by a respectable minister for her honesty: after this woman had put the light out when going to bed one evening and before she slept, she heard loud banging on her bedroom window and a voice calling her by her name: 'L_, rise, there is a spirit in the house.' She recognised the voice as that of her father who had passed away. She was frightened at first and hid under the bedclothes; after a little while, there was another loud banging and the same voice calling as before: 'L_, rise, there is a spirit in the house.' This time she plucked up courage, got up and went towards the window and saw a vision of her father standing outside and she heard him say to her the third time: 'L_, rise, there is a spirit in the house.' When she looked across she saw one end of her house ablaze. She aroused others from their beds and milk and cream, the most accessible liquids, were thrown on the fire. After fetching a great quantity of water, the flames were extinguished before too much damage was done. Thus, by means of a spirit from its own sphere, the family was rescued from what could have been an awful tragedy. This family had experienced a similar ordeal previously when the entire house and furniture had been destroyed.

By travelling beyond this region to Oshkosh, our train travelled faster than usual because it was thirty minutes late. However, two malicious boys caused the train to be delayed another thirty minutes whilst the conductor and others removed the barricade of wood and stones these boys had thrown across the rails. The conductor then ran across three fields to catch the rascals. The chase was successful and the lads were crying when they were detained in the train. Where they were taken and what happened to them I never discovered but they had a free ride to somewhere as a reward for their misdeed! If they had done this atrocity at dusk, the consequences could have been very serious.

In Winnebago County

This county is situated on the west side of Lake Winnebago which is thirty-five miles long and half that measure in width. There is very pleasant countryside surrounding this beautiful lake. After visiting the agricultural regions where one finds a great number of Welsh people, I went to the attractive town of Oshkosh (population 16,000) where there is a flourishing wood-market.

About fifteen miles further north, one finds Neenah and Menasha, two towns on the highest point of Lake Winnebago – one on each side of the Fox River in which Dotty Island is situated. This island is one and a half miles long and half this distance in width. The railroad station is placed on this island because of its accessibility to both towns. These towns, because of their idyllic positions, are of great interest to visitors in the summer. Some of their entities are historical; one of them is 'Treaty Elm'. The chiefs of the ashen complexioned Indian tribes, who were associated with this treaty, used to meet and conduct their 'big talk' and draw up covenants here. It would be an eye-opener for anyone to visit the wood factory on this island, to see a spill being made in just a second, sixty every minute, as well as objects such as train wheels, wheel rims and the like; all made in less time than it takes you reader to read about them.

The Revivalist

This man is a remarkable character when one considers the power which engulfed him at one time and the fact that he is known to millions of people in Wales and America. He lives near the house I used to stop over, in the district of Oshkosh and I decided to send for him. He came without delay. He was of a large and heavy stature and the small amount of hair remaining on his head was completely white.

He appeared well groomed, in his late forties, very lively and cheerful. At my request, he delivered a summary of his life. After narrating about his work which involved previous religious revivals he added:- 'After this I became too weak to preach in public. I spent four years in lodgings in Aberystwyth without preaching at all; afterwards I would occasionally preach in that catchment. In the year 1868, I started reading the Prophets and writing my viewpoint of them. I had no relish for anything else at that time. At the end of that year I wrote letters to the Pope and to Napoleon III. They were published at that time in *Baner ac Amserau Cymru* (Banner and Times of Wales). It was at that time people started saying that I was losing my sanity.'

'What were the letters you wrote to the Pope?'

'I told him he was either going to die soon or there would be a swift end to his temporal power in the world. I wrote this at the end of 1868 and at the end of 1869 my prophecy became reality because all temporal sovereignty on earth was snatched from him.'

'What did you write to Napoleon?'

'I wrote three letters to him. I told him in one letter that I could see him sitting very dignified in an armchair with a sharp-eyed, nasty-looking man standing behind him; that I could see him (Napoleon) contemplating standing up but if he did so, then this other man would take his place and he would lose his seat for ever more. This sharp man, as I understood afterwards was M. Thiers, the man who occupied the presidential chair after Napoleon.'

'How were you able to foresee such things?'

'The Scots call it second sight. At that time I was unable to think seriously about anything without seeing whatever it was in some shape in front of me. Whenever I thought of Napoleon, I would see him in some form and with this detailed conviction in my mind, I realised that the image portrayed of him was an omen of what was in store. I was so vexed by these mental impressions that I had to write to him again and as a reward for my work I was given a home in Carmarthen and there I stayed until Napoleon was defeated and all my prophecies regarding him were substantiated. When my family discovered that all these premonitions had come to a conclusion, they invited me to join them in America. I therefore lived with my parents for two years in America but since I was at that time sending letters to Mr Gladstone, my family began to think that I was taking leave of my senses again.'

'What did you write about to Mr Gladstone?'

'I wrote to tell him that the thousand years were drawing near and I gave a description of them from the Prophets. As a consequence of this, I was taken to a hospital in Oshkosh. I spent my time there reading and writing on the Prophets. Dr Kempster (the institution's supervisor) said I was normal in all aspects except on the subject of the Prophets. Of course, he did not understand anything about them. He said he would release me within two months so long as I completely abandoned these issues. To be totally honest, I was very comfortable in this hospital and since I had such a passion for the Prophets, I did not feel like retreating from either. I only had to ask for a sheet of paper to write something on the Book of Revelations for them to consider me totally unbalanced.'

'One of the many people who visited me in this place was Father O'Malley (famous for his stalwartness to the Catholic Church). He was an ardent abstainer and as he approached me I said to him: "ostendo nobio misseracordium Domine" (Lord show us mercy). We had a very friendly chat. He, asking me questions and I reciprocating. When he was leaving, the ward's assistant asked me to say goodbye to him in Latin.'

'I said to him: "Dominus vobiscum" (God be with you). With a wave of his hand he replied loudly: "et cum spiritu tuo" (and with thy spirit also).'

Mewn dirgel ffyrdd mae'r uchel Iôr yn dwyn ei waith i ben.

(The Lord accomplishes his work by incomprehensible deeds).

It was 'by an incomprehensible deed' that He led this servant of His to see me. There are people in the community who have sprung forth to supervise large churches without any talent for the vocation and are utterly useless. They enjoy prosperous livelihoods and are regarded as high and mighty people whilst this young, striving minister who has converted many people from their evil ways, has had to toe the line as if sedges had been entwined around his head and his feet were in stocks. He is, at present, a minister to a small, insignificant Church. It is said of him, however, that he is a remarkable man and that his prayer on a Sabbath, the other week, was outstanding. Who knows, the Lord may generate more work for him to accomplish.

To Waushara County

In Neenah, I boarded the train to travel about fifty miles west to Waupaca. Changes in landmarks were visible on this route – new clearings, new farms, new buildings and new villages. However, old forests were still throwing their dark shadows over the black bogland which covered part of the terrain. For the first time, I saw hedges or fences or whatever they were called; they were made entirely of tree stumps which had been dug from the ground and placed in long lines, parallel with each other. Their roots, some interwoven, others in upward and outward directions, made such a complex entanglement, that I would imagine it would be impossible for a four-hoofed creature to jump over them. Waupaca is a small, flourishing town and is surrounded by beautiful countryside alongside a chain of four lakes.

Since I did not keep my appointment to meet my friends in the Welsh settlement of Wild Rose the previous day – friends who had asked to meet me, I had no option now but to walk there, a southerly journey of fifteen miles. The weather was warm and the road sandy. I perspired a great deal and drank water from wells owned by people living along the way – very refreshing water it was too. Just before I reached my destination I was so glad to come across a lake located in a particularly pretty glade. In it I bathed and with exception to the man who regained his sight in Lake Siloam – (John 9,7), I doubt very much whether anyone has had more satisfaction than what I experienced in this welcoming lake. I proceeded thanking the Good Lord for the beneficial water and for the freedom to embrace amiable nature without being hampered by man's commandments. Three years previously, I had intended bathing in a river, near a town in England, only to find at every entrance large signs posted on white boards with the warning 'Trespassers Will Be Prosecuted'. If the Giver of all goodness, kind Father of all His children, had planned that this free-flowing river on its way to the sea, should be a source of enjoyment to all creatures, then I was denied that privilege. I went forth that day with bitter feelings and I thought of the day when many impudent gentry would see the phrase 'Trespassers Will Be Prosecuted' in another light.

The settlement of Pine River or Wild Rose or Indian Land, as it is known by some, is the most northern of Welsh settlements in Wisconsin. From this area I travelled through another Welsh settlement, towards Berlin, a town twenty miles east and from this town to Milwaukee.

Towards and on the Wisconsin River

Next, I journeyed across the state of Wisconsin, that is, from Lake Michigan towards the Mississippi River. After travelling through captivating agricultural land, passing the small, pretty town of Beaver Dam on Beaver Lake and through the villages of Randolph and Cambria, I descended in Portage City (population 5,000). There is a canal, one and a half miles in length, alongside the city and at one point it joins the rivers of Wisconsin and Fox and thereby forms a navigable route from Green Bay, Lake Michigan, to the Mississippi River. The Welsh settlement of Caledonia is about five miles south of Portage City, on the other side of Baraboo River.

Seventeen miles west of Portage City lies Kilbourn City. This one like many cities in western America is in reality just a village. It was here I descended from the train to board a quaint little boat, the *Dell Queen*, in order to see the wonders of the Wisconsin River; a remarkable river for sure, not because of its size or its historical and commercial importance but because of its inexplicable formation in a romantic bed of sandstone. The rocks which rise high and steep each side of the river have formations of all kinds of images, such as: buildings, pillars, people, ships, chimneys and various other shapes. Some were quite bare whilst others were covered with moss and fern. The river itself is quite impressive; in some parts it appears as if it is lying on its back with its dark, large face reflecting heaven's cheerful, blue sky. In other places, it is narrower and deeper and appears as if it is lying on its side. Its depth is about one hundred feet in these parts and dark shadows of silent rocks are cast on its banks. This river also has very sharp bends with sections of its waters rushing through openings and creeks, creating fords and amazing cascades. It would be too much of a task just now to describe them all. The different sites are called: Romantic Cliff, The Rock's Chimney, The Echoing Cave, Allen's Tavern, the Chapel's Ridge, The Ship's Harbour, Elin the Devil, The Demon's Armchair, the Witches' Valley, The Phantom's Room, Pity the Fat Man (this is a narrow passage between rocks) and many other suggestive names.

How were all those wond'rous objects formed among the pond'rous rocks?
Some primeval grand upheaval shook the land with frequent shocks;
Caverns yawned and fissures widened, tempests strident filled the air
Madly urging foaming surges through the gorges opened there;
With free motion toward the ocean, rolling in impetuous course,
Rushing, tumbling, crushing, crumbling rocks with their resistless force;
And the roaring waters, pouring on in ever broad'ning swells,
Eddying, twirling, seething, whirling, formed the wild Wisconsin Dells.

From the Wisconsin to the Mississippi

Surrounding Wisconsin River, mainly the west side of it, I found terrain of a completely different nature to any I had ever seen. It comprises a vast plain with upright rocks arranged in an orderly manner scattered on it. Some of them are hundreds of feet in height and vary from slim, lofty columns to all kinds of shapes and sizes; some are in clusters, others miles apart; some beautifully covered with greenery whilst others are bare. They have appropriate names such as: The Lonely Rock, The Twin Cliffs, The Devil's Chimney and so on. How did these amazing rocks form and when? What were the views of the old inhabitants about them? If they resembled our ancestors, they probably thought that a massive giant, whilst travelling this way, found them in his waistcoat's pocket, or else they were in his boots and hurting his feet so much that he shook them out in this area! However, these rocks give the appearance that they were washed and eroded thousands of years ago. The ground is very sandy in this district with shells and other aquatic objects revealing themselves occasionally, thus confirming quite clearly that this land was once a seabed or formed the base of a large lake or, maybe different parts, in different eras, created a bed for the Mississippi River. At that time, the rocky formations must have been islands. The earth is sandy and of poor quality with only weeds, wild vegetables and wild herbs growing here. In a place called Camp Douglas, thirty-two miles west of the Wisconsin River, there is such a cluster of rocks that they would be ideal as a strong, military fortress, if one was ever required.

I had often been in this region and on one occasion had a nasty experience here. I wanted to go to St Paul through countryside that I had not visited before. I therefore transferred from the *Chicago, Milwaukee and St Paul* (I had a licence to travel on all branches of this railroad) to another one, thinking it was the *Chicago and North Western* since I had a licence to travel on this one also. After a little while I discovered that I was on the wrong train and rather than pay to go on this railroad, I decided to walk a distance of ten miles, back to Camp Douglas, to board the train that I was on earlier. It was dark with no moon or stars to help me on my way. I did not come across an abode at all and since I had read in the 'Guide Book' the previous day the following report about these parts, my trek was not a very comfortable one: 'of game, there is superabundance of bears, wolves, deer, foxes, &c.' If they were that plentiful they were courteous enough to leave me pass through without attacking me and I found refuge in Camp Douglas about one o'clock in the morning.

Tent by Lake Spirit, Iowa

The next place I arrived at was Sparta, a small, clean town in rich countryside, full of natural beauty. It stands on one of the highest peaks in the state where the air is cool and refreshing. The town has famous medicinal waters and from the summit of Castle Rock, the highest of the surrounding craggy hills, one experiences a panorama of brilliant views in all directions. Eight miles south, lies the Welsh settlement of Blaendyffryn. From here I travelled through the Welsh settlements of Fishcreek and Bangor to La Crosse (population 15,000), a place situated on the banks of the Mississippi River, one hundred and ninety six miles west of Milwaukee. Whilst approaching La Crosse, I almost thought I was on one of the railways of Wales; such was the 'Welsh' greenery everywhere, namely: fern, broom, harebells and so on. The hills, the woods, the stones, the soil and everything imaginable, apart from people, spoke Welsh and I was so glad to hear them!

Upper Mississippi

In La Crosse I boarded the train that ran along the west side of the Mississippi to go northwards as far as Minneapolis. After crossing a long bridge, I found myself on the Minnesota side of the river. I was unable to see its eastern side because of wooded islands obstructing the view. These islands vary in size and formation and they reflect a paradisian presence. It would be heaven on earth to put one's roots down here in order to keep company with beautiful nature in its glorious simplicity and be able to survey the various leaves and flowers in order to observe their joyful smiles whilst, each day, receiving a mystical revival from the sunshine. Listening to the birds praising their Creator with songs that blend with the melodious breezes is a blessing in itself. Below this harmony, the roar of the deep river is heard. Oh! Lord, give me strength to enable me to enjoy your boundless accomplishments. These islands differ from the Susquehanna ones inasmuch as one is unable to find any farms or houses on them. The reason, no doubt, is the fact that the islands are prone to flooding at times.

When the entire width of the river was visible, I noticed that it was, on the whole, about a mile wide with beautiful scenery comprising rocky and wooded hills rising on each side. Steamboats, rafts and the like were to be seen floating on it. Beside Minnieska, a little below Winona (population 11,000) there are rocks of exceptional formations and towards Wabasha the river appears like a lake – about five miles wide. It is known at this point as Lake Pepin. It stretches as far as Frontenac, thirty miles higher up and here it is seen again in its usual width. The land close to Lake Pepin was home to the old inhabitants, the pre-Indians, who were known as 'mound-builders'. Their strange gravestones are spotted around this area today. Wabasha was at one time the capital of the Sioux and Dakota tribes. Here, in their typical wigwams, sat their chiefs in serious discussions concerning wars and rights. Of all the famous cliffs found between Wabasha and Frontenac, the most famous is the Sugar Loaf, near Lake City. From this cliff one can see the extent and splendour of Lake Pepin.

There are many historical accounts and fables associated with these districts. For instance, the Maid's Rock, where it is maintained that beautiful Comona (after the Big Chief, her father, decided to hand her over as a wife to a brave warrior; alas, one she was unable to love) drowned herself in the silent bosom of the Mississippi. After travelling through Redwing (population 6,000) and on to Hastings, where the La Croix River flows into the Mississippi, the latter becomes leaner and the wilderness which once surrounded it decreases. In my assessment though, the tenderness and beauty it reflects is enhanced at this location.

St Paul

I shall not forget in a hurry my first glimpse of the exalted city of St Paul as it appears in the distance. The beautiful valley of the Mississippi overspreads towards the hills whereupon St Paul is situated. The seemingly thin, white veil of the horizon, the light beaming between the city's pinnacles on the crystal river, the green valley and the scattered trees make the entire scene appear as if it had dropped from the sky. It was more like an illusion or a dream than a real terrestrial locality. One hears about the works of designers and artists but the prowess of the

Almighty is such that he is incomparable amongst the gods nor are there deeds like His deeds. If you reader will have difficulty in experiencing the described spectacle, the fault will be yours or on the unfavourable quality of the atmosphere at the time; the whole scenery can change so sudden that I myself failed to experience the same vision when I returned to the area at another time. St Paul (population 42,000) is the capital of Minnesota. It is situated on captivating hills on the banks of the Mississippi. Across the river is a very strange bridge which reaches upwards from the top of a high rock on one side to the top of another on St Paul's side.

Lake Calhoun (Minn.) and Scene on the Dalles of St Croix.
Reached via 'Albert Lea Route'.

I had seen Red Indians, albeit only a hasty glimpse of them, at an earlier time. Here, in St Paul, I had the opportunity to concentrate on them. They came to this city to sell skins of wild animals or to exchange them for the merchandise of white people. Their squaws endeavoured to dress in clothes worn by white women. They appeared shabby though and were shod with moccasins while their heads were covered with lengthy, coarse, loose hair. One could see, even from a distance, that they were Indians by their mannerisms. They always walked quickly, one preceding the other. When they stopped, they did so very suddenly, holding themselves as erect as poles; then they would turn their faces to look over their shoulders before proceeding very briskly again as if they had found something of importance to focus on. They would approach the wall of a dwelling, then stoop and look around the corner, the same way as they lurked behind trees or rocks to spy on an attacker or when hunting. Instead of sitting, they would crouch down with their knees touching their chins. They have large, ruddy faces and thoughtful, serious and determined expressions. There are variations in their facial lines though, each one depicting different thoughts, abilities and tendencies. They differ from the Negroes in this instance since the Negroes' habits are more consistent.

Minneapolis

Scarcely ten miles further up the Mississippi, where one finds the remarkable waterfalls of St Anthony, is situated a sister to St Paul; a younger but stronger and cleaner city. Yes, here she is, Minneapolis (population 48,000). This city was very fortunate in its location inasmuch as it lies in a very beautiful and flourishing area. The city has presented itself in a very appealing fashion with its clean, wide roads and impressive buildings. It has the most brilliant advantages because of its abundant supply of water which is used to turn the numerous mills and here is found the largest flour-mill in the world. Apart from the mills, one also finds in this city, high elevators and they are outstanding spectacles. One census conducted three years ago came to this conclusion:

> there are in the city twenty-one mills with the capacity of milling 15,000 barrels of flour daily. Most of it is exported to Europe with seven trains leaving the city towards the east daily – every train transporting 125 barrels in each carriage. Wheat from the Red River region is the main commodity and 1,650,850 barrels were dispatched last year. The amount of wheat received was 8,103,710 bushels. The complete length of all the trains transporting merchandise from the city last year would measure over three hundred miles. If the trees in Minneapolis' timber market were made into tables, one foot in width by one inch in depth, then placed on top of each other, they would encircle the earth.

The quantities have increased by now though, since this is a city expanding rapidly.

The producing fields of Western America, with storehouses and mills like the ones found in Minneapolis, are the means of sustenance for the poor folk from England and Wales as well as immigrants from other countries of the Old World. It is said that these people create a threat to the farmers of this land because they ask low prices for their produce in the markets. My opinion is that the farmers should be quiet on that score. Maybe the landowners are at a disadvantage by these storehouses, but it is of no significance to the person who pays rent for land in this region whether the harvest is plentiful or in short supply or whether the market price is high or low. Most of the revenue goes to the bottomless pocket of the landowner; the remainder he gives to his tenant, his employees or as payment for nourishing fodder for his working animals. There may be honourable exceptions of course.

The surroundings of Minneapolis are rich in natural, scenic beauty comprising waterfalls, lakes and so on. Tourists come here in their thousands to fish and amble during the summer months. About three miles from the city, one finds a lively and delightful stream called Minnehaha – not unlike the streams found amongst the hills of Wales. It has acquired fame mainly because of its Fall known as 'The Fall of Minnehaha'. The name has been translated from the language of the Indians and means 'The Fall of the Laughing Waters'. It transmits an appearance of laughter and inflicts a chortling sound as it meanders, flows and jumps over large rocks and tiny gravel. As it approaches the Fall, the stream broadens its stratum and bounces widely in one thin, white veil and thus creates a safe pathway between it and the boulders. It sings:

I come from fields of frost and snow – my winding way I follow;
I come from where the wild woods grow, I come from hill and hollow;
I foam, I flash, I leap, I dash, I glide with music merry,
O'er pebbles bright, with rainbow light, along the lovely prairie
Minnehaha, Minnehaha, laughing, laughing Minnehaha,
Minnehaha, Minnehaha, ha ha, ha, ha, ha, ha, ha, ha.

I tremble on the rocky brink – my winding way I follow,
I gleam, I pause, I plunge, I sink into the hidden hollow;
I loudly roar along the shore – I tremble and I quiver;
I rush along, with joyous song, to greet with mighty river;
Minnehaha, Minnehaha, laughing, laughing Minnehaha,
Minnehaha, Minnehaha, ha, ha, ha, ha, ha, ha, ha, ha.

The main lake is Lake Minnetonka meaning 'massive waters'. It is fifteen miles from Minneapolis and contains a series of twenty-five bays where large numbers of pleasure boats float. It is surrounded by spectacular forests and grand guest-houses are situated on its shore. Visitors make a point of coming to this area to gaze at the splendid scenery.

Lake Spirit, Iowa

The West

After returning for about one hundred miles along the Mississippi riverbank as far as Winona, I boarded the *Chicago and North Western* train towards the west with the intention, if possible, of seeing the 'West'. In the states of New York and Pennsylvania, people speak of the people of Ohio, hundreds of miles westward, as people living in the 'West'. After arriving in Ohio, I was told that I would have to travel through the states of Indiana and Illinois to Wisconsin, hundreds of miles farther again, in order to set foot in the 'West'. To Wisconsin I went, but what did the people of Wisconsin know about the 'West'? It wasn't to be found there. The people mentioned it constantly and whilst pointing in the direction of the Mississippi, they said that it had crossed the river many years ago. I also crossed the Mississippi but the 'West' had left its banks for some distant region towards the land of the sunset. I started my journey from Winona about midnight, thinking that I would be on a vast plain by sunrise, far from any habitation – without any farms, houses or tame animals visible. In spite of travelling very fast, with the 'iron-horse' bellowing and sparking indefatigably, it was the same scene of farms, buildings and people I discovered in the morning and that was the way it continued until late in the day. By now, I was beginning to doubt whether there was such a place as 'West' existing. Was it a mythological creature existing in the imagination of men after all!

However, about noon the 'West' came into view and this is how it

Minnehaha Falls Between Minneapolis and Ft. Snelling
Reached via 'Albert Lea Route'

appeared:- a large drove of cattle, around a hundred more or less, were being driven from St Peter's, near the Minnesota River, through countryside with no fields, hedges or fences, only a few houses scattered here and there. I asked a Westener who sat by me, why were so many cattle to be seen together? 'They are the town's cattle going out to the grassland,' he said. 'Over there you can see a man on horseback; he is the one responsible for them. The cattle-owners pay him per head of cattle for his work.' It was the same setting, in general, afterwards on the prairies because there are no hedges or anything else dividing farm from farm or field from field. Every farmer turns his animals onto the common land, whilst men or even some children, together with their dogs, look after them. The cowmen have to make sure that the corn and oat crops are not trampled on but apart from this exception, they are allowed to claim the entire land. They can drive their animals wherever there is good pasture. The sight of one drove after another reminded me of the anecdotes held about the people from the Orient and the patriarchs of yore directing their flocks to places where the grass was plentiful.

Oh! such expanse of land I could see from Minnesota! Land, land! land! as far as the eye could see – in all directions; limitless land, yes indeed, much greater than the ocean. The sea can disappear from sight and the horizon can show up close, yet the prairies extend further than the eye can see. It is amazing how this gigantic land was planned when time began. The eye does not have complete satisfaction when looking at the sea. There is always that feeling that it could see further if the edge of the sky could be lifted or drawn to one side. However, one look at this vast surface of land is adequate to make one say: 'enough'. Eyesight's scope can only stretch so far; it has no power to see further. The outlying visible distance vanishes without ceremony, not immediately as happens with the sea; it just gradually melts away tenderly and lovingly. Nature arranges a thin grey veil embellished with an appealing yellow tint over the far outline and at dusk it blushes into a delightful, loving and serene 'goodnight'.

The land is not completely flat. It rises into hills or rather gradual mounds, undulating gently like the ocean's waves. The few buildings one sees are encircled by bushes or rows of poplar, cottonwood, maple and other trees – all planted by man, apart from some shrubs which nature has provided alongside the streams. All this scenery conveys a pleasant impression. It is around these parts that one finds the immigration flow these days. When the region will be well populated and brought up to a high level of cultural standard with farm boundaries created and fields, buildings, towns, main roads, mansions and fruitful orchards arranged on the land, one can be certain that this area will be quite outstanding. St Peter's (population 4,000) is a fairly new and beautiful town and is arranged in a scattered format in a paradisean glade full of groves, four hundred and thirty six miles west of Chicago. We crossed the Minnesota River with its hilly surroundings and splendid trees. This valley has a very pleasant demeanour inasmuch as it cuts off the monotonous uniformity of the prairies.

Troublesome Events

About twenty-nine miles west of St Peter's, New Ulm is situated (population 3,000). Within and surrounding this town there is a colony of Germans. It is said that the first settlers consisted of 'Freethinkers', a race of atheists and that their hatred towards all kinds of religions was so great that they vowed that they would oppose any religious building being erected in their midst. After a time, when people who were religious moved in, such was the opposition of the atheists towards the suggestion of a place of worship being built, that the military had to be brought in to repress them. By now, there are two Protestant Chapels and one Catholic Church in the town. The ungodliness of these people, according to some, was the cause of heavy judgements being imposed on the inhabitants from time to time. It was here in 1862 that the terrible massacre by the Indians occurred. Many men, women and children were killed in cold blood. The people fled from the vicinity. The Indians too, afraid of reprisal, did not come near for some time. Because of this episode, the town was made up of furnished houses, shops and warehouses full of goods but without a living soul in it. It was the white people, escorted by soldiers, who ventured back first of all. A fortress was built but the Indians kept attacking ferociously but unsuccessfully. After defeating the Indians and capturing three to four hundred of them as prisoners, General Sibley was afraid to take his captives through New Ulm in case there would be a riot; therefore, he took an alternative route. However, they encountered crowds of women and children and in spite of threats from the General, these women and children managed to shower the heads of the redskins with stones.

Swarms of grasshoppers (locusts) had often descended on this region, as well as other parts of the north-west, causing much destruction. The 'Cincinnati Commercial' correspondent describes them thus:

the following day I travelled through three swarms of them, each one covering a spread of around half a mile. In the house where I stopped for lunch, the farmer was in utter despair whilst his wife and daughter wept and clapped their hands in deep anguish. Their farm was in the path of the destroyers and as I walked with the family towards the ripening wheat field, I saw thousands and thousands of the insects plummeting down upon the crop with a roaring commotion. In front of them were green prairies and yellow meadows full of corn. Behind them blackness, desolation and demise transpired. I saw them at another time in larger swarms, flying higher up in the sky, shining in the sun's rays like pieces of white and yellow paper.

Hurricanes and hailstones had also brought disaster to these parts. The most violent storm was when New Ulm was battered by ferocious gales on the afternoon of 15th July 1881, only a few days after I had left the area. Roads and buildings were shattered almost completely. Terraces of three or four houses were wiped out without any trace of foundations. At least, thirty-two lives were lost then and many more were injured. Six people were so affected that they went mad because of the turmoil, the panic and the tension. Animals were killed and horses flung through the air by the force of the storm. It was reported that one live horse had been found trapped in some branches the following morning. The storm peaked about five o'clock in the afternoon when complete darkness prevailed throughout the town. A thunder and lightning storm erupted with such uproar that it sounded as if the clouds were scrambling and groaning. Soon afterwards, different objects were whirling through the air, namely: houses, hayricks, dishes; also animals, chickens, geese, turkeys – all tangled up. Shingles, rafters and furniture also hurled about in the gales, thus creating a rattling pandemonium. Suddenly, the rain poured down clashing with the lightning and the clatter of the thunder. The roar of the wind, the screams of men, women and children, the bleating of animals and the neighing of the horses created such a horrendous scene that it made the satanical situation appear like the end of the world. The great uproar lasted about twenty minutes and the destruction covered an area of approximately two miles.

About seven miles from here is the most western point of the Welsh settlement of Blue Earth County. The Welsh here as well as many other good people in the surrounding area were at the periphery of the turbulent events and they did suffer losses as a consequence. They lost lives in the massacre inflicted by the Indians and were affected by the plague of the locusts and the storms. As far as the locusts were concerned, they had retreated many years ago. They had vanished instantly, not gradually like in other districts. I asked what was the reason for their disappearance? All they could tell me was that something strange, mystical and unexplainable had dispersed them. They had all disappeared together as if by agreement. One man stated that he thought they went away because the saints' prayers had been answered. 'Did the saints pray in a particular manner for them to disappear?' I asked. 'Yes,' he answered. 'The state's governor sent out a proclamation that a day of obedience and prayer be kept to ask God to redeem them of this plague and after that we were never troubled.'

Western Towns

On this line of railroad one finds a village almost every twelve miles and although they have only recently been built, one finds that all merchandise in their shops is comparable in price to that found further east, with produce (corn and animals) being despatched to eastern markets. As well as dwellings, there are workshops, shops, storehouses, inns, chapels and schools in these hamlets. Two local weekly newspapers, affiliated to the two political parties in the country, are printed in the area. The residents are diligent, enterprising and honest; maybe the last adjective should not describe all land merchants and innkeepers! The people in these remote areas are aware that this land is being populated very rapidly and that there are opportunities here in all kinds of occupations. Moral standards are high, mainly because the people are happy, industrious and committed to living honourable lives. They have plenty of space, therefore they do not have to intrude on each other and consequently no jealousy or malice erupts. There is no tendency in their midst for pilfering. People who are that way inclined, as well as other kinds of wrongdoers, prefer to lurk in cities or other more populated areas where spoils and takings are more plentiful. Be mindful that the area described covers new towns in the western agricultural region. As far as new towns in industrial areas are concerned, ones which are developing into important centres for commerce and traffic, the scene is different. Although the majority of people in these areas are also honourable, these places do have 'nests' where wild characters such as drunks, thieves, gamblers and the like settle.

Somewhere, on the other side of New Ulm is 'Sleepy Eye'. This place is situated near a lake of the same name. Some locations have very strange names. In Pennsylvania, I travelled through 'Bird in Hand' and in Iowa through 'Last Chance'. In Nevada one finds 'You Bet a Red Dog'; very euphonious names also, such as 'Shickshinny' and 'Kittakattakon'. For that matter, we ourselves have place names that are unsurpassable. One supervisor, when I was handing my licence to him on the train, asked me for my address. I gave it to him: Llanfihangel-y-Creuddyn. 'Thlan what? Say it again, please, if you can remember it,' he said with an expression of surprise, laughter and puzzlement. On offering to write the name down for him, he pulled out a sheet of foolscap paper and asked if it was large enough!

As we approached Walnut Grove, the homesick travellers hoped to see some woodland but it appeared that nobody had thought of planting any trees along the way. The name Walnut Grove, a delightful sounding name, was a wishful-thinking prophecy in this barren region. If the village had been named Walnut Grove City, the American element would be absolutely correct! Near Tracy, a young expanding town, there is a small colony of Welsh people. Eight miles south of this town one finds a lovely scene of many lakes, maybe the best in the state. This is the homestead of the water-duck, the Turkish kite and numerous blue herons.

In Search of a Domain

After departing from Tracy, we were facing lands which had come on the market recently. The land supervisors of the railroad companies walked through the train to get accustomed to the passengers who were focusing on viewing and purchasing land. Most of the passengers had this objective in mind. Apart from a few young couples, the majority were young men. I enjoyed observing the expressions on the faces of these people as I tried to understand their feelings and hopes on this journey. They were on the verge of settling on these uninhabited, distant prairies with only land and sky to welcome them. I can see a young lad and a young girl, a couple so it seems, well-attired and presenting an appearance of good upbringing. They both appear as a solemn, serious pair, especially the girl. She spends most of her time sleeping beside the lad. Occasionally she peers through the window at the vast landscape; thereafter leaning back with her eyes shut. When the supervisor comes through, they show him their land-inquisition tickets. They revealed themselves to me as a couple who had left comfortable homes in a populated suburban area; a pair who had said goodbye to guiding, watchful parents in order to row their own boat on life's large ocean. Another seat was occupied by a more modestly dressed young couple, nevertheless they were jolly and full of mischief. It was the girl who was most excitable though. They also had land-inquisition tickets and they appeared to me as diligent and thrifty youngsters on an adventure that involved spending money they had previously earned on a piece of land in order to be in each other's company. Again, sharing the same seating area was a family – young parents with four small children. The two older ones had their eyes and noses fixed to the window with their never-ending 'whys' and 'wherefores': how were they able to build houses when there were no trees or stones anywhere? How were they able to have apples, peaches and cherries, as well as innumerable other questions. I was amazed at the mother's ability to answer all these questions so competently. Another two men with the same mission were also in our compartment. I judge these passengers as pioneers whose experiences and ventures will be recorded in future times – father and mother settlers in these localities. It is much easier to purchase land now than in times gone by. A generation ago, people who had crossed the ocean had to dwell in woods and live very far from conveniences such as railroads, towns and markets. The first period had to be persevered, living close to nature and sustaining themselves by cutting down trees and cultivating the soil. Nowadays, many parts of the country are linked by railroads.

Gwneir cerbydau cyn bod teithwyr, gwneir gorsafoedd cyn bod nwydd,
Gwneir o'r dwyrain i'r gorllewin yn dramwyfa ryfedd, rwydd.

(Trains are made before there are travellers, stations are built before the availability of merchandise,
Nowadays there is an amazing user-friendly passageway from east to west).

There is arable soil in these regions, ready for cultivation and farmland can be purchased either by the government, the railroad companies or land merchants. A field of sixty acres belonging to the government costs one and a quarter dollars or two and a half dollars per acre, depending on how near or how far it is from the railroad. A one hundred and sixty acre field can be purchased as a deal for planting trees on ten acres of it, or again the same acreage as a deal for residing on it for five years. Government land is the one that is grabbed first. I elaborate more extensively on this subject in my book: *HANES TALEITHIAU UNEDIG AMERICA A'R CYMRY YNDDYNT.* (THE HISTORY OF THE UNITED STATES OF AMERICA AND THE WELSH LIVING IN THEM).

Dakota's Territory

The area that joins Minnesota and Dakota is more hilly than other areas I have noticed on this railroad. To me, the territory appears mountainous although one cannot say it is an actual mountain either. It appears so, I believe, because of the absence of buildings and distributed and cultivated land. After passing Gary, the first town in Dakota, the land surface becomes more level again. Whilst standing in Chicago and Milwaukee stations and seeing crowds of foreigners: Germans, Norwegians, Swedes, Poles, Irish and so on, cramming train after train for the west and on reading in the newspapers that as many as 20,000 such foreigners travelled weekly through Chicago alone, I became concerned that the country would be overflowing very soon. However, after arriving in the West and witnessing the unlimited land surface, I wondered where people would come from to inhabit this sector. I was also curious to know the destination of the Norwegians, Swedes and others since I could only find Americans in these towns and villages, that is, apart from a few newcomers.

After travelling ninety-three miles beyond Tracy, a distance of six hundred and nineteen miles from Chicago, I found myself in Watertown, on the banks of the Sioux River, a place where this branch of railroad terminates. This town's first building was erected in March 1879 and when I was here in June 1881, there were 30 shops, 2 journalistic offices, 7 hotels, 3 churches, 2 banks, 1 grain elevator, 5 timber yards and 1 school – an aggregate value of four thousand dollars. Every amenity was accessible to the townspeople and the folk of the surrounding area. Orderly streets and even mansions were being constructed. Watertown is an example of a progression of new towns which are built alongside the railroads that infiltrate through the various districts in the West. The townspeople and people residing in the surrounding area are well provided for.

There is fertile countryside and beautiful scenery around Watertown. Amongst the many lakes there is one not too remote called 'Punished Woman's Lake' – a translation from an Indian name. An Indian Chief had a beautiful daughter who was loved by two young Chiefs. She was in love with one but her father made her marry the other one. She instinctively fled with the man of her own choice resulting in her husband arming himself and mounting his horse to hunt down the two runaways and he vowed that he would not give up until he had delivered revenge on them both. After being unsuccessful in his search for months on end, he ascended a hillock to have one last glance before returning to his own district. He saw nobody but after descending on the other side he came across the couple sleeping lovingly in each other's arms. Maybe too magnanimous to attack them while they were asleep, he shouted at the pair to arouse them and forewarned the young man to prepare for battle. The young man clutched his weapon and jumped up. He strived to overcome his opponent. Alas, he was not strong enough to hold out against his enraged rival and he was fatally wounded. The man, thinking that he had also killed the girl, returned to his kinfolk and told them what he had done. The old Chief, very vexed to hear this news, hastened towards the location of the bloodshed only to find that the girl was not there. He followed her trail of blood until he came to the lake and there he found her body. He consecrated the bloody path with paving stones and henceforth the lake has been called 'The Lake of the Punished Woman'.

The Journey to Huron

To reach the other branch of the *Chicago and North Western* line, I had to return as far as Tracy, then journey west two hundred and fifty-five miles to Fort Pierre on the banks of the Missouri River. Beyond the James River, the route as far as Huron exposed magnificent views. Some parts consisted of vast level plains as previously described. However, it was towards Lake Benton, on the border of Minnesota and Dakota that I observed the most beautiful scenery – crystal clear lakes, lovely bushes, open prairies, small plains, sloping hillocks and captivating peaks which the Welsh admire so much. The entire landscape was a symmetry of natural delights complementing each other in a homely manner, thus pleasantly portraying the wonderment of nature. Oh! if only the Welsh had come over early enough to seize these places. No doubt similar regions are still available from the government but one thing is sure, they have to be snatched immediately, otherwise it will be too late.

We were asked, as usual, which travellers wished to have supper in Huron and an order for the people requesting the meal was handed in. Alas, supper was not meant to be that evening. When our train was crossing a large, waterlogged bog – a place where it is impossible to step outside – we were prevented from proceeding because a goods train had derailed a few hours earlier and was blocking our pathway. We were held up at this point from six o'clock in the evening to six in the morning. There was not a single light as an indication of a dwelling in any direction. Many people were having hunger pangs and much food was waiting to be served in Huron. We were too remote to do anything about the situation that evening. The cooks in Huron were peering through their latticed windows and thinking: 'why was the train so delayed? Why had the wheels slowed down?' The moon was looking down on us and took it upon itself to amuse us by calling on the earth and the stars to join it in a game of 'hide and seek'. By midnight, the moon appeared to have pulled a purple covering over its surface and it was impossible to see a fraction of it for a while despite a clear sky. I believe the earth reciprocated too, because its light also diminished before thousands of stars emerged as if trying to find them both. The stars opened their eyes and twinkled fervently. I saw stars that I had never noticed before, even when there was a full moon. They seemed to be playing and dancing but when the moon reappeared, they passed out of sight. Dawn broke and the earth was full of cheerfulness and by the time the grand sun, father of all time, emerged out of its sphere, both moon and stars had disappeared. The route was now clear for us to proceed and we felt the wheels turning and after hours of fasting we delighted ourselves, not with the moon and the stars playing bo-peep with us, but with thoughts

77

of the cooks laying the breakfast tables in Huron.

A little before reaching Huron we crossed James River or Dakota River by its old name. There is much reverence towards this valley because it has excellent soil for immigrants. It is towards this river that the flow of many nationalities focuses these days. As far as the Welsh are concerned, they are usually the last to come forward to seek such privileges – 'the day after the fair'. Railroads are constructed along the valley from north to south. If several families from Wales agreed to emigrate to a western part of America and settle as a large colony in one of the fertile glades of the West, where there are railroads and towns and where every necessary convenience will soon be available for everyone's benefit, it would be one of the best blessings that could come their way. Several men of intellect and experience should visit the different regions in order to make wise decisions in this respect. I shall elaborate more on this subject in my next book. At present, let's continue with my travels.

Prairie, Prairie

Soon after we departed from Huron, we started a long journey over a bare and unvarying prairie. Between Huron and Fort Pierre, a distance of one hundred and twenty miles, there were only eight stopping places for the train – ones numbered: Siding No.1, Siding No.2 and so on, with nothing in these sidings except a tiny house for use by track workers. Apart from the house mentioned, there was no dwelling or hayrick, no earth or woodland, no field or hedge, no sea or mountain, no hill or valley, no lake or stream, no human or animal – only land, land, massive land within eyeshot in all directions. I overheard someone ask where were the birds; another answering that birds prefer to gather in populated areas. I do not know whether this is true or not. I can say that I do not remember ever seeing a bird in these distant lands. Because of this fact and the absolute silence, stillness and uniformity of the landscape, I felt as if I was in a world stranger and more inaccessible than when on the ocean. On a sea voyage, one observes the birds, the fish and the movement of the waves with its many variations. This territory compared more to a large, still oceanic bed than a sector of Minnesota. When on water though, one can view a few buildings, woods and other objects that transmit a picture of life and activity in the distance but because of the deprivation of such sights on these prairies, the horizon continually appeared near to us and we were assuming all the time that we were travelling along a valley. The terrain appeared to be gradually rising away from us in every direction. At one time, I believed that we had proceeded as far as had been visible, that we were at the farthest spot and that we would start our downward journey on the other side soon. Yet, in spite of advancing and advancing, the furthest point did not appear nearer at all. Alongside this route, a variety of herbs and beautiful flowers were growing – an assortment unique to that landscape.

Since this road did not disclose any alteration in scenery, there was nothing at all to amuse me for the present and my mind wondered back to the past to seek what subject matter would flash before my eyes. Alas, I could not think of anything worthwhile apart from the creation of the world – no earthquakes, no volcanos and no floods – only the progression of nature and the occasional visitations of herds of buffaloes with some barbaric people hunting them. My thoughts then steered towards the future. I visualised the scene in the twenty-first century: the entire countryside is adorned with towns, roads, farms, small and large buildings, trees with birds singing on their branches; orchards with boughs curving with the weight of fruit. I envisaged fields full of corn undulating in the ticklish breeze, similar to the ocean's waves; animals grazing and frolicking nearby; elderly people and youngsters filling the roads; the sound of song and acclamation rising from the temples; success and joy, sadness and sorrow descending on this country, the same as in other countries. Amongst all this, I imagined a mother having a conversation with her two small children whilst sitting outside her house in the shade of a maple tree.

'What is a hill, mother?' asked one of the children.

'I have never seen one,' was the answer. 'Granny saw some when she was little though. A hill is an elevation similar to an earth-mound where potatoes are kept underground to shield them from frost in the winter, except that a hill is much larger than that. It is higher than this house; higher than Owen Pugh's barn. A mountain is higher than that even.'

'Well,' said the child, after considering his mother's reply: 'the potatoes kept in hills must be as large as pumpkins and ones kept in mountains as large as barrels. What is a river, mother?'

'A river is a large stretch of water which has made a bed for itself along a valley in order to flow over the land, similar to water in a wheel's track after it has rained. I remember when I was a little girl, whilst on a visit to Aunt Mary, seeing the James River; this one was an exceptionally large river, as wide as this house.'

'Dear! dear!' Johnnie remarked: 'where do you find a well so big that it contains that much water and where do you find a wheel so powerful that it can be brought to the surface? May I go to see Aunt Mary so that I can see a river, mother?'

'You and Susy can go when you are older, that is, if you are good.'

After an exchange of questions and answers about lakes, rocks, waterfalls and many other phenomena, away went the two children to create mounds – pretending they were hills. To invent rivers, they let water run through the finger-marked ridges they had created.

Ranches

A few miles before we arrived near the Missouri River, the landscape became a mixture of rocky hills, sharp ravines and narrow valleys with rapid streams running between steep banks. A farmhouse appeared on a high slope on the right and on a fertile meadow on the left, a large herd of cattle came into view. The cattle were owned by a Mr Read and this area as well as the herd were referred to as 'Read's Ranch'. A ranch is a large farm owned by one man or a company. On some there are thousands of cattle; on others thousands of sheep and on some thousands of a mixture of animals. They are kept summer and winter on the prairies, the same as the sheep of Wales are kept on Welsh mountains. Some harsh winters claim heavy losses and it was said that the owner of the ranch that was not in view had lost over five hundred cattle the previous winter. Many of these ranchers are being robbed by Indians and white people alike. The animals are taken to the markets in summer and in spite of huge losses, ranching is a very profitable business. Where there is no boundary on the grazing meadows, many animals wander afar.

Once a year they have a 'round up' when the ranchers gather all the animals together in different locations. Afterwards, they are all taken to one central place where the animals are claimed by their owners according to the stamp-mark on their skins. The life of ranchers is a strange one; they live in remote places, scores of miles from the nearest neighbour and although they are targets of much danger from Indians and others, they themselves are also considered dangerous and troublesome as far as new settlers are concerned. When land that has been farmed by ranchers, but owned by the government, is sold, the ranchers feel anger towards the incomers who arrive in their country and unless the settlers constitute a strong colony able to defend its rights, it is not entirely safe for settlers to meet up with ranchers.

Fort Pierre

We ascended alongside the bank of the Missouri River and arrived in Fort Pierre. Not much can be said about the river in this place apart from its slow flow and brown colour. It is about a mile and a quarter in width. What a town Fort Pierre is – both ends of it: such toil, such buildings, such seizing of opportunities! Less than a year ago, I was told, it was a mere village comprising about half a dozen houses. I believe I can count hundreds, if not a thousand, homes here now. Some are made of brick and some of wood; they are of varying shapes and patterns: some with frames, some with boarded sides, some with planks or intertwined wood as roofing material: some held up with poles pounded into the ground and intertwined with branches before being covered with clay. Others would have been built entirely of turfs.

Many families lived in tents as well as in waggons covered with white canvas. I was there on a Sunday and the sound of construction work was heard even on this day. Wood was being sawn and transportation of building material was taking place. Movement of mules and horses was apparent too. Shouts, cracking of whips and all kinds of noises were heard until the whole neighbourhood resounded. One large shop was full of boxes, sacks, furniture and other goods, all piled up like peat-stacks; in the meantime, the shopkeeper and his staff were organising the house. Furniture could be seen stacked up in many places and in front of one shop a carriage was being assembled. Adjacent to the town or campsite or any other place of dwelling, pet animals of every colour and size could be seen; some in fine shape, others not so well cared for – the entire scene resembled that of a fairground. Amongst people living in this region were Dutchmen with their waggons full of merchandise. Dutchmen! Who are they! They are not Germans but Indian farmers. These people are judged by another Indian tribe (ones of a more savage nature, who spend their time warmongering) as a subordinate class of people because they take on the work of squaws. I do not know why they were called Dutchmen, unless they thought they were similar to German settlers – tilling the land. These people, especially the ladies, in spite of having ruddy complexions, paint their faces with some kind of bright red colouring. The government allocates land to these people and they are provided with houses, animals, furniture and everything necessary for agricultural purposes; some of them make a very good living. Their reservation is on the other side of the river. The reason for this amazing assemblage of people in Fort Pierre is the construction of the railroad through to the Black Hills where very profitable leadmines are now in operation. Deadwood, the nearest place west from Fort Pierre, is the town that people aim for. As yet, the railroad only reaches Fort Pierre, the remainder of the journey is accomplished in stages. Heavy commodities are transported from Fort Pierre to the Black Hills in a line of large waggons – six or seven connected to each other as one train, with eight or nine pairs of horned oxen pulling it. Joggle, joggle is how this conveyance travels along, night and day over the lonely, remote prairies. I was surprised to see the whips which the drivers clasped – a kind of rough, heavy rope made of leather, tapering towards the front and about fifteen feet in length. The driver held on to a long piece of wood which had this narrow strip of tough leather connected to it. He would whirl this rope two or three times around his head before flinging it until it landed on the back of one of the animals until the poor creature writhed from the swipe. Fort Pierre was a very ungodly place then. The inhabitants' faces characterized the appearance of cold-bloodedness and drinking, gambling and other vices were conspicuous everywhere. Most of the residents had come from all quarters of the globe during the previous four months – nobody knowing a soul beforehand but were to be neighbours from then on. This town, situated on the bank of the Missouri and on the line which connects the Black Hills with the east, has a very promising future. What a marvellous place for adventurers, a place of great potential for commercial opportunists and people with special skills. The eagles also converge where there is carcass! This location is seven hundred and eighty-one miles west of Chicago.

The Journey to Mitchel

Mitchel is only fifty-five miles from Fort Pierre. In spite of this short distance, it was not possible for me to travel between the two towns without making a detour of almost eight hundred miles. I returned on the same road as I had advanced as far as Waseca – a journey of three hundred and eighty miles. I then went south to Albert Lea, a young town in beautiful country with vast hunting grounds and lakes full of fish. Indeed, this line to Iowa is surrounded by amazing scenery. In Mason City I decided to go west, passing Clear Lake – a fascinating and well-known place. I travelled through Algona, Emmetsburgh and other smaller locations. I arrived in Spencer and went on a journey of twenty miles north to observe spectacular countryside comprising crystal-clear lakes and exceptional scenery. Spirit, East Okoboji and West Okoboji are the most famous of the lakes – each one about six miles long. Their waters are encompassed with coarse, minute gravel and in some places by rocky, steep banks. The landscape is adorned with verdant bushes of maple, oak, cedar, elm and other attractive trees. The waters are alive with different varieties of fish and the adjacent area with quails, wild geese, herons, swans and pelicans. Occasionally, the light-footed stag can be seen leaping about over the prairies or amongst the woods.

The view from Lake West Okoboji is equal to any on earth. About twelve miles south of Spencer there is a prosperous Welsh colony in an area commended for its good land which can be purchased for a reasonable price. There are also many seasonal and spiritual opportunities in this district. From Spencer I went to Mitchel Dakota, one hundred and fifty miles west. This town, at the time, was only a little over two years old, yet it was progressing rapidly towards a more sizeable place – forever extending its boundaries. It is located in fertile land about seven miles west of the James River. The landscape is neither level nor hilly but 'rolling' – entirely without trees though. Slightly west of Mitchel there are several Welsh families who have acquired their entitlements and soon there will be a settlement in this region too.

From Mitchel to the City of Columbus
Returning on the same road, I stopped in Rock River Valley in order to be able to walk on my own over the prairies of Sioux and Lyon counties – the north-west corner of the state of Iowa. After throwing a satchel containing food over my shoulder and holding a walking-stick in my hand, I turned my back on the town and very soon only my head and shoulders were visible in the long, undulating grass. I could not help thinking of the prairie wolf, the badger and the coiled snake. I did not encounter any living animal though, only birds. I ended my adventure near the Rock River. I am not sure how many rocks are embedded in this river in other areas, but there are not many in this location. The ground rises gradually and splendidly on each side of the riverbanks. Herbs and other plants were growing on the surrounding land making it obvious that the land was fertile.

After reaching the train I noticed two gentlemen distributing literature. One approached me and asked: 'Are you travelling in the cause of temperance?'

'No.'

'Are you a preacher?'

'Yes, is that what you are?'

'We do not appoint preachers but are of the opinion that if one of us has the talent to evangelize, then he is at liberty to do so. Therefore, I am the one who preaches whilst my brother is not a preacher.'

'To what denomination do you belong?'

'To the Comrades, or the people who are called Quakers.'

'You dress the same as members of the public.'

'Yes, this is how George Fox[4] himself did; he dressed according to the fashion of the times. Living without any egotism, in the simple style of the period, is the belief of our religion. Some people hold on too long to the homage of the George Fox era, losing sight of the religious principles practised by George Fox.'

'It is said that you, the Quakers, are very righteous and honest people. Is this part of the country of such calibre that people from the east and overseas consider it to be a sound location for settling?'

'Yes, without a doubt, especially towards Millcreek in O'Brien county. You should see this region. It is good because the land is so fertile. Admirable people live there and the settlement terms are very acceptable. You must forewarn people in case they are tricked into buying land without acceptable regulations attached to it.'

By now, I was tired and ready for a rest. I hoped my aunt, my father's sister, would be able to accommodate me and with this in mind I travelled two hundred miles off course to Columbus City. After reaching McGregor, I went south along the west bank of the Mississippi, through Dubuque (population 23,000) to Davenport (population 22,000). This route disclosed a variety of scenery – craggy rocks on the right and amiable islands on the left. After arriving in Columbus City, I discovered that my aunt and her family had left years ago. I did not feel like staying with strangers, therefore I resolved to keep going and devote myself to my mission.

The Speech of the Train

By now, I was travelling towards the north-east. In Muscatine I found myself again on the banks of the Mississippi and of all the sightings of it, this is where I saw the river at its best. Its amazing width dotted with attractive green islands impressed me as the most beautiful river I had ever seen. Through Rock Island (population 12,000), Savana, Freeport, Beloit and Elkhorn I eventually arrived in Milwaukee. After experiencing such inconsistency in the level of the ground on this journey and having exercised my duty of socialising with new passengers, I became entirely oblivious of my surroundings. I was in complete limbo, engrossed in meditation. The continuous and monotonous clacking of the wheels and the rails fell on my ears in apparitions of words. How did the perception materialize that American partridges said 'Bob-Bob-White' and other birds 'Whip-poor-Will', and the owl in Wales was saying '*ceirch-du-du-du-yn-fy-nghwdyn-i?* (black-black-black-oats-in-my-sack)?' How did it come about that thousands of people were so foolish as to believe that trees, rocks, buildings, images and so forth spoke certain words and were able to communicate with mankind. Everyone seemed to be under the illusion that they were superhuman oracles or gods? One ˙can be bewildered for a long time by the ceaseless noise of the train and wonder why it is possessed with such folly. The never-ending words some trains would chant would be: '*paid-bod-yn-grac; paid-bod-yn-grac* (don't-be-angry, don't-be-angry).' The speech of another would be: 'rattle-and-rout-the-rat, rattle-and-rout-the-rat.' On my travels I heard many such utterances, full of hard consonants. After realising that the train was bound by certain words, it was impossible to imagine it saying anything else. The endless words this time were: 'a-Yankee-trick, a-Yankee-trick.' Whilst I listened to these repetitive dictions clacking away every second and at the same time half-heartedly watching objects rushing backwards, I suddenly saw a horse brandishing his front hoof in the air whilst the rest of his body was totally immobilized; at the same time, another horse could not stand up. The passengers rushed to the windows. The train stopped for a minute. A doctor stepped out and then we immediately went on our way. A man and two women travelling in a waggon pulled by two horses were crossing the railroad when our train crashed into them. They were thrown into different directions by the impact. No-one was killed on the spot but what transpired afterwards I never found out. I was disturbed by this accident for a while but when my emotions calmed down, I realised that the wheels and the rails were still taunting each other or someone else by such utterances as: 'a-yankee-trick, a-yankee-trick,' because of what had happened. That is a summary of my journey. A wiser man would report less dissipation. There is a saying though that it is the dunce who discloses the truth!

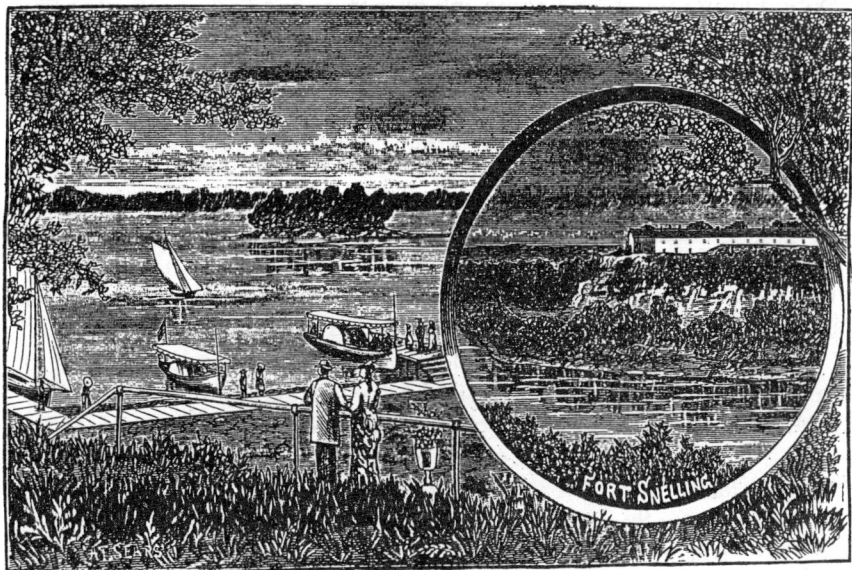

Cedar Lake and Fort Snelling (Minn)
Reached via 'Albert Lea Route'

A Journey to North-West Michigan

From Milwaukee I proceeded across the borders of Winnebago to Appleton (population 9,000), a place situated on the banks of the Fox River, where there is a good source of water energy for practical purposes. Consequently, there are different kinds of mills and many manufacturing plants employing manual labour established here. Twenty-nine miles northwards, after passing De Pere, I arrived in Fort Howard and Green Bay (population 8,000) – the two places facing each other over the Fox River as it flows into Green Bay on Lake Michigan. From this place I travelled another twenty-nine miles to Oconto (population 4,000). There was nothing interesting to view on this route, apart from an occasional village. We could only see trees and more trees for scores of miles. For quite a distance tree stumps and relics of dead wood were the scene. The grass was green and saplings fifteen feet high were posing full of esteem and joyfulness of summer – all with green, healthy foliage. As far as the old trees were concerned the seasons did not affect them – be it summer or winter. Their gentleness had left them; they appeared lifeless: 'they shall not awake, nor be raised out of their sleep' – (Job 14,12). These trees are positioned in large groups and their foundations are charcoal-black in colour with their thin, bare, long branches reaching out in a very weary manner in all directions. They continuously mutter: 'over here and over there and that way the big fires occurred in 1871' – blazes which destroyed hundreds of miles of Wisconsin and Michigan woodlands. About the same time also, the large city of Chicago was burnt down. Right in the centre of this massive forest fire stood the town of Oconto as well as many other villages that had been totally destroyed. I could not see any traces of fire-damage in these places now though. Nevertheless, fire was still a danger and could play havoc if it happened again in this area since the houses and many other possessions were made of wood. The roads are paved with sawdust and near every station piles of beams, boards, shingles, posts, railroad ties and so on, are packed ready to be transported to the markets.

Many of the villagers are employed in the production of charcoal for the blast-furnaces which appear in the region bordering on Lake Superior. The charcoal houses have white exteriors and are arranged in rows – ten to fifteen in a line – each one circular as if the upper halves of the cornstacks or ricks found in Wales had been placed on the ground. Around their footings there are holes for the smoke to escape. Charcoal is produced somehow by burning wood very slowly in these buildings. The other side of the utilized woodland, pine, cedar and other evergreen trees grow in abundance – their beauty prevailing both in summer and winter.

These parts are known as the pineries and most of the pinewood used in this country comes from this area.

After travelling through Peshtigo, Marinette and Menominee (where I crossed the river from Wisconsin to Michigan) and several other villages, I arrived in Escanaba (population 3,000), a lively, small town but an important one, thriving by means of its wood-markets but mostly through its ironworks. The region from this point northwards to Lake Superior is rich in ironore. Escanaba is situated two hundred and forty-three miles north of Milwaukee. Its harbour, on Lake Michigan, could contain all of the world's battleships. Its three iron dockyards are almost two miles long and have the capacity to hold 55,000 tons of ironore and 1,200 cars can be loaded there daily. The railroad company, *Chicago and North Western*, has 2,700 cars and 55 steamengines used entirely for these purposes. As well as the mentioned industries, these surroundings also attract tourists. Amongst the dense woodland, stag hunting is popular as well as the hunting of bears and other animals. The children of Nimrod[5] like to hunt them all!

My next journey was through rough, hilly countryside and although trees grew everywhere, iron was the product the government was interested in. By the time I was in Negaunee (population 4,000) sixty-two miles north of Escanaba, it appeared that the inhabitants only worked in the iron industry. Most of the ironore was dispatched as soon as it was mined. Ishpeming (population 7,000), a town nearby, is the most productive of all the places supplying this metal. Another forty-two miles farther and I was in Marquette (population 7,000) on the banks of Lake Superior, the father of all waters, and the largest of all the lakes in the world. This town is beautiful, clean and flourishing and the encircling countryside – the lake, its waters and the grounds are of immense interest to anyone interested in nature. The wilderness and the simplicity are the way they were devised by the Creator. Over on the clear lake one sees many wooded islands and fishermen's boats with some steamboats belonging to visitors sailing along too. The shores have not been affected, as yet, by man's intrusion. The red man, child of the forest, can be found without going very far. He is harmless in this region as a result of the teachings delivered by the Catholic missionaries here. Many generations of these missionaries lived very patiently in wigwams in order to educate these people. On my return to Milwaukee, I landed in Fond-du-lac (population 13,000) at the south side of Lake Winnebago. I then went east to Sheboygan and back – a round trip of eighty-six miles.

The Circuit of Minnesota's Festival

After almost a month of travelling from place to place to see the formation and wonders of the countryside, I resumed my preaching duties throughout the catchment of 'Minnesota's Festival'. Where I began is called 'The Institution of the Large Forest'. As it happens only half of the area has large trees, the other half is a prairie. From this area I travelled twenty miles south to the Welsh settlement of Blue Earth. I was in Lake Crystal, nearby, when the news reached us that President Garfield had been shot and I was in Mankato (population 6,000) at the east end of the settlement on the noted date of July 4th, 'The National Day of the United States'. On this day the 'Declaration of Independence' is read out; patriotic speeches are delivered and exhibitions depicting happy situations are set up. This time, however, there was no rejoicing in Mankato, nor any other town throughout the Union. It was more like a funeral day. The entire country was grieving because this important man, its Prince, had been injured.

From these parts I had something like a hundred miles to travel before reaching the settlement of Lime Springs which is between the states of Minnesota and Iowa – a region with very beautiful countryside. Whilst staying in this area on July 15th, New Ulm was destroyed by a whirlwind and I endured the most atrocious storm of thunder and lightning which was followed by a gale and torrential rain. A cloudburst had occurred and I had never experienced anything like it. As a consequence of this storm, I could see the saplings and the maize spread out flat on the ground. From this place I went north for one hundred and thirty-two miles to Minneapolis wherefrom I undertook: ANOTHER JOURNEY TO DAKOTA, across the state of Minnesota, through an amazing expanse of wheat fields – crop after crop and meadow after meadow – as far as the eye could see in all directions. These parts were more hilly than the most southern part of the state, therefore my vision was limited. In a very short time, a small workforce would transform a large field of rolling wheat into round sheaves stacked on the ground. The cutting machines are pulled by three horses standing side by side. Two types of machines are used; both are operated by wheels made of similar planks except that the ones used to fan the winnowing machines are larger, higher and lighter. These planks, whilst they rotate, cause the straw to tilt forward and fall onto the machine's platform as it is being sliced. On this platform two men stand, ready to tie the straw into sheaves. The staff are just two harvest workers and a driver; both machines are called 'the harvester'. There is another kind called the 'self-binder'. Only the driver operates this one. He tends to the horses and the machine controls the wheat – its cutting, gathering into sheaves and the tight binding. The most objectionable aspect of this machine is the wire used to bind the sheaves. The wire is an obstacle when threshing and also a problem when the animals are fed with straw. Nowadays, string is used instead of wire and the machine operating this invention is very useful.

Along the banks of the Minnesota River I travelled over the most western area of this state and after crossing the line to Dakota, I went quite quickly to the young, beautiful and developing town of Millbank where I descended and saw a vast expanse of very interesting grassland. Although I had travelled one hundred and ninety miles from Minneapolis, I still had eighty miles to go before reaching Brown county, the other side of the James River, where there is a young colony of Welsh people. Parts of this journey were over hills and rocks completely bereft of trees. Only occasionally were there any signs of inhabited dwellings.

Since the train stopped for quite a while in one place, I attempted to do a deal with an Indian for a pony he hoped to sell. We failed to agree on a price of course. He paraded on the pony's back while I praised him, through an interpreter, for his showmanship – thus we were both satisfied. There were more signs of habitation as we approached the James River. About two miles west of this river, the village of Bath is situated. It was only a month old at the time and there were only a few houses made of rough boards nailed haphazardly together there; other abodes were just tents. The main shop was a tent made up of white canvas, nevertheless it contained a variety of merchandise. Another building, with its lower half made of wooden boards and the upper half of canvas, was the hotel – a place always popular with travellers. Another long, low building is called the livery-stable, a very necessary building in the West since the land agents need to travel on horseback over the regions when deciding which farmlands to recommend.

Settling Down – The Beginning
Four miles north of Bath one finds a Welsh settlement, consisting mainly of people who had come from the region of Cambria, Wisconsin. On my journey to this area I saw a man ploughing some virgin land with a sulky plough drawn by three horses. The first house I called in was Mr Robert Rowlands' home. He was looked upon as an old settler since he had been there for more than a year but his family had only joined him two months before my arrival. His house was large and grand and much talk was made of his abode. It was considered big because the ground floor could be divided into two rooms by a partition made of canvas! The floor

was covered with boards and the inner walls were panelled with rough planks which were attached to a thick outer wall made of turfs in order to keep the family cosy at wintertime. The turfed roof also rested on a layer of planks. On another farm I met a man busy building an additional house with turfs so that he could transform the house he had already erected a few months earlier into a shelter for his animals. The next house I visited was occupied by six young men. They were recent newcomers; each one had acquired a farm and had agreed to build one dwelling to be shared by them all. In this house they would cook their meals, do their laundering and the reprimanding of each other! Their vision, however, was profit and reward since they hoped to transform each farm into a Garden of Eden which would be their paradise on sunny mornings after their retirement from hard, tiresome labour. I was informed that there were other houses of the same nature in the area. My next lodging-house was comparable, as far as comfort was concerned, to the one owned by Robert Rowlands. The head of the household told me that he himself had built it and he was of the opinion that he had planned it better than any skilled architect would have done. He stated that the boards he had used had dried out and shrunk after they were fitted and therefore half-inch grooves had appeared between the panels throughout the building and along the roof. Because of this occurrence, the house was well ventilated during the summer season. What about the winter? Cladding it with turfs of course and making it as secure as a wren's nest.

What kind of winters are experienced here? Stormy ones, so say people from afar; winters easily endured say the people who have lived here. Firewood and other fuel are not plentiful. Wood from the riverbank is sold for a high price and coal is obtainable at the station. The inhabitants plan to plant some bushes and rows of cottonwood, poplar, maple and other trees in the region – saplings which grow quickly. After a few years, the trees can be felled and the fuel problem will be solved. There is nothing to differentiate one farm from another except for some posts placed on corners by the government's land allocators and in some places by furrows marked out by the landowners' ploughs. As far as fields are concerned there are none yet. A length of maize can be seen here, a section of wheat over there and another crop yonder. Haymaking takes place without anyone's permission; it is a case of where hay can be found. The animals are released to join the communal herd as was before mentioned. One or two cows and a few working-horses are kept near the houses and very often they are tied up by a forty foot long lariat. They are the most pitiful of sights in the West when the weather is hot since they cannot escape to the shade. The land is flat with occasional gradual hillocks and the scenery, at times, is spectacular. The town of Columbia and other distant, obscure places, sometimes appear on the horizon as if they were quite near.

In Nebraska

My next destination was the state of Nebraska. After a roundabout journey of about nine hundred miles through Farmington, Austin, McGregor, Davenport and Des Moines, I came to a large and strange station called Transfer, near Council Bluffs, on the east side of the Missouri River. It is approximately at this point that the western and eastern states meet. On the east side of the station are the terminals of five or six of the largest railroads. On the west side, the famous railroad of the *Union Pacific* is based. Its route is over the Missouri to Omaha and along the Platte valley to the Rocky Mountains, the land of the saints and the vast West! Omaha (population 31,000) is situated on the west bank of the Missouri. In 1854, only a log cabin was here and it is said that a Welshman by the name of Jones was the town's first postmaster and that he kept the post in his hat. Apparently, he was a keen huntsman and people who were expecting mail had to chase the hat very often! Nowadays, the town has a proper Post Office and the adjacent buildings are very attractive. From here I travelled south for over a hundred miles to visit the Welsh settlement near Blue Springs. Although this settlement is youngish yet, it is progressing well and expanding rapidly. The countryside is beautiful and the area enjoys a very favourable and healthy climate – not too hot in summer and not too cold in winter.

I proceeded west for one hundred miles as far as Red Cloud and indeed, the scenery was spectacular. I returned through Lincoln (population 14,000), the state's capital, to Omaha. From here I took the *Union Pacific* line along the fertile and famous Platte valley as far as North Platte City, about three hundred miles west, before returning on the same route. I saw crops of maize and excellent grazing lands.

An Eloquent Boy

Whilst waiting for the train on the transfer, a boy of about fifteen from the 'boot-blacks league' ran towards me. After agreeing to a 'shine' he questioned me intensely about the western towns I had visited – their successes and expectations. He then asked: 'where are you going?'

'To the east,' I replied.

'That is God's land,' he said.

'Whose land is the west?' I asked.

'The devil's land,' he answered.

'Why are you choosing to go from God's land to the devil's?'

'Because I prefer his family; his children are all genuine. As far as the people who claim to belong to the other, half of them are bastards – their black noses are covered with white cloaks, repugnant to the people who honour truthfulness and purity.'

'Oh! you little rascal,' I said to him. 'Do you realise what you are saying?'

'Maybe not, maybe I am speaking religiously since I notice that not many people who proclaim to be religious understand their own belief. The language of religion is the language of Heaven and is splendid. Only the one's that have been in Heaven or were taught by Heaven's spirit can understand it. The religious rigmarole listened to by many is only the language of parrots, whereas the saintly fashion of our time resembles monkeys in a dingy habitat. I have respect for religion if it is genuine. I honour truthfulness. I prefer candid devilry to sanctimonious charades. An absolute fiend is more honourable than a false angel.'

'Where are you heading to?' I asked him.

'Anywhere, maybe I shall go where I'll make my fortune.'

'Where did you come from?'

'From all directions as far as I can make out. In how many places I was before I was old enough to remember, I can't tell you but I do remember being in London, Paris and many other major European cities. I came here half an hour ago from Chicago and soon I shall be boarding the train to Colorado.'

'You must be very rich to be able to travel this way.'

'No, I do not travel by the source of money. I have privileges that many people know nothing about. I have a special compartment that others are not allowed to enter.'

'Where is this compartment?'

'You see that small seat under the train between the wheels. I sit there – you shall see in a minute.'

'What if you were seen by the authorities?'

'What about it! All they can do is pull me out. The law does not allow them to kill or harm me; however, they will not see me. I have not been spotted yet.'

'What if the train collided with a cow or horse?'

'Well, I would be better off than the poor animal. I do not go out to meet difficulties; if I was that way inclined, adversities would have devoured me long before I was born.'

'Well,' I muttered, 'there are many roads one can take on life's journey.'

'Yes,' he replied, 'and I am going to follow them all. I have already travelled through parts of two continents and I am going to seek what is in store for me in this part of the world.'

'Are your parents alive?'

'Maybe and maybe not. What I do know is that I have no information about them. I am probably the son of one of London's "street-walkers", or my mother could have been an honourable, dear girl who was betrayed, or maybe a noble lady came purposely to some corner of the city to hand me over as a gift for my mother. Maybe, one day, I shall discover that I am heir to a vast fortune and will have titles bestowed upon me. Maybe people will write about me and sing my praises. Will you recognise me then as the boy who shone your shoes here today?'

Before I could answer, the bell rang and the train was about to move. Very nimbly the boy placed himself, his box and brush tidily on the seat under the train, as he had said he would. Away he went, poor little lad. He was handsome with an abundance of talent and impudence.

In Iowa

Ensuing all that, I started on my journey to preach through the states of Iowa, Missouri and Kansas. The place where I began was Long Creek, near Columbus City and then on to Iowa City (population 9,000) and Old Man's Creek; then to Welsh Prairie where it had been announced the previous Sunday that: 'a preacher from Cardiganshire will be with us, therefore remember, all of you, to turn out.' From there I went to Williamsburgh. In all of these settlements, robust and successful farmers appertaining to our nation had colonized. From Marengo, I travelled west for ninety miles to Des Moines (population 23,000) – the state's capital. Nearby, Sevastopol is situated and it was here that I started to visit and take an interest in the miners of Iowa. Thereafter, I took the south-east route through Knoxville and came to the regions of Beacon and Givin, near Oskaloosa (population 5,000); then onwards to Ottumwa (population 9,000) and Belknap.

On the journey between the last two places I remembered the illusion I had of the twenty-first century on the plains of Dakota because when the train was passing a rock the size of a haystack, a man joined me and others on the rear platform and shouted in dismay: 'What a huge rock.' Since no-one answered him, he repeated: 'Has anyone ever seen a rock as big as this?'

'Yes, some,' was the answer.

'Well, I haven't and that is the truth. I see this rock as one of the world's wonders. Don't you then?'

'Everything in the Creation is a wonder and no doubt a rock of this size would be amazing in your country.'

'How do you know my whereabouts?'

'You live in the northern part of this state, don't you?'

'Yes, but how do you know that?'

'By seeing the plains of your countryside in your eyes and the amazement on your face when you saw that piece of rock.'

'Isn't it a mighty one then!'

'By comparison to the molehills of your country, it is big but when you compare it to some of the rocks we shall see on this route, that is, if you are going further, it is merely a molehill.'

After gazing for a moment at the person he was chatting to, just to determine whether he was jesting or being serious, the man sat down. I noticed that he was peering long and hard into a mirror to find out, I presume, whether he could see the reflection of the plains in his eyes!

From Belknap, I went west as far as Allerton; then on to Lucas and Cleveland, where I was presented with some works of the Mormons and I was informed of the differences between the two branches of the Latter-day Saints.

The Hog Back, Lake Spirit (Iowa) Reached Via
'Albert Lea Route'

In Missouri

From Cleveland, I went south for about one hundred and fifty miles through Centerville, Kirkville and Macon City to Moberly (population 7,000) and Huntsville where there are many Welsh coalminers. The Americans of these regions are usually slaveholders or people of such traits. They speak as if through their noses and pronounce the letter 'h' in a very peculiar way. To some extent they regard a white man who labours with contempt and believe that black Negroes should be the manual workers. There are many black people living in this area.

From Huntsville, I decided to go north to Bevier, a village comprising a large percentage of Welsh people and a place where much coal is mined. When several people in this area were providing me with information about the locality, one of them asked me whether I would be reporting the facts exactly as they were conveyed to me. 'I shall aim at correctness,' was my answer. He then said mockingly: 'we do not want to account for anything that is not proper with regard to our lives. I ask you, therefore, is it proper for a Welsh minister to baptize Negroes?'

'One of the commands taught to us Ministers of Religion is that we should baptize all nationalities. Negroes are not excluded and it is completely acceptable for a Welsh minister to baptize these people.'

'Since we are on the subject,' the man said: 'I shall disclose to you what has taken place in the past. Many Negro families came to reside in this region and since there was no Minister of Religion amongst them and since the consensus of the white ministers was (many from these parts were of the lineage of the old slaveholders), that it was improper to baptize Negroes, the Negroes approached Welsh ministers and asked them if they would condescend to baptize them.'

'Condescend to baptize,' the Welshman said: 'I consider it a supreme honour to baptize any living creature, even if they were mules, as long as they showed signs that they believed in Christ.' Thus, without any more ado, he baptized them.

Ten miles further west lies New Cambria and its surroundings – a hilly setting consisting of farmland and also the most extensive Welsh settlement in the state. About fifty miles further, I descended in Utica to join another Welsh settlement named 'Dawn'. Here one finds more favourable land. Slightly south-west of this region one finds the 'Low Gap' Welsh settlement where beautiful countryside and good land can be purchased quite cheap. From here, a kind friend took me at midnight in his carriage to Moresville in order to catch the train to Kansas City. As we were passing one house, he said: 'this is where a good and virile Negro lives. At the time of slavery, slaveholders used to bring the slave women here in order to breed a good stock of slaves – offsprings of the man living here. This man was considered of such calibre that slave women were brought hundreds of miles for their contact with him.'

The train travelled through an area very much plagued by robbers. Gangs squatting in remote places, would cause trains to stop whilst they burgled the passengers. This was a recurring occurrence this summer in this area. A few days before I travelled on this route, they had shot dead the conductor and one of the passengers and also robbed all on board. They would pounce in a cohesive fashion. It was hands up for everyone or else be shot on the spot. In the meantime one of the robbers would wander around with a sack to collect the spoils such as pocket-books, watches, cash, jewellery and many other valuable items. After robbing the express trains and the mail compartments, they would gallop away. These villains are usually rebellious people from the South. I now understand though that some of the savage leaders have been arrested and as a result, the country is a safer place.

Kansas City is a flourishing urban district situated on the picturesque banks of the Missouri. The population of the city increased in ten years from 5,000 to 56,000. This was the third time for me to cross the Missouri. I crossed it the first time by Fort Pierre, about six hundred miles to the north and again near Omaha. The annual county fair was held near Kansas City when I was there. These fairs are held in every county for three days. Their purpose is to exhibit, rather than sell and award prizes for the best animals, corn, fruit, machinery, horsemanship and many other attractions. The main event in this fair was a fifteen mile horse race between a Miss Williams and some other Miss. Miss Williams had beaten her competitor in a previous race but it was the other Miss who won this time. One prevailed as rider whilst the other excelled in speed, especially whilst changing horses – a spectacle that had to be accomplished six or seven times.

Kansas

From Kansas City I travelled south for four miles to Rosedale where many Welsh people are employed as furnace operators. After returning to Kansas City I went west on a thirty-mile journey to Lawrence (population 9,000), a place which was the centre of bloody battles between the border ruffians during the big rebellion. The place was occupied and robbed by the notorious thief Quantrell and his bandits. Another twenty-seven miles and I was in Topeka (population 16,000). The state fair was held there and it caused congestion on the railroad leading to and from the town in all directions. There were many natural and artistic objects exhibited, all well worth travelling hundreds of miles to view them. Nevertheless, the main event of this fair again was the horse race between Miss Curtis from Kansas and Miss Pinneo from Colorado. The length of the race was supposed to be twenty miles but one of the girls became unwell and it was shortened to ten miles. The sick girl finished the course though and then fainted. However, she won the crown.

Another phenomenon of this fair was the temperance victory. Amongst the thousands, yes, hundreds of thousands of men who had travelled hundreds of miles to this fair, not a single drunk was to be seen and there was no-one selling or buying alcoholic drinks throughout the fairground. Kansas has adopted temperance laws and it is illegal for anyone, except druggists, to sell alcohol within its boundaries. There is however, throughout the entire state, a great deal of sly drinking and trading taking place. I witnessed two, only two, showing off their Dutch courage in a town that was supposed to be alcohol-free. Who were they? Indians? No. Irishmen? No. Germans? No. Yankees? No. Not Welshmen, surely? Yes, indeed, two Welshmen who had only just arrived from Wales!

Since I was expecting my belongings to follow me to Kansas City, I was unable to leave Topeka before two in the morning. I arrived in Osage City by five and after much difficulty I found some Welsh people. I was so tired though that I came to the conclusion that a bed would be more fitting than a pulpit – although it was a Sunday. I was escorted that afternoon for twelve miles to the Welsh settlement of Arvonia, where I met the Reverend M.B. Morris from Colorado together with his wife and daughter. If it had not been for this visitation, the most astonishing and exceptional part of my journey would probably not have been completed. After receiving Mr Morris' heavenly tonic which lubricated my ailing spirits, I departed with renewed energy!

To go from Arvonia to Bala, in Powys, about eighty miles towards the north-west, I had to return to Osage City where I heard about the death of President Garfield, about three months after he had been shot. I passed Peterton, where there are many Welsh coalminers, through Burlingame and on to Manhattan. A man from Bala had come to meet me with his carriage but since he went to a different station to the one I had arrived at, we failed to see one another. Therefore, I trekked along the 'Valley of The Wild Cat' for about twenty-six miles. The countryside reminded me of the terrain in some areas of Wales. I almost believed that I was walking near the sea in Merioneth whilst observing the stone-built houses and the stone hedges erected on rocky hills.

From Bala I journeyed on to Junction City, about twenty miles south. There was a dispute there between the drinkers and the temperance people. If there was a problem in getting twelve jurors to pronounce a guilty verdict on a man who was prosecuted for selling alcoholic drinks, the considered opinion was, that the alcoholic drinks market would win the day and that it would be safe and proper for anyone who wished to sell the cursed liquor to do so. It was said that some towns in the state had won the argument this way and were able to challenge the law.

From here I advanced to Emporia (population 5,000) – about sixty miles to the south-east. Near this town one finds the largest, most prosperous and most important of the Welsh settlements. I stayed here for over a week and found the inhabitants very friendly. After a long period of drought, it rained heavily there on 29th of September and everyone was overjoyed by this gift. However, destruction followed because a ferocious gale blew over the northern edge of the town. Several houses were shattered and four people lost their lives. I saw two corpses – a young lady and a child aged eighteen months.

I proceeded to Burrton, ninety-three miles south-west, where there is a small Welsh settlement. As an example of the welcome extended to new arrivals, the following was published that week in the Burrton Monitor:-

> We now have a tailor, in the person of Mr Owens, just from the old country (Wales). He comes well recommended, has a good face upon him, and we are all going to patronize him and help him along. We want every fellow that strikes our town to 'stick'.

The countryside in this region is very flat but about twelve miles further south, towards the banks of the Arkansas River, the terrain is more undulating. It is excellent ground and is being sold by the first-rate railroad company, *Atchison, Topeka and Santa Fe*, for very reasonable prices and favourable terms. If anyone is seeking such land, no time should be wasted because it will be snatched up quickly. The soil becomes less fertile from this point – poorer still towards the Rocky Mountains.

Fifteen miles from Burrton lies Hutchinson. From this town onwards the railroad runs along the Arkansas River. Only expansive plains are visible with towns and villages scattered here and there. These are habitations which have been created and supported by means of the railroad and the hope is, that these districts will expand and become as famous as their guardian – the railroad. The inhabitants of the town of Sterling, for example, exaggerated that their town was as big as New

Kansas Avenue, Topeka

Kansas Sheep

York although construction work had not been completed! Farther on, stands Pawnee Rock, an amazing place with a history of Indian wars. Robert E. Lee is one of the many names carved into the rock. He was Commander-in-Chief of the South during the great rebellion. He carved his name here when he was a young lad.

Soon after passing Larned, we started going over quite barren land, Mount Gilboa being one area. This region experiences very little dew and hardly any rainfall. It is said that a strange phenomenon takes place here: that black clouds move towards the west over an area of eighteen miles every year without releasing any of their contents. Mother Nature does not allow her blessings to be wasted where they are not required. Where there are just sand or rocks to be found, no rainfall occurs. In contrast, where greenery and trees appear, Heaven ensures that there is enough rain to sustain the vegetation. There is a scriptural message here too:- 'And it shall come to pass in that day, I will hear, saith the Lord, I will hear the heavens and they shall hear the earth; And the earth shall hear the corn, and the wine, and the oil, and they shall hear Jezreel' – (Hosea 2 – 21,22).

The School at Larned, Kansas

The geographers of old mapped out Nebraska, Kansas and Colorado as the great barren land of America and only a generation ago, it was believed that nothing could be grown west of the Missouri. I do not know what gave this belief validity then, the reality today is that it is no longer correct. In the year 1866, Kansas was rated twenty-fourth in the States of the Union League as far as agricultural produce was concerned. In the year 1878 it was first in its production of wheat and fourth in the Indian corn harvest group.

Colorado

Colorado is the youngest of the states. It became a state in the year 1876, a hundred years after the 'Declaration of Independence'. For this reason it is called the 'Centennial State'. It lies on the rough slopes of the Rocky Mountains and is full of amazing natural beauty. The state's underground prosperity of gold, silver, copper, iron, lead and the alloy bronze have attributed to some of the best craftsmanship. I travelled a great deal in this state but my account of the journey from Erie through Denver and Pueblo to Leadville summarizes my experiences.

I shall start at Erie – a village in a plain glade within sight of the mighty mountains. There is a settlement of Welsh people here, most of them working in the lignite industry.

Denver, (population 36,000) is the state's capital and considered the most spectacular city between St Louis and San Francisco. It stands 5,240 feet above sea level. Although it is a young city it has excellent roads and buildings including a cathedral, a theatre and a railroad station. One stands in amazement when observing them. Many Welsh people reside here but are very scattered. It was here that I decided to travel on the *Denver and Rio Grande* railroad in order to proceed southwards. The railroad's proprietors call this route 'The Scenic Line of America' and I do not believe that this assertion is over-exaggerated either. It would be quite appropriate to call it 'The Scenic Line of the World'. It is here that one finds the longest narrow gauge railroad system in existence; it has to be narrow to enable the carriages to tackle the tortuous track full of ascents and descents – all wild and daring. After ascending 2,260 feet within fifty-two miles, we came to a place called 'The Divide' – the highest point on this branch. A lake is situated here where pleasure-seekers are to be seen rowing, fishing and shooting wild ducks. After passing the lake we came to the vicinity of red sandstone rocks. Their frontage resembled rows of pillars in straight lines as if they had been created and adorned by a craftsman. They emerged in such a regular and orderly style as if they had been placed there by man to cradle the hills.

I descended in a village called Monument, with the purpose of travelling five miles east to visit a small settlement of Welsh farmers – a place called Gwilymville. Here, without a doubt, one finds Welsh farmers in the highest of localities because Gwilymville is twice the height of Snowdon.

The Surroundings of Colorado Springs

Colorado Springs is a young, prosperous and virtuous town situated at the foot of a high mountain called Pike's Peak. Its streets are a hundred feet and avenues fifty feet wide, respectively, with rows of leafy trees shading them. This town, as well as many other American towns, is a temperance town. No landowner is permitted to sell alcoholic drinks on his estate and he cannot allow anyone else to do so on his behalf either. Should this take place that person would, according to the conditions of the deed, lose all rights to his land.

Five miles from Colorado Springs, Manitou is situated; another very fashionable town enveloped snugly in the mountain. Many visitors come daily to these two towns to enjoy the fresh air, the medicinal springs and the wonderful scenery. These amenities make this locality a truly spectacular place.

A few miles north of these towns lies Monument Park, a place where evergreen bushes grow amongst rocks and pillar-like red and white sandstone formations of every size and shape – all towering over the landscape. Some are so decorative that one could be tricked into believing that they had been created by man by means of his chisel. Some appear like arched gateways, some like spears, others like a blacksmith's anvil; some like carved busts and others like gravestones.

Nearer to Manitou is the 'Garden of the Gods' where one finds stones depicting men, others portraying women draped in veils, others resembling the images and gods of the old Orientalists – their heads similar to that of birds, lions or oxen. Some stand alone whilst others are in small groups; many are in clusters, appearing quiet, sad and sombre. When one observes them from one angle, they appear like particular species of live creatures. Examining them from another spot, they appear as different breeds of animals. Other rocks would resemble buildings, pinnacled churches and towering fortresses. If a stranger slept in the open here on a moonlight night and he happened to wake up before dawn, I am sure he would be engulfed with very strange sensations. He would not be afraid of lions or bears, although he could have reason to fear such animals; no, he would be wondering what his plight was. He would be in a dilemma as to whether he was waking up in this world or the next one! Whilst walking in this area, I witnessed intact wooden stumps transformed into a solid mass. One could spend several days here and yet be fascinated by astonishing phenomena arising continually. About a mile north of Manitou the 'Cave of the Winds' is found. Its interior consists of seventy-two halls and large rooms through which man can walk unbending. Basalt is to be seen in abundance; also stalactites hanging from the ceiling like icicles. Trampling along by the light of a lantern in this cave and listening to reverberating sounds whirling through rooms and fissures is like listening to the voices of spirits uniting together to embrace someone. It is the same eerie feeling as one would experience if one stood alone, on a moonlit night, in the Garden of the Gods.

Nearby again is Ute Pass which is a picturesque gap between tall, straight majestic rocks. Amongst these rocks are caves, tunnels and amazing waterfalls – Cheyenne Canyon, Williams Canyon and Glen Eyrie – to name a few. Other landscapes in these regions are well worth travelling from afar to see and appreciate.

The Start of the Journey to Pike's Peak

Pike's Peak in Colorado, although not the highest, is amongst the highest and by some estimates the most outstanding peak in the Rocky Mountains. It is renowned for the fact that it is the highest habitable place on earth. The peak is 14,147 feet above sea level, therefore, it is almost four times higher than Snowdon. At one time, this mountain was the chief destination of people seeking gold and the main site of the government's land allocators. The summit is still a base for government officials studying atmospheric and weather conditions.

In the summer months, many people strive to achieve their great ambition of climbing to the summit of this famous mountain. I was also possessed with this enthusiasm and I was so keen that I decided to be engaged in the foremost category, namely, people who accomplish this attainment through stamina and the strength of their limbs. Those pertaining to this group spend one night at the peak in order to see the sun rising in the morning. Most people ride on horseback to reach the peak and the horses used for this purpose are kept in Manitou which is 6,000 feet above sea level. This means of ascending the mountain is classed as secondary though. The mountain's summit is about 8,000 feet above Manitou. The ascent is about ten miles long with a gradient of 800 feet per mile. To understand this account of my journey, reader, think of a steep hill a quarter of a mile long with its top 200 feet higher than its base; then imagine you are climbing such a hill for ten miles – not on a road which has been suitably constructed, like the main roads of Wales, but on a narrow path of uneven fine gravel; a surface that would cause your foot to slide back a little every time you stepped forward. Other sections of the path's surface are made up of small, sharp stones and one would have to wear very tough boots indeed, to prevent any of these shingles from penetrating through one's footwear. At other places one has to step from boulder to boulder as if climbing a stairway and extra care has to be taken not to be absent-minded in case it would be one's last movement!

I started off early from the paradisean town of Manitou and walked on a delightful, straight road and drank from the beneficial springs of iron and soda, a refreshment probably unequalled in the world, I eventually found myself at the base of the ascent and here the most colourful and amazing scenery welcomed me – the phasing out of the beautiful valley and the appearance of huge rocks, which were adorned with evergreens, each side of the roaring, clear river which plunged downwards from a great height into a colossal depth below. It frolicked and bounced from rock to rock and bubbled playfully as it reached its abysmal bed, a place where it experienced merriment in abundance. Nature was at its best, entertaining and delighting me on my journey; the sky was clear and the climate favourable. I was too heavily clad though and my backpack was weighty because I had prepared myself for the harsh wintry weather which I would be experiencing by the evening.

The First Stage of the Ascent

I began the task of ascending and by doing so I saw the massive boulders above me on both sides and rocky crests peering downwards in such a sinister way as if they were ready to fall any minute. Between them were the affectionate cedars and the delightful pines nodding to tell me to venture forward and not to fear anything. On my right was a chasm with depth engulfing depth by the noise of the torrents below. Beyond the waterfalls and ravines I could see stratum resting on stratum, rocks hanging on rocks and an array of columns and pinnacles towering above peaks until they appeared to be touching the azure heavens. Upwards and upwards I plodded, up the narrow, winding path; along such a zigzag route that I could not see behind, ahead or any other way apart from directly above because of the density of the trees and the rocks. I was ascending through fissures between steep rocks. Sometimes, I would cross the river from one bank to the other. Most of the time though, the path was along the edge of a deep gorge. Although the journey was arduous, I was grateful I was not on horseback since I had more faith in my own two feet. I was also glad that I did not have a guide since the fact that I was alone enabled me to communicate with wonderful nature in all its fascinating ruggedness and murmur praise to: *i Dad y trugareddau i gyd*. (Father of all mercies) – [A line from a hymn by the Reverend B. Francis, Horsley].

There were some metallic pieces such as lead or clear silver, reddish copper, bronze and maybe gold amongst the stones and gravel, thus making the path and its surrounds glisten in the sun's rays. Beyond the footbridge, where I had crossed the river, was a very large boulder, the size of a house, blocking the path. Luckily, a thoroughfare had been created underneath it and this escarpment was called 'Sheltered Falls'. Farther on I saw a large felled tree with its roots facing upwards. Its base measured four feet in diameter and was much larger than the trees growing there now. Time and erosion had consolidated it into a massive rock-like object. However, its bark, grain and roots had kept their natural appearance.

After ascending another four miles without meeting anyone or hearing anything except the roar of the waters, the chanting of the breezes and the melodious chirp of the birds, I came across a new house made of stocks. Near to it were two saddled horses. These animals were tied up and there were two guns leaning against the wall. I found two young men sitting inside the house. They told me they were honest and peaceful people, cultivating the land, providing animals with fodder and hunting wild creatures for their skins. They said that they had built their house in that location because they preferred the wilderness of nature and liked the tranquility of the place. I asked them how were they able to till the land and feed animals amongst such craggy rocks. They replied that there were areas of plains higher up where they planted potatoes and where they could take pleasure in the company of their cattle. They were surprised to find that I was travelling alone and on foot, without a weapon to defend myself if I was attacked. They said that bears, jaguars, mountain-lions and panthers were inhabiting that region and that all lone travellers really should have some means of protection if a dangerous situation arose. I had heard that such animals lurked on the outskirts of Pike's Peak and what these two gentlemen said, made such knowledge more realistic. Something made me suspicious of these men though. I started puzzling as to why they were living in such a remote place. Anyway, my aim was to reach the mountain's summit and since I had already accomplished a great deal of the project, I decided to proceed. Upwards I ventured, following the rapid river through narrow clefts and between rocks more monstrous than the ones I had seen earlier. Suddenly, I found myself facing an open space, an area maybe of around forty acres that was almost flat – a green and pleasant spot covered with patches of verdant bushes and a sprightly small stream traversing along, chanting a little tune. I had now distanced myself from the main river. This delightful location is surrounded on all sides by the mighty rocks, thus making it a very serene and secluded patch. Here, on a green lawn, I rested to drink some of the clear waters from the stream. I have thought many a time since, that I would have liked to have lived in such a tranquil place.

Monument Park, Colorado

Hotel in Manitou, Colorado

Equilateral Rock

Anvil Rock

The Last Stage of the Ascent

After travelling through this paradise I proceeded to climb the rugged acclivity. The remainder of this journey was not so pleasant, not only because of the craggy landscape, but the entire ambience was drab and gloomy. The pleasant scenery previously observed was diminishing and all vegetation appeared far below and to crown it all, the path veered away from the friendly stream. I had to climb the last six miles without any water to drink and I became very thirsty. I had reached an altitude where no plantations thrived so I bade farewell to these companions. Whilst continuing to climb these steep gradients, extreme exhaustion set in. I still held on to a small fragment of energy though and was able to plod on although the wind was strong and the temperature very low. Some flowers were visible – ones smaller but more delicate and distinct than daisies. Their colour was dull grey, similar to that of lead and they were so fragile that they would disintegrate if handled. I was now in a region where the air was so thin that some people would experience difficulty in climbing any further owing to breathing problems. People who are prone to such difficulties often develop conditions such as swellings, nose-bleeds, bleeding from ears and sometimes they vomit blood enforcing them to descend very quickly. Luckily, I was not affected by the high altitude. As far as my lungs were concerned, I felt that I could keep up the same pace from the base to my goal. However, my legs were crippling me and I had to stop for several minutes after almost every two dozen strides. I started to hanker like Richard III on Bosworth Field: 'A horse! A horse! My kindgom for a horse!' I had reached a place where no plants or flowers could grow. I was amongst bare rocks and stones and I could see the nearby peaks beneath me and way down in the canyon most of the landscape had been transformed into a screen of fog. I could see the streets of Colorado Springs in the distance; they were like thin threads crossing each other. I also believed I could see some lakes which appeared like tiny, white spots. Apart from this view there were no hills or valleys and no forests or prairies in the vicinity.

As far as the unending, hazardous assemblage of reddish, angled, sharp and spiky rocks were concerned, it was obvious that they were constructed (cut and thrown haphazardly against each other) when they were forced out of the earth's crust in some bygone era. They vary in size from a pebble to a rock hundreds of feet in height. My perception was that if all the blocks, trunks, stocks, buildings, quarry stones and seaside rocks of Wales were all painted red and bundled together they would resemble the steepest cliff in this region. The strange nakedness of the rocks made me feel uncomfortable, as if I was in another world.

I believe the combination of harshness and the blazing redness of the area attributed to my thirst becoming more acute. This mountain's attitude towards me was quite different to what it had promised. When I was about fifty miles away from it, it invited me to a leisurely hike and even when I was at its base in Colorado Springs, it seemed to indicate that it was not higher than the other peaks and that the ascent would not be too arduous. At this moment though, its red and rough children were riding slipshod over its surface as if they were mocking me in my exhaustion. After walking, walking and more walking in order to go round a cliff's corner or a high, rocky peak, thinking it would be the last one, another huge rock would reveal itself, and another, and another, resulting in my disappointments turning into absolute despair. I had never experienced such delight as when I saw two donkeys approaching me on the narrow path. Both of them had a load which had been secured by frames on their backs and this cargo was transported with great care. I came across a small frozen lake which had been formed as a result of rainwater turning into ice between the stones. I broke the ice into tiny pieces and placed them in my mouth and the words: 'cold waters to a thirsty soul' were thus defined – (The Proverbs 25,25). Soon, I saw another four donkeys coming towards me followed by two men. These men told me that I only had a quarter of a mile further to go before I reached my stopping-place. I found this last lap very gruelling but when I saw the 'Signal Station' sign I was overjoyed. I was welcomed by the two occupiers. I had reached my destination and accomplished the eleven miles of laborious trek within nine hours. The sole of one of my boots was totally worn off with only my sock to protect my foot from the stones.

A Night on the Mountain
After drinking water, warming up and unwinding as well as tying a piece of leather under what remained of my boot, I went out to view the scenery. The summit of this peak was probably two acres higher yet; everywhere was a mass of red rocks the same as previously described. Towards the centre of the spot that I had reached was a low and plain building constructed from the surrounding stone. It contained four rooms and was used as an observatory. The occupiers were Sergeant O'Keef and Major Criben, both government officials who had a big bloodhound to keep them company. All around, I could see mice, striped chipmunks and birds similar to house-martins. This building was connected by a telegraph line to Colorado Springs and Washington, where weather conditions and wind directions were recorded daily. A short distance from the building was a fine gravestone made of white marble and the following inscription carved in black letters on it:

Fair Cynthia with her starry train
Shall linger o'er thy silent rest,
And waft one soft sweet spheric strain
To Erin dear, among the blest.

ERECTED

By Sergeant John and Norah O'Keef
in memory of their infant daughter,
Erin O'Keef, who was destroyed by mountain rats at
the U.S. Signal Station on the summit of Pike's Peak,
May 25th, A.D. 1876

Unfortunately, low cloud and mist resulted in poor visibility in what would have been a magnificent view for hundreds of miles otherwise. In spite of bad weather conditions, I was able to see some peaks in the Rockies and the main chain over in the west. They were all snowcapped and appeared very glorious in spite of their cold and rough exterior. I witnessed the sun setting in the west but it was towards the east that the most spectacular scene was appearing. The black shadow of Pike's Peak could be seen on the skyline with two shining, bright beams of light emerging from the darkness, one pointing north and the other south.

After we dined, an amusing meeting consisting four sessions, was held – an hour for each session. Firstly, the two observers described the way they lived to me. Two miles beneath this place there were trees and a small stream where another small house was situated – an abode for two other men. These men owned donkeys (known as burros) and they were the ones I had met on my way to the observatory. The occupiers of these two dwellings were in communication with each other. It was on the backs of these donkeys that wood, water, food and other necessities were transported to the station. The donkeys were always laden and had to carry enough provision during the summer to last all winter. During the winter, weather conditions would only allow these people to communicate with the outside world by means of the 'wires' alone. They showed me many treasures, luxuries and requirements which they possessed. They had a splendid library and appeared very happy.

The second session was an attempt by myself to put across a good word for Britain against vicious attacks from the Sergeant. Besides, I can mention, that I had had to keep up this defence many a time in several areas of the country. I am known in Cardiganshire as an ardent American whilst in America I am judged by many as a too zealous Briton. Some obtuse British people hold absurd views about America and assert misleading comments about the country whilst some narrow-minded, ignorant Americans have an unfriendly attitude towards Britain. Meetings with such people could disturb the peace sometimes. The Sergeant at one end became ferociously aroused and I almost thought that he was about to armour himself, go down the mountain, cross the Atlantic and give England a good beating! It was a good job the Major was calm, cool and wise since it was his approach to the matter that rescued the mountain from a conflagration that day!

The third session composed of comparisons in our different languages since the three of us represented different branches of the Celtic stock. Sergeant O'Keef was an Irishman, Major Criben from the Isle of Man and myself a Welshman, of course. It was a pity that I had not known of this agenda before I set off from Wales since I could have invited Professor John Rhys[6] to accompany me in order to credit him further. Although

Professor Rhys held a high position as a Celtic scholar, I am sure that chairing this Celtic discussion at the top of Pike's Peak would promote him to a higher level than any held by all of the world's scholars! We came to the conclusion that the idiom of our three languages had similarities with some words almost identical. Although we were cousins, each with his own language, we had to converse in the alien language of English. These proceedings were concluded by the Sergeant reciting some poetry in Gaelic, the Major reciting the 'Parable of the Ten Virgins' in Manx and myself delivering the 'First Psalm' in Adam Jones' language!

The last session of the meeting was accomplished by educating me in the intricacies of telegraphy and atmospherics:-

Pike's   – Name of the Station
Noddy   – The level of the barometer: 30-04
Female   – The level of the thermometer: 18°
Grief   – Total moisture: 70
Head   – Wind direction and weather conditions: southerly and clear
Lawyer – Wind speed: 36m per hour, unvarying

Thus were the weather conditions that day and the data was telegraphed to Washington when I was there. I was told that I was extremely lucky since I was there on the finest day they had experienced that year. After these pursuits, we decided to bade 'goodnight' to each other but I could not drop off to sleep. To begin with my shakedown (*howsal*) was not very comfortable; this in combination with other factors such as: the day's fatigue, the thinness of the air, emotion about the gravestone, the noise of the mice and the sound of the Sergeant swearing at the dog – whilst asleep as well as when awake, resulted in a totally sleepless night for me. I became ill as if I was seasick and was told that every newcomer to those heights experienced such disorder.

The Following Day
I got up early in order to see the sun rising in the sky but it was foggier and cloudier than the previous evening. It was early morning with stormforce winds blowing the fog and clouds over the multitude of craggy rocks which were appearing and disappearing as if the entire expanse contained boiling yeast; the scene was more horrible than the roughest sea I had ever seen. Luckily, the largest clouds started to disappear, others remained, whilst some would play around mingling with the sun's rays, thus displaying a brilliant array of colours – bright

red declining to a lighter shade as well as all the varying colours of the rainbow – each one blending into the other over an area so immense and varying. This area incorporated the most extraordinary mixture of clouds – some white, some black, some in layers, some in rolls, others woolly and some in rows. It was amazing how this magnificence increased as the invisible sun was setting towards the horizon – a sight that no bard or artist could ever portray. When the sun eventually emerged, the fog lifted and I was able to see the entire scene. An astonishing shadow of the mountain reflected in the sky towards the west but without the two beams of light this time. Why this happened, I do not know, unless the beams seen before were reflections of the snow covering the western ridge of the mountain.

The next exploit was descending. With brass wires, pieces were cut from Major Criben's high leather boots and tied under mine and so I set out. The tales I had heard from the two men at the observatory about the strength and brutality of the jaguar and how a man had disappeared from that very place the previous week, the same as others who had been lost at other times, made my descent more agonizing than the ascent even. This fear increased when I came down as far as the trees, where I met two men on horseback on their way up. I was seeing paw prints along the path; they were much larger than those of any dog and they were so recent that they obliterated parts of the horses' hoof-prints. I thought the beast had gone to the riverside, perhaps to drink water and that maybe, I would meet it when it returned, but thank heaven, I never saw a glimpse of it. I would much prefer to pay to see it in a menagerie! I walked steadily without taking any breathers, not even in the flat and lovely glade. Sometime before I reached the base my legs were giving way. As a result I had no alternative but to throw them in front of me the same way as a man with a cork leg would do. The intense fatigue that I had felt, resulted in a stay in bed for me for three days afterwards. This was the worst weariness I ever experienced. I had been to Pike's Peak! I was glad of this but I do not think I shall ever attempt such a trip again.

Strange Mounds

Here I am again on the railroad from Colorado Springs to Pueblo. What are these multitude of mounds in clusters of around a dozen? Apparently they serve as habitats for ants. In one place that was all I could see each side of the railroad – large red ants with tough jaws. Thousands of them dwell in curious rooms and galleries in the same colony and on observing thousands of their habitations, so close to each other, one realizes that the number of occupiers must be tremendous. Since there is not a single, idle, slow or incapable one in their midst, the work they accomplish is beyond any comprehension. No doubt that describing all their rules and customs and chronicling their wars, adventures and movements would amount to several volumes.

What are these other mounds with holes in their centres and more unsightly than the habitats of the ants? I am told that they are the living quarters of the prairie dogs which are small, tawny creatures. These dogs are larger and heavier than rats and love to run and play. The moment they see the train approaching they all run towards the entrances of the tumps where they sit and bark with all their might. When the train nears them, they disappear completely. They are butchered and eaten by the Mexicans. It is said that the prairie dog, the prairie owl and the prairie rattlesnake like to share the same home. No doubt the dog is the 'commandant' and it is dubious whether the other two are really comfortable.

Again, what are those compact, conical hills one can see, similar to the mounds occupied by the ants but much larger? They too appear in the same area and are called wind-hills or sand-hills. It is said that they originated when the spiralling winds caused mounds to form and with the progress of time, more sand adhered to them until they compared in size to large snowdrifts. Time has by now established and solidified them until they are like the land that surrounds them. They are covered by the natural, sprouting vegetation of this region. Hills formed by water are found in many countries and ones formed by landslides in other lands but only at the base of the Rocky Mountains have I discovered hills formed by winds!

Pueblo, Coal Creek and Canyon City

Pueblo is a word meaning town and later on I shall describe other pueblos in New Mexico and Arizona. Concerning this pueblo, it compares to an Indian or Mexican town – very old and comprising adobe housing, the same as the ones in Santa Fe which I shall describe in another chapter. On the outskirts of the town there is a village of dugout homes. These are dwellings constructed in fissures or openings in hills or rocks with their outer walls made of poles plaited together by narrow sticks; these walls are then dubbed with clay and the earth itself functions as roofing. It appears as if the earth's core is on fire when smoke emerges from these houses. I have heard some Welsh people, now living in mansions, saying that they lived in dugouts when they first settled in the West. I only found dark-skinned Mexicans here now and it was my first encounter with these people. Their presence reminded me of the Biblical pictures I had seen of elderly people from the Orient because the women wore long shawls which covered their heads, shoulders and backs and they carried their water pitchers in their hands or on their heads in the same way as Rebecca did by the well – (Genesis 24,16).

Pueblo, a new town inhabitated by white people (population 9,000) has two divisions, one named Pueblo and the other South Pueblo with the Arkansas River flowing between them. Most of the buildings are quite new; some large and elaborate, others mere boards nailed together quickly and haphazardly. Scores of tents had been pitched by the riverbank and it was amazing to find that they were arranged so orderly and were so well-kept and clean inside. They were fitted out with floor coverings and furniture – furnishings comparable to that found in more luxurious homes. From Denver to this point, I had travelled southwards for one hundred and twenty miles. Then, I decided to go north-west on a journey of one hundred and fifty-eight miles to Leadville.

Pueblo is thirty-five miles from Coalcreek, where there is a large settlement of Welsh miners. I stayed here for several days as a guest of the Reverend M.B. Morris, a gentleman mentioned in my comment on Arvonia, Kansas. I am indebted to him, his kindly wife and angelic little daughter for their hospitality. Nine miles towards the west, Canyon City is situated where it is reported the best coal in the state is mined. Mineral springs of iron and soda are also in the locality. This town, with its coal and water commodities as well as its natural scenic surroundings, is rated as a very fashionable place as well as an important commercial one.

The Grand Canyon[7] and The Royal Gorge

Talk about gorgeous scenery. What a sight! Scenery that cannot be compared to Niagara Falls or any other landscape on earth. People from all corners of the country and from the entire civilised world come to witness the grandeur of this locality. We boarded the open-top observation car in Canyon City in order to see the marvellous scene. The Grand Canyon is a very steep pass in the mountain; it is two hundred and seventeen miles long and was formed by the Colorado River. The most spectacular part of this pass, the Royal Gorge, is a narrow fissure between the rocks and measures a mile and a half. These deep clefts created in the earth's sandstone are prominent features of the Rocky Mountains and constitute the most wild, magnificent and exciting scenery that one can ever envisage. The river meanders underneath, sometimes flowing rapidly; at other times jumping, falling, raging and thundering over, between and alongside huge rocks like the Towy near Ystrad Ffin!

Each side of the Gorge – straight and upright – emerge the largest rocks I have ever seen. The sun's rays never reach these lowlands but way up, hundreds, or to be more accurate, thousands of feet above us, an azure strip of sky can be seen. One can think that it would be the easiest thing in the world to throw a stone from one bank of the river to the other but there is no record of anyone succeeding in doing so; yet there are only thirty-five feet between the sides at one spot. The best way of picturing the depth of this fissure is to imagine Snowdon being split down the middle, thus creating an even surface from Beddgelert to Llanberis! Only a few venture to look down into this gorge more than once; one glance is enough to install in the mind such a concept of 'depth' that had not been conjured before and never to be forgotten whilst in the land of the living.

The railroad ran alongside the riverbank at the lowest point and at one place our train travelled over a bridge – not crossways but forward over a stretch of river because the gorge was so narrow. Since the river often veered suddenly making it impossible to see much of what was behind or ahead, we continually imagined ourselves being confined in a deep pool. Yet, our train had room to proceed and proceeding it was too, not slowly and sluggishly as was customary on bends on wide railroads but journeying forward like a crazy Jehu[8] – advancing helter-skelter, haphazardly, away and away. Sometimes it would appear that we were about to be thrust against a huge rock which emerged in front of us. Almost simultaneously though, the small, brave and fierce steamengine would accelerate and go round a corner like a lightning-flash whilst pulling the train like a coiled, swift snake. Once, I felt sure that we were going through a tunnel because it seemed that only the rear part of the train was outside the rock. Soon, the engine became evident again and it was obvious that it had discovered a passageway to enable it to proceed ahead like a frightened hare, with us passengers clinging on as if for our lives. The train sped frantically uphill while the wild and raging river surged downwards and every moveable object appeared in great haste to flee to safety in case the engulfing rocks would capture them! Great amazement showed on the faces of the passengers; some were wide-mouthed as well as wide-eyed; others had their arms up in the air and then without a word being muttered, everyone would burst out laughing. Maybe some corner or strange peak had come into view amongst the high mountains or a sudden corner had been masterly tackled. The entire experience affected our emotions in a very strange and amusing way. Who, indeed, could not help laughing whilst watching romantic nature and a wild, affectionate construction playing such serious jiggery-pockery with each other! Nature is beautiful, majestic and appealing in its glorious wilderness; indeed, ingenious accomplishment is also bold, excellent and venturesome. Both intertwine in blessed matrimony.

The Journey to Leadville

After journeying through the Grand Canyon, we left our surveillance carriage and boarded a warmer train. However, I was so absorbed in the pleasure of being transported along such a scenic route that I was oblivious of weather conditions. I stayed overnight in Salida and on my return journey, in Buena Vista, in case I missed something of importance and also to take advantage of the sunlight.

After rising early in Salida I looked out towards the north. What a cold and wintry scene I was setting eyes upon! Is it possible for eyesight alone to conjure up a feeling of coldness or any other feeling in one's body? I believe so, because I felt quite comfortable when I stepped out onto the road that morning. Thereafter though, I started shivering from the effect of the raw, wintry weather. I saw the lofty, black mountains of Ouray, Shavano, Yale, Havard, La Plata, Grizzly and others with their upright, gloomy, still, silent and majestic peaks. They appeared quite near, although they were quite far really. They were like a line of hulking mules, all covered with snow and encased by clouds. Some clouds moved at a slow pace, pretending to play between the peaks, others whirled by the force of the gales, making a roaring sound high up in the heavens. These surroundings made me aware of the freezing weather conditions in this area and I was feeling the cold by now.

Farther on, I reached the twin lakes; ones that are 9,000 feet above sea level and here is the highest point on earth where boats can be seen. Many visitors come to this desirable spot during the summer months. It is a place paternally shaded by Mount Elbert and others. The highest point in this mountain range reaches 4,000 feet above the lakes.

I arrived in Leadville; this town's existence and the speed by which it turns out its products is miraculous. It is a place that seems to have been constructed overnight. It started as a village in the year 1877. Now it is a city of more than 40,000 inhabitants with well planned streets and marvellous buildings. There is no record of a city growing so large in such a short time. It possesses prosperous mines of gold, silver and other minerals. These minerals have made many a poor person very rich in a short time. On the other hand, some wealthy people have become very poor too, since a land of gold and silver, wherever it is found, is sure to be a resort for all kinds of adventurers – shrewd people as well as

The Denver and Rio Grande Railroad through Toltec Pass

foolhardy ones. This city has been a gathering place for a variety of scoundrels and it is said that only as far back as three years ago, seldom a day dawned without someone being murdered here at night-time. Although it is much improved regarding morality and religion, there is still room for more reformation. I understand that many Welsh people reside in the city itself, as well as in its surroundings. It is situated over 10,000 feet above sea-level. Of the numerous people that come to Leadville to make their fortune, only a few contemplate staying here to enjoy their wealth; most prefer more temperate climates.

Colorado has a dry, salubrious climate – so dry indeed, that animal skeletons are seen in the meadows – not rotting away leaving a nasty smell but all shrivelled up. The skin is attached to the bones long after the flesh has perished. Visibility is so clear that far-away places appear quite near. Many an unfamiliar rambler from the east has been tricked by this illusion. He would start his journey early in the morning, hoping to reach a visible hillock by noon; however, in spite of trekking steadily until late afternoon, the hillock was as remote as when he started off. People who are affected by breathlessness, indigestion and the like, find relief in these parts. The rocky surface of the countryside is amazing too; some trees have been transformed into a complete stone-like mass but have retained their grain and woody formation. Human corpses are similarly affected and no doubt the mortal remains of some of you readers will solidify in the cemeteries of the Rocky Mountains one day. Your bodies will be better preserved than those of the old Egyptian mummies!

The Scenery at La Junta
There are, by now, two routes from the Missouri River towards the Pacific Ocean; one appertaining to the *Union Pacific* and *Central Pacific* railroads through Nebraska, Wyoming, Utah, Nevada and California. The other one is connected to the railroads *Atchison, Topeka and Santa Fe* and *Southern Pacific* through Kansas, Colorado, New Mexico, Arizona and California. This is the latest line and it covers more natural and ancient fascinations than the other one. I decided to take this route with the intention of returning on the other one. However, I changed direction in Leadville and arrived in La Junta, a distance of two hundred and twenty-one miles, in order to reach the road leading towards the south-west.

It is customary in these parts to carry revolvers – maybe as much of a fashionable habit as a practicable one. When a group of people were waiting for the train at La Junta's station, four drunkards arrived around midnight. They immediately surrounded the fire whilst muttering argumentative chit-chats amongst themselves. Two stupid ones were trying to give an unintelligible explanation about some incomprehensible matter to the other two crazy men and since they were sinking deeper and deeper into a farcical dilemma they decided, without any hesitation, to try their prowess in gun-handling. They made sure that nobody stood between them and the door but to their astonishment, the signalman, accompanied by a giant of a sheriff, arrived and without as much as a 'how d'you do' out they were flung, topsy-turvy through the doorway like four footballs. They eventually came to the conclusion that it was a blessing to find their long-lost feet again. They had more faith in their feet than in their hands. The leather soles of their boots were more beneficial to them than their pistols because when they were released, all four of them ran gleefully to face the four different points of the compass. However, since they also wished to catch the train, they returned quite sober and quiet. By now, everything made sense to them and they behaved like good children afterwards. The people present, who were spectators to this event, thoroughly enjoyed the excitement. It was an incident that compensated for the tiresome waiting time.

A New House in Colorado

From La Junta to Raton

Since it was night-time when I travelled through the south-east regions of Colorado, I cannot describe the countryside but it is said that it is very fertile with good crops of hay and flourishing grassland. Cattle and sheep are the main animals reared here. Trinidad, a young and flourishing town, is the centre location and main market-place. We arrived there at dawn. However, about half an hour before we came to the station, I witnessed what I had always wanted to see which was a prairie on fire, because half a mile from us, the land was alight. Large gaps appeared every so often, no doubt caused by sections of barren moorland. Between some openings, bright red flames emerged – straight ones sweeping upwards, fluttering and rattling like a row of fiery swords being held by invisible cherubs. The fire appeared quite massive, yet it was said that it was small compared to some that occurred there at times.

After leaving Trinidad, we started to climb Mount Raton. What an ascent! We were not going up gradually, as was customary for trains, but climbing the hill like a waggon. The steamengines were visible (two of them had to be in operation) way ahead of us with their wheels like the hooves of hinds clasping with all their might to get us to the top. It was not practicable to take a straight route, only one in a zigzag manner – from right to left and from left to right, similar to a horse climbing a hill; thus we proceeded round the bends. Eventually, the patience of the iron-horses depleted and instead of continuing with the climb to the top of the mountain ridge, they forced themselves, with us behind them, into a black cavity in the ground and here we entered a two thousand feet long tunnel. I completed my journey through Colorado in the darkness of this tunnel and when it dawned, I was starting a pleasurable journey in New Mexico. I felt that my last experience symbolized the inevitable magnanimous transformation ahead of us all. Our earthly mission terminates in the shadows of the Dark Mountains. However, it will be wonderful to start a divine excursion on the Other Side, in the Land of the Eternal Light.

We started to descend from the mountain on a different face. If the ascent was astonishing, the descent was absolutely dreadful. I cannot describe my feelings when travelling in the train during this descent because not only was I seeing heavy soil and hideous rocks each side of us, as well as a deep ravine on one side, but the train had its front part hurtling downwards, while its rear part was up in the air. We travelled over several bridges and high trestle-works with the winding railroad resting on these thin crutches and since the carriages were large and heavy – all leaning sideways when the train was whirling around bends,

I dared not stand on the lower side of the corridor, in case my noteworthy weight (125 pounds) would result in the train toppling over. The thought of it! What if a wheel became loose at that point or a trestle gave way. Well, we would just nosedive; how long it would take us to tumble down to the very bottom, I do not know. I was nervous and felt shivers going down my spine. At the base of this descent lies a young and lively town called Raton, a place surrounded by coalmines and a distance of one hundred and four miles from La Junta.

From Raton to Las Vegas

From Raton onwards the scenery was quite picturesque. On our far left we could see large drums of hills or mountains and on our far right, extending in the direction the train was travelling, was the backbone of the continent – covered with a thick layer of snow and dazzling in the sun's rays. Its various high peaks displayed amazing peculiarities. Our train puffed along what appeared to me as a wide plateau between these white mountains and the other rugged hills. Only a few buildings were visible because not many people inhabited this area; the few that did were generally ranchers. As many as 25,000 cattle would often belong to one owner.

We proceeded to a most appealing location, known as Park Grounds, where green shrubs, pine trees and bushes of evergreens grow – similar to the way trees are planted in the parks of the gentry in Wales. In between this greenery, red and white rocks and strange columns of sandstone appear – many depicting buildings, figures and the like; they are comparable to the ones in Monument Park and the Garden of the Gods in Colorado. It was a hot and pleasant summer's day. This weather, together with the green and gentle landscape, presented an astonishing contrast to the wintry conditions seen on the far-away mountains.

After travelling one hundred and eleven miles south from Raton, we came to Las Vegas (population 6,000) – an old Mexican town where one finds adobe housing and men and women strolling along in the old Mexican manner – (I shall have occasion to describe these people later on). The part of the town nearest to the railroad station has developed as a consequence of the rail network and therefore has a more recent facade. Nearby stands an old, grey, round-headed rock known as Hermit Mountain – a place where a hermit resided for many years. Apparently, he never ventured from the mountain and survived on nuts, roots and alms brought to him. He quenched his thirst with water from a nearby well. There are in this town, as well as most of the towns in New Mexico and Arizona, people known as Penitents – an association that originated from the papal Church. It appears that they emanated from the third order of the seraphic father, Saint Francis of Assisi. They have a tradition throughout passion week, the days preceding Easter, to travel along a rough and rocky road to a mountain top where there is a Cross. Whilst walking thus, they whip and wound themselves and each other until they bleed. At the same time they groan, sigh and weep – yes, cry loudly and pityingly. This is their idea, poor souls, of following their Saviour!

Las Vegas is most famous for its hot springs which are only two miles away. One can see the 'Cross of Penitents' on a high hill as one approaches them. There are twenty-two springs in total, varying in temperature from 110 to 140 degrees. Sick people from all parts of the country come here to be healed. People suffering from tuberculosis and some agonizing with other ailments come throughout the year and between the delightful climate and the healing waters, it is a genuine fact that there is better hope of recovery from ill-health here than anywhere else on earth.

The train appeared to be enjoying the surroundings by the way it dawdled through a large part of Park Grounds and the enchanting countryside. At times it coiled itself, similar to a snake twisted in an octave fashion and many a time it emerged in the shape of a horseshoe. We were, by now, commencing on a long climb with hills and small mounds encompassing and decorating the whole way.

Hills and Yet Stranger Rocks

We came to a mountainous area which appeared so sculptured and symmetrical that I almost thought, although I knew better, that they were the work of craftsmen. Some would be quite round, others square, others triangular, others 'L' shaped, others star-like with a high point in the centre and five or six arms extending outwards. Bernal Point was the one which drew most attention though. It is situated apart from the others, has four sides and rises steeply to a great height. Its height is twice its width and on top of it stands an upright rock rising to about 100 feet. Not only is the mountain underneath this rock four-sided but encircling it is the most picturesque curvature, similar to the top of a pagoda. This strange mountain has a historical interest too. During the war between the United States and Mexico, almost four hundred Indians, the ones that waged war on the side of the States, invaded the village of Bernal where Mexicans lived. Twenty-six of the Mexicans escaped to the highest point on the rock and since this spot was only accessible from one track, the Mexicans could defend themselves from any number of Indians. The Indians, however, instead of retreating, decided to keep watch until

Rocks in New Mexico

everyone sheltering on the rock perished from famine. This was what happened and from then on the rock has been called, in the ordinary dialect of the people, as 'Starvation Rock'. Two Crosses have been erected as memorials to the tragic incident. One can also see Crosses in fields in this area wherefore religious inhabitants ensure protection and blessing on their possessions.

Farther on, there appeared a long chain of high rocks. Going by stature, form, colour and decoration, they were as spectacular as any rocks I had yet seen. I would imagine that some of them were hundreds of feet high. Their fronts were similar to pillars, as if a craftsman had created them and they were of two contrasting colours – their lower halves in scarlet and their upper halves in mottled white. Regarding decoration, green twigs emerged from their sides and appeared as a source of delicate adornment. When peering through the green branches, the red and white colours of the rocks presented a most effective scene. It was along this narrow valley, hedged in by towers and colourful shrubs, we were now travelling. If one prefers gigantic rough scenery, one should take the *Denver and Rio Grande* railroad. However, if one chooses to see, in addition, the beauties of nature with winter and summer simultaneously chuckling at each other, then one should opt for the *Atchison, Topeka and Santa Fe* railroad through New Mexico. When one considers the many ancient relics located in this territory as well as in Arizona and that the railroad runs through warm, enjoyable climatic conditions, it is easy to establish that it is this one which is most popular with travellers going towards the Pacific Ocean.

Strange Territories

For many reasons, one can consider New Mexico and Arizona, the regions I am now travelling through, as the strangest territories in the world. They are strange in their natural scenery and include large areas of sand that appear like lakes of crystal, wavy waters; mountains so equidistant as if they had been placed there by human hands; rocks resembling buildings, towers, towns, images and even musical instruments; one had to be quite near them to realise that they were not real sometimes. Their summers match their winters, one is as evident as the other. Their rivers are also extraordinary – the ones that move their beds overnight. They meander between sheltered sandstone banks that are as compact as the ones they leave behind. Occasionally, they disappear completely and after miles of flowing underground they emerge again. The sensation they create is curious and is similar to a shining mirror which reflects and brings into view strange objects, although a mountain range is between them and us. The two territories have remarkable potentials, inasmuch as they contain a wealth of silver, gold and other valuable treasures – turquoise being one of them. It is considered that a piece of best quality turquoise, the size of a shilling, would be worth £300. The history of these territories and their ancient relics are very peculiar. When personifying these lands, they resemble someone waking up from an important dream and failing to discern its relevance. The mighty ruins, the huge walls, the long canals, the vessels and odd tools found here are proof that these parts were once populated by a nation or nations more sophisticated and civilised in their activities and skills than those of the Indians living here at present. Who were these people? Where did they come from? What was their history and what became of them? One yearns for answers to these questions but they are not obtainable, mainly because of the last query.

However, it is believed that it was Cortez, the brutal Spanish conqueror, who was responsible for bringing extinction upon these people and obliterating their empire and history. He saw the gold they wore on their clothing and eyed their tools. In the year 1514, he first of all enticed Montezuma, their king, into his clutches; then he marched through the land with a strong army, killing thousands of inhabitants, grabbing the wealth and proclaiming the land as part of the Spanish realm. The Aztec[9] people, overpowered by Cortez, had believed that Quetzalcoatl[10] was their founder and god. He was a handsome, tall man with a long black beard and when he was departing from the Gulf of Mexico, he hoodwinked the natives into believing that they were the chosen people. He promised them that he and his descendants would visit them again. All this enabled the thievish Spaniards to achieve an easy victory as well as ownership of the land.

After travelling twenty-nine miles beyond Las Vegas. we came close to Pecos, a place which used to be an important village inhabited by the Aztec people. Tradition has it, that Montezuma, their last king, was born here. He is now worshipped like a god and it is also claimed that it was he, who built this pueblo and the three-storey temple. He also built in his *estufa* (a place where the chiefs congregated) a holy fire with his own hands – one which never failed to burn during night or daytime. Before he left, he planted a tall tree with drooping branches[11] near the *estufa* and instructed his people to keep the holy fire continuously alight until the tree would wither; that would be the time when white people would come from the east to occupy the land and drive the Spaniards, their invaders, out. He proclaimed that he, himself, would return to build his kingdom; that the land would become productive and that the mountains would yield great wealth of silver and gold. Brave warriors endeavoured to keep the holy fire alight for more than three hundred years. In 1837 only forty-five persons of that lineage were alive with only seven of them warriors. Since it was impossible for them to keep guard any longer, three of them took the fire into the woods and it is believed that Montezuma revealed himself to them and released them from their troubles. Afterwards, they joined their friends in Pueblo Jemez, on the west side of the Rio Grande River. Near Pecos, some stones are to be seen with human footprints clearly imprinted on them and legend has it that they are the imprints of Montezuma's feet when he was departing. His worshippers look towards sunrise each morning as they wait for Montezuma's return. In Pecos, stands the remains of an old, large cathedral, 118 feet long – erected in 1628. Nearby is La Glorietta, where a bloody battle was fought between the Northeners and the Southerners during the last uprising.

Arrival in Santa Fe

After the train had descended a steep slope on a gradient of 180 feet per mile similar to the drop on Mount Raton, we came to Lamy, sixty-five miles south of Las Vegas. There I took another branch of this railroad to go another seventeen miles west to visit the old, strange town of Santa Fe. Ascending, we were now making continual turnings on the pleasant park grounds. The most spectacular scene was the sunset. I had witnessed other magnificent sunsets from mountain tops before, but I had never seen anything so impressive as this one. Oh! what awe-inspiring sky was above us; what brilliant clouds floated about! Stating red, scarlet, purple, yellow, green, blue, shot, silver, gold and so on, would only partially describe the spectacle since there were such redness, such blueness, such transparency, such tenderness, such purity, such amiability and affection in all these colours. Only the heavens could possibly display such a variety of intermingling splendour and enchanting fascination. No language except the one of an angelic bard could describe it perfectly. Oh! for the sunshine of our lives to come to rest like this! Such magnificent reflection beautifying even our clouds – a clear symbol that our souls do swim in a sunny environment on the Other Side.

In contrast, this glory was followed by darkness and by the time we arrived in Santa Fe's station it was night-time. Looking down at Santa Fe, with its adobe housing, is like looking at the ground. It is difficult sometimes to realize that it is there at all, even during the day. To discover it at night was quite baffling because unless one is in the centre of town, its candles and lanterns appear like chafing-dishes. I came to a river that was impossible to cross. I therefore retreated and after coming to some black mounds, I discovered that they were homesteads. I knocked on the door of two or three of them but instead of opening the doors, the women shouted something in Spanish from within. Whilst I was walking along a narrow, dirty lane between rows of low, dark houses, a piece of advice I received from a friend in Kansas came to mind: 'whatever you do, don't wander far from the railroad in New Mexico and don't stay out alone at night.' At last I came to a corner where a surge of light shone through an open doorway of a grogshop or saloon. Inside were several men – Americans, Mexicans and Indians. They carried pistols and long knives fastened to belts tied around their waists. They spoke loudly and seemed agitated as I ventured into their midst. However, there was silence when they saw me and they peered at me awkwardly. I asked the barman the way to the town and I was directed by him. Although that encounter was very frightening, embarking into the darkness again was almost a worst experience because I would not want to face one of those long knives when alone. I was told the following day that I had been in a very dangerous place; that robberies, murders and the disappearance of people were rampant in that area.

The Old Town

After crossing a bridge and getting confused sometimes amongst the houses and the narrow, dark roads, I came to the plaza – the centre of town, where some light gleamed through the shop windows. I felt that I was in a strange and unusual place. I lodged in an hotel which had a loft; such hotel is considered a high building here. I went upstairs to my room – one with a veranda. On peering through the window the following morning, I saw a thick layer of snow on the flat but potholed grassland. As I glanced more precisely, I realised that the flat grassland was, in fact, the roofs of houses and that the potholes were indeed the spaces between the houses. Whilst ambling along the streets in bright sunlight, counting the turrets and judging the bulwarks, Mark Twain's words about Tangier came to mind:-

What a funny old town it is! It seems like profanation to laugh and jest and bandy the frivolous chat of our day amid its hoary relics. Only the stately phraseology and the measured speech of the sons of the Prophet are suited to a venerably antiquity like this. Here is a crumbling wall that was old when Columbus discovered America; was old when Peter the Hermit roused the knightly men of the

Middle Ages to arm for the first Crusade; was old when Charlemagne and his paladins beleaguered enchanted castles and battled with giants and genii in the fabled days of the olden time; was old when Christ and his disciples walked the earth; stood where it stands today when the lips of Memnon were vocal and men bought and sold in the streets of ancient Thebes! (Section of Chapter 8 – 'Innocents Abroad').

It is not known whether Santa Fe is as old as Tangier but it is believed to be the oldest town in America. It was the main town of Montezuma's people before the white man (apart from the old Welsh settlers, maybe) had any knowledge of the continent.

Santa Fe (population 7,000), like most of the Spanish towns (the name when translated means 'the holy faith'), has been built around approximately two and a half acres of land called 'plaza'. The dwellings, similarly, have been built around open land, called 'placita' and many people use areas of the placita as a garden in their home. The narrow roads are requited by the plazas and the placitas. Housing is of the adobe kind and the dwellings are one floor, four-sided structures, made of large bricks of earth and straw and baked in the heat of the sun, the same method as bricks are made in Egypt. The drab walls are several feet in thickness and erected higher than the flat roofs. The roofs are covered by earth, about a foot in thickness and when grass and weeds grow on them, they appear like small fields. The inhabitants can be seen walking, playing and dancing on the roofs. There are holes in the upper parts of the walls to allow rainwater to run through and to enable this water to fall about four feet away from the foundations, there are troughs or wooden pipes projecting outwards. The decoration above the fireplaces is an indication of the people's religion.

I happened to be in the town on one of its most spectacular days, although it has a very, very strange history spanning over hundreds of years. This was a day which will be remembered by the inhabitants as well as by myself because of snow that had remained on the roofs. It rained heavily inside the houses whilst a cloudless sky and sunshine were the order of the day outside. Although water ran off the roofs through the holes in the upper parts of the wall, the melting snow had seeped through into the living-area, causing great inconvenience and chaos for the residents. Beds, cupboards, chests and everything the people owned were saturated. Nobody remembered snow falling there before. This is surprising since the town stands 7,000 feet above sea level.

The most famous building in the town is the Palace – a large adobe house with its length on the north side the same as that of the plaza. The roof's extension, held up by a long row of pillars, juts out far beyond the building itself. It was built over 300 years ago and it was here that the old Spanish generals governed with dictatorial power and unrestrained cruelty. The Mexican rulers followed them with a similar degree of disdain and it is here that the present Governor lives. Here, some of the continent's noblemen were imprisoned and from this place also, many people were led to their execution by order of the 'man in the palace'. Many battles took place here at one time and if I chronicled them all, they would amount to several volumes. Events, which would now be considered incredible, occurred in this region in the past.

It is said that the history of the Palace is the history of Santa Fe, the same as the history of Santa Fe is the history of New Mexico. On the other side, opposite the plaza, a low, old, rusty and heavy door was shown to me. Through it many pitiful people had entered never to return because they did not hold the same religious beliefs as the priest! There are many other old and interesting buildings in the town and the ones more recently erected are becoming noticeable. In these latest buildings there are tools and Aztec dishes with images of Indian gods depicted on them as well as jewellery – bracelets, necklaces, chains, combs and such like, all of them so skilfully made that it is a joy to look at them.

Santa Fe is a strange town – strange in its design, strange in its history and strange in its inhabitants. Three languages are spoken here, Spanish, English and the language of the Pueblo Indians. Everyone expects everyone else to understand Spanish. The women wear loose shawls over their heads and shoulders leaving only a small area of their faces visible. Men can be seen pulling water pitchers up with ropes from wells using the same mode as the patriarchs of old. Outside houses, women can be seen stone-grinding. The dark-skinned Mexicans return from the mines wearing low hats with wide brims and a variety of tools hanging from their waist-belts. The Red Indians would also come in from the rocky regions or the forests with red napkins tied like ropes round their heads; they have coarse, long, black hair reaching over their shoulders. They wear striped blankets over their backs, wide trousers and yellow moccasins on their feet. They are the ones who provide the town's residents with firewood brought in on the backs of mules. It is said that it takes a day for an Indian to cut down a bundle of wood, another day to bring it to town, the third day to hang around trying to sell it and the fourth day to return home with only a quarter of a dollar (one shilling and a halfpenny) for the bundle.

The First Bundles of Wool Leaving Santa Fe

The Palace in Santa Fe

Mexican Earthenware

The Old Churches

The churches are numerous here with Catholicism being the main religion although there are some Protestant denominations being founded. I visited the ancient church of San Miguel, an adobe building erected over 300 years ago. On one side of it, stands the oldest house in America in all probability; it is older than the church and it is reckoned that it will be standing a hundred years hence. There is a splendid building, called The Academy of the Christian Brethren, on the other side of the church. People continually visit the church, cross themselves with holy water, kneel in front of the images, say a little prayer and cross themselves again before leaving. They were very kind to me and willing to show me many sacred items. Nearby, the Institute of the Loretta Sisterhood is situated.

I proceeded to the cathedral. This is a large adobe building also. Its walls are six foot wide and inside one finds a number of large images, many brought over from Spain. Carved into one of the walls is a reconstruction of the grave of the Lord Jesus with an effigy of him inside. Jesus' side, hand and foot show the bloody wounds created by the spear and nails. The image is covered by a thin sheet of cloth. I had heard beforehand that people worshipped in this cathedral at all hours. There were two women dressed in black there when I was paying a visit; one was reading and the other praying in front of the image of the Virgin Mary, despite the unexpected rain pelting down on them. It is expected that a grand building, made of stone, will be built around the present place of worship and on completion of construction work, the old adobe will be demolished. I sat for a moment on top of the building, day-dreaming that I was in a meadow, out in the country, at the end of March three hundred years ago!

I also visited the old chapel of Our Lady of Guadalupe. This chapel's roof is constructed of large wooden blocks; its floor is full of dented gravestones and the interior walls have a few old pictures adorning them. Nearby, is the adobe chapel of Our Lady of the Rosary. This one is almost two hundred years old. Once a year, an 'Eight Day Prayer for Rain Festival' is held here. On the first Sunday – the first day of the festival, Mary is carried from the cathedral by four priests on an elaborate scapular conveyance. Firstly, she is carried by four young girls dressed in white, then by Mexicans and Indians and lastly by just anybody. The best carpets are brought out from houses and lain over the road, Mary is requested to rest for a little while; then the priests kneel down around her praying for rain and the people throw their money into the collection box. After they all enter the church, the Virgin is placed in a niche and kept there for eight days while the prayers for rain continue. Since it is at the beginning of the rainy season this festival takes place, the prayers are usually answered!

There is a tale that one year they had to be cruel to the Virgin before the rain came. Although the priests continued to pray and the people kept handing over their offerings, the Virgin kept being obstinate and there was no sign of rain. Eventually, the patience of these people depleted, but different to the disappointed Baal worshippers on top of Carmel (1 Kings 18 – 19 and 28), instead of cutting themselves with knives, (although there were some knives quite handy) they pulled the image down, stripped her of the ornamentations, kicked her over the rocks and threw her into the river. That night a deluge occurred, the largest ever experienced there. It proved to be a judicial downpour; the river overflowed its banks and the town was almost drowned. The people hurried to restore the Virgin and position her in her proper place.

They adorned her more admirably than before and promised double obedience to her thenceforth.

In front of the church there is a small tree which used to be the marker for a cockpit. Cock-fights became such attractions that they induced many Indians, Mexicans and others to the religious services on a Sunday. It was a great misfortune to the Cause to let these religion-sustaining games decline, because there are no services in this Church any longer, apart from the annual ones before the rainy season. The Protestant Churches better take heed from this consequence, not to eradicate lotteries, other games and holy wiles which enable the Almighty to sustain his Cause in the world!

The Occupants of the Rock

There are in New Mexico and Arizona extraordinary people called Pueblo Indians, namely village Indians. They are different to the nomadic, quarrelsome, looting tribes of the Territories and they prefer to live in villages. They till the land and they are of a quiet and peaceful strain. It is possible that they are descendants of some of Montezuma's people or of other native people who occupied the country before the Aztec race arrived.

The lower classes live in holes and caves. 'The conies are but a feeble folk yet make they their houses in the rocks' – (Proverbs 30,26). The hairy heads of some peering from the rocks and others waving their brown arms, make one think that the mountain is pregnant with human beings and that some, like locusts, are about to free themselves in order to walk about like us. An adobe like this is called a pueblo and the residents go down to the valleys to cultivate the land. There were similar people, or maybe worse ones, in the country where Job lived: 'Who cut up mallows by the bushes, and juniper roots for their meat. They were driven forth from among men (they cried after them as after a thief) to dwell in the cliffs of the valleys, in caves of the earth and in the rocks. Among the bushes they brayed; under the nettles they were gathered together' – (Job 30, 4-7). Isn't there any hope for such people? 'Let the wilderness and the cities thereof lift up their voice, the villages that Kedar doth inhabit: let the inhabitants of the rock sing, let them shout from the top of the mountains' – (Isaiah 42,11).

It is the disreputable members of these tribes that live in caves and holes in the rocks. Normally, they dwell in villages, with houses of the same style as the adobe dwellings of the Mexicans. Some of these villages are erected on the ground whilst others lean on a rock and some on top of a large stone. It is obvious that security against the quarrelsome tribes was a feature when designing the houses since they comprise one, two and sometimes three storeys. I went with a friend through rough pastures and over craggy rocks to see a pueblo, with the intention of knocking on the first door we came across. There was no door however, no entrance nor exit, no side nor gable; only a blue column of smoke spiralling upwards from a pipe that was sticking out of the flat roof. We could hear chatter though, a kind of unhappy complaining conversation; it seemed to come from underground – deep and distant. This confirmed that there were humans there, drawing breath and not completely silent even if they were in a bad physical state. As we looked up to observe the column of smoke more closely, in order to see if there were any spiritual images appearing from the area where we heard the strange, distant voices, suddenly a large black tuft of straight, coarse, long hair emerged onto the roof. It stopped for a moment, the same as a seal does when its head is above the wave; only for a moment though; suddenly there was a shake, a stretch of shoulders and a body showing! We thought it looked like a man. It stood on its feet as straight as a pole, as still as an image, as quiet as a phantom, as pale as death, as sullen as a grave and as serious as if it had just left Hades[12]. Was the light so dazzling that it was difficult for it to see us closely? We believed so, since it stood facing us with a look of dismay on its face. We were trying to guess what would happen next – whether it would sink back into its hole or spread out its wide blanket and fly away or maybe disappear in that very spot. We saw it bending low and again we heard noises from underground. The creature had expanded to its full length by now and behold another similar being comes up, and another one and another and another until we could see standing on the roof a crowd of creatures – amazed and silent. Lastly, a ladder was pulled up and placed against the building and one by one these images came down from the roof and walked towards us. We knew by now that they were men and we shook hands with them. We could feel that they were of flesh and bones. Our superstition subsided and we turned to have a closer look at the buildings and behold the whole village was alive with Indians; some on the roofs, some descending and some approaching us. There was hardly any exchange of thoughts since we could not speak Indian nor Spanish and they could not speak English nor Welsh. All we could do was look amiably at each other. Their skin resembled decaying bones in a grave and their attire was ugly and untidy. It made me realize however, that we were all from the same beginnings and that we were all of the same making. The quotation from the Bible came to mind: 'for dust thou art and unto dust shalt thou return' – (Genesis 3,19). Some, by painting themselves, made their already rosy cheeks flame-red. They enter their houses through a hole in the roof and they pull the ladder back after them in case a criminal would make improper use of it. Other pueblos, constructed more recently, have a door in the wall and a certain kind of window to let light in. The houses with more than one storey are not the same as the ones we have in our country. The idea here is to put one house on top of another more often than not. Measurements are not important – just that the upper house is slightly smaller than the lower one. Some of these houses are built with spaces between the two layers. These buildings are mansions compared to the wigwams that other American Indians dwell in. Some people have houses not unlike beehives, only of necessity of course, they are larger than hives.

A Warm Dwelling

Agriculture

The farmers of this land are indeed incomparable. They, their animals and their furniture are truly amazing. A description of them with their mules was made in the wood-market of Santa Fe. Mules are only used to carry packs. Their pulling animals are oxen – small animals with a shabby appearance. Their plough is made of two pieces of wood. One piece is a piece of trunk and the other a warped branch which is held by the left hand of the ploughman. The end of the trunk which has been hewed to a point is the part which is in the earth acting as coulter and ploughshare. Attached to this pliable piece of wood there is another length which is called 'the pole'. It stretches between the two oxen as far as their heads. There, it is connected to the yoke which rests, not on the necks of the animals, but on their heads. It is tied to their horns with tapes and then attached to straps which cross their foreheads. Therefore, it is with their foreheads the oxen pull the plough. The ploughman holds a stick in his right hand in order to egg the animals on and sometimes only one ox or one cow pulls the plough.

Ploughing in New Mexico

The haulage vehicles of these people are just as inventive as their ploughs. Some farmers are wealthy enough to own large transporters. These so-called 'vans' consist of two wheels, an axle and a pole or cradle. The wheels are made of two round pieces of wood sawn from the stump of a large tree – six inches or more in depth with a hole in their centre to connect them to the axle. Attached to the axle is the pole which is then secured to the yoke on the oxen's heads. Resting on the axle and pole is the box or large cradle, where the transported contents are kept. When one considers the weight resting on the heads of these oxen, one feels so sorry for these animals. Such is the commotion between axle and wheels that when the vehicle moves, the rocks echo by the noise created. This vehicle is similar to the *twlyn* or the *wagen-druck* mentioned by Wisconsin's Welsh people as their means of transport when they first settled there. There is not a single piece of iron in the plough, the vehicle or anything else. They thresh their corn by making the oxen stamp on it. These people have very strange habits. Although they are of the same colour as other American Indians, they are quite different in their ways and customs. They are ardent idol-worshippers, possessing their own small, ugly gods made out of soil, using the same method as for earthenware pots. They have suffered a great deal of maltreatment from their oppressors, namely the Indians, the Spaniards and the Mexicans but their history proves that when the need arises, they can protect themselves quite effectively when it comes to self-defence. They are being eradicated quickly from the earth's surface though and in no time, the land that knew them so well, will not know them at all.

An Old Church in New Mexico

The Welsh Indians

It is not my intention when declaring these tidings to argue or oppose the old doctrine about the lineage of people from Wales on the American continent and the flow of Welsh blood in the veins of the old Aztec people. Since I have collected a few mites[13] in these parts, I shall now throw them into the kitty. They can be sent to the mint to be validated and used towards the cause considered most worthy.

Pecos, for instance, is a town, believed by some, to be the birthplace of Montezuma, the most famous of the Aztec kings and where the holy fire lit by him was kept alight for hundreds of years. It is said that the meaning of Pecos, in the language of the natives, is 'spotted complexion' signifying that the inhabitants had fair pigmentations with freckles on their faces and limbs. Therefore, it is symbolic that Pecos is almost synonymous with Picts – ancient pre-Celtic people who inhabitated parts of Scotland in the ninth century. If a large number of people from Scotland as well as from Ireland and Wales, as was claimed, joined Madog, son of Owain Gwynedd, on his voyage to America in the twelfth century, it would not be impossible for them to build a city and for that city to be named after them.

Of the few Aztec words that I know, most of them are very similar to Welsh words. The Aztec people called the places used by them to hold large national, political and literary meetings in their cities as 'estufa'. Isn't this the same as *eisteddfa* (seating) or *eisteddfod* even? The original name of Mexico City, which is situated on a mountain 7,000 feet above sea level, was 'Tenochtitlau'. Could this mean *Tŷ'n ochr taith i'r lan*? (A place in the direction of the shore)? The large pyramidal temple which belonged to them was called 'Teocalli' Isn't this *Tŷ o allu*? (A house of power) or *Tŷ y Galluog*? (The house of the Mighty) (The Almighty)? A cathedral is now situated on the foundation of this temple. Many of their town names start with 'Te'. Many places on high ground are called 'Tehua' – *Tŷ Uchaf* (Highest House) maybe! Other place names in the English form start with 'Tla' since it is 'tl' or 'thl' the English use as equivalent to the Welsh *ll*. It is probable that *lla*, *llan* or *lle* were the origin of these names. Tlacopan – *Llancopa neu Lle'r gopa*; Tlapallan – *Llanbellaf neu Llepellaf*; Tlascallans or maybe Llascallans was the name of an Aztec tribe. Cayman – *Caeman* or *Caufan* was the name of a river. Pueblo – *pentref* (village) could have originated from *pobl* or *poblfa* or a *poblog* (populated) place.

About two hundred miles west of Santa Fe, along New Mexico's border with Arizona, one finds the Zuni Indians – the last traces of the old Aztec natives. Folk who have mixed with these people say that they have fair hair and blue eyes and that it is difficult to understand why they are indeed Indians. Another trait about them is their astuteness when bargaining. It is also said that these Indians describe their origin thus:

> that a crowd of Welsh miners and their wives accompanied Prince Madog over the ocean in the twelfth century and made their way to the land inhabited by the Zuni tribe. The Welsh people had such a warm welcome that they decided to settle amongst the Zunis. Before very long, however, the Zunis killed off all the Welsh men and took on the Welsh womenfolk as their wives.

That is their explanation of the existence of fair-haired persons with blue eyes belonging to them.

About one hundred miles west of the land of the Zunis, towards the

Colorado Chiquito River in Arizona, one finds the Moquis Indians (Madocians possibly). According to some they are more like the Welsh than the Zunis. They live in pueblos or sometimes a town above very rugged rocks – places where the Navajos, the Apaches or any other violent tribe cannot reach. They speak a language that is unique to them. The inhabitants of Harro, the largest town, also speak a language that only they understand. These people are bilingual though and can speak the language of the others. It is likely that the people who live in this particular town are descendants of the Scots or the Irish who crossed the ocean with Madog. It is said of the Moquis Indians that they have a culture unique to themselves. When I was in Salt Lake City, the elder, John S. Davies, said that he had met and spoken to some of these Moquis people and that they could repeat some Welsh words after him quite eloquently. He believed that their appearance was very similar to the Welsh and going by the photographs he showed me, I am also convinced that they were of the same lineage as Adam Jones and his wife Eve! Well this is my bulletin of historical occurrences anyway. I do not want to come to any definite conclusion regarding my account of what existed centuries ago, the reader can decide what he or she thinks fit.

The Valley of the Rio Grande

From this region – towards the Pacific Ocean, there was at one time a civilization consisting of towns, buildings, meadows, gardens and orchards. It has been discovered through distinct perceptible signs that there was an ancient race here once who had attained a cultured lifestyle and were constructive in many ways. However, the unopposed Spaniards invaded and demolished the entire community by bloodshed and fire. That historical era was wiped out almost in one day. Such was the blind bigotry of the Catholics that they destroyed every written article and all insignia that could have been handed down and be of historical value. All that was left was ruin and the wrecked remains have decreased and faded into oblivion; the paths are overgrown and all signs of habitation have ceased with the erosion of time.

After travelling sixty-seven miles southward from Lamy, I came to Albuquerque, one of the largest and the most important town in the territory. This town and Santa Fe were in competition as to which one would be the capital of the state. Twenty miles south of Albuquerque lies the village of Isletta, where twenty years previously, the river played a confusing trick on Mr S.W. Cozzens, his companion and their servant Jimmy – an Irishman. They had camped on the bank of this 300 foot wide river with the intention of crossing it the following day. There is no such unpredictable river in the world as this one. Its bed is nothing but dangerous quicksand. They had been made to understand that they should be in a particular spot and were very concerned about the crossing because of their mules and heavy waggon. When morning broke, Jimmy woke the other two by shouting that no amount of money would persuade him to proceed one step further in that bewitched land. He was not afraid of the bloodthirsty Indians but of something else and he was about to return home immediately – indeed 'that very blessed moment'! He prayed intensely to the holy saints for protection. It was some time before his boss was able to reason with him; he was so upset. At last he asked: 'Where is the river then?' The river was pointed out to him when Jimmy started crying again. 'That's it – it is no longer there. How did the devil take it to the other side, I'd like to know?' When the other two companions went over to the riverbank to try and perceive what Jimmy was saying, they had to look around to find the river flowing behind them as compact, as quiet and as leisurely as if it had flowed along that bed for the last hundred years. They were then able to cross the old riverbed as safe as Israel going through the Red Sea – (Exodus 14,22). The banks of the river are so sandy that the river can decide to move its bed whenever it chooses. It has no consideration for meadows, orchards, the corrals of the ranchers, the villages or anything – everything must give way to it at short notice. There was a big conflict between the towns of La Mesilla and Las Cruces at one time. The cause of the friction was their position on different sides of the river – a kind of hostility that would have occurred between two parishes in Wales in days gone by. When this disagreement was about to reach a fervent point, the river decided to change its bed again and both townspeople found themselves on the same side of the source of the controversy. They then decided to be friendly towards each other and united as enemies of the people who were left living on the other side of the river!

After reaching Rincon, one hundred and seventy-eight miles south of Albuquerque, I took the south-eastern branch of the railroad that I was travelling on, in order to go seventy-six miles to El Paso Del Morte. On my left, I could see the Organ Mountains, named thus because of their perforated high cribs similar to pipe-organs. I was now in the territory of the violent Indians, the Apaches, who at that time were rebelling against the government. There were rumours, far and wide, about the barbarity of these uncivilised people, so much so, that different to the Pueblo Indians, I did not have any desire to see them or their villages. The Apaches have never been defeated properly. Soldiers have been unable to follow or trace them in their shelters amongst the rocks. Fear of them in times past, and to this day to a certain degree, has prevented the valuable minerals of New Mexico and Arizona from being mined.

Before I proceeded on that particular route, I was told that a train had come to a stop in a remote area further along the line, resulting in a long delay for the passengers since the fault would take some time to be put right. To kill time, some people strolled about in order to view the landscape. Apparently, one couple wandered too far and when they returned, they found that they had been left behind. Since the Apache tribe could spot them and descend upon them, their plight was anything but safe. They actually saw a troop of Indians coming down from the mountain – hurrying towards them. Their fear, by now, was intense. Their only hope was that another train would appear but alas they could not see one although visibility was good. The Apaches were approaching fast. When all hope of escape had almost diminished, a small puff of smoke appeared on the horizon – just the size of a man's fist. However, it was some time before it showed any increase or advancement. To the couple, now, it seemed that it would take an hour for the smoke to come near them and that it would only be a minute until the Apaches reached them. They were in a state of great despair. Since time was on the side of the enemy, hope was fading fast. They had not realized the power of the smoke though because the Apaches had also seen it and it had made them decide to slow down since they were not enough in number to cause any villainy in full view of the train. The couple had some comfort from what they saw but since there was no station at that point, what if the train did not stop? They came to the decision that the woman would stand in front of the approaching train to make signals for it to halt. A woman is queen in America, not in the same fashion as Victoria is Queen of England, it is true, but her power and authority is far greater, although her salary is less! Wherever she is seen, she demands and receives homage, obedience and respect. That was the way it was this time too; the train slowed down and stopped, the couple got on board and the bloodthirsty Apaches lost their prey.

El Paso del Norte

By the time I reached El Paso in the south-west corner of Texas, I felt I was in a very remote spot but as *Siencyn Ddwywaith* (Jenkin Jenkins) used to say when anyone told him that his farm was very far: 'far from where do you mean?' Well, in my case, far from anywhere I had been to before and far from where I intended going. I was one thousand seven hundred miles from Chicago in the north-east and almost one thousand three hundred miles from San Francisco in the north-west. The ranchers of

Texas, ones called cowboys, are awful men. Their main amusement is shooting and if they kill a man they are not bothered. After crossing the Rio Grande, I was in El Paso Del Norte, Mexico – a place as the reader knows, that is in another country and has a different government to the United States. This is a very strange town. Its buildings are of the adobe style and Mexican in appearance and everything and everyone there seemed ancient. The dark-skinned men wore light-coloured flat hats with brims as wide as their shoulders. These hats were decorated with thick, decorative ribbons ending in tufts. They wore tidy jackets and wide-bottomed trousers. Leather belts were worn by most men. Each belt was full of cartridges, held a revolver and a sheathed double-bladed knife. The women were clad in striped shawls which covered their heads and shoulders. They dressed in light coloured gowns, plain in shape but flowery in pattern and on the Sabbath and holiday time they were always tidy and clean.

The houses are surprisingly plain and dull outside. The roofs are of wood and easily constructed. It was an exception to find chairs or tables in the rooms of the genuine Mexicans. Floors were used as tables and chairs and they preferred hands to knives and forks. The shining knives hanging from their belts were not for the purpose of eating or carving. Their diets consisted of tortillas (thin flat cakes made of maize-flour baked on a flat ironplate not unlike griddle cakes or fresh bread found in Wales). They also use cayenne pepper made from their chilli pods. I was surprised to see so many of these tied onto red and green ropes beside their houses. Red pepper is used here more often than onions are used in Wales. Fréjoles, namely peas, broad beans and garlic form part of their diet. Meat is seldom eaten since it is not readily available. When it is included, it has to be cooked with plenty of red pepper and garlic. It is said that Mexicans are quite happy whilst they have a string of red peppers and a packet of broad beans handy and that they refuse to work if they possess a granule of one or the other!

These people are more skilful as farmers than the Pueblo Indians but I do not recommend that it would be profitable for any farmer to come over from Wales to practise the industry their way. Their 'threshing machine' is made up of several sheep or goats – fifty more or less, but sometimes as many as a hundred. They are made to trot and jump over the corn in a circle. These animals are so well trained that when they move, they all move, and when they stop, they all stop – as regimental as soldiers.

I visited the barracks. The soldiers wore white uniforms making their skins appear much darker. Nearby, there were scores of them washing themselves and their clothes in a murky lake – one which had been purposely constructed for that use. The most amusing event I witnessed in this place was a fight between two men. I am somewhat convinced that anyone thinking of taking up this sport would gain if he had instructions from either of these men. One of them would hold the other with his hands and shake him about with all his might. Then the other one would have a go using the same method and that was the way they continued until they tired out. The one to flag first or the one who had been overcome was the defeated one. Fighting with fists is not an option with them. Pistols and knives are the weapons used when things get too steamed up by shaking alone. With the exception of this serious fight, I never saw anything disagreeable amongst these people. They have shapely figures and many of them are quite attractive.

The town was so bereft of window displays and signs that it was almost impossible to distinguish between shop and house. Amazingly, the hoteliers do not go out of their way to attract trade. They are possessed of a surly humility and sometimes pretend that things requested are not available, when in fact, they have everything appertaining to the convenience and fashion of the people. They do not consider that artistic decoration is important except when it applies to their churches and Sunday-best clothes. Their churches, although old, have columns and towers on the outside and many images and pictures inside. When one realizes that every place in their country has been named after a Guardian Saint or the Holy Cross, one would think that they are quite religious. Yet, as far as the boundaries of belief are concerned, their religious practices are quite indistinct. They are dim in their intellect and sinful in their conduct.

Arizona

In Arizona I found the terminus of the new railroad to California – the *Southern Pacific*. I started my journey towards midnight and after being on wheels for eighty-eight miles, I found myself in Deming where passengers from the north-east enter on their way to California. About forty miles west of Deming a clear and beautiful lake came into view with the overshadowing mountains reflecting brilliantly upon it. It was called a mirage. There was not a drop of water in the vicinity since the 'lake' was just hot, deceiving sands. After travelling scores of miles yet, I crossed the line to the large territory of Arizona; the name when translated means 'the beauty of the sun'. It is said that a vast amount of Arizona's land will be quite productive once an efficient irrigation system is in operation. It is in its underground assets that Arizona can

Tomorrow's Man

take pride though. It is prophesied that one day this state will be recognized as the richest place on earth. Millions of dollars have been offered for some of its gold, silver and copper mines. Complete pieces of boulders, half a ton in weight, are worth between three and four hundred dollars (£60-£80) per ton. One lode, ten miles long, has produced a quantity valued at 200,000 dollars (£40,000) per month. These new productive veins have only just been opened.

Spanish adventurers settled in this area as early as 1540. Twenty years later missionary stations were established here by the Jesuits. By the year 1725 they had thirty such stations with seventy-one Indian villages also under their superintendence. They began to reform the savages who were quite willing to be educated by them. The contempt the papal teachers expressed towards these people increased to such a degree though, that the pupils started to revolt against them. They killed the missionaries and burnt their stations. This territory was also a sanctuary for white criminals for years. The most wicked of people: thieves, murderers and the rejected of society were able to do whatever they wanted to and the inhabitants were more afraid of these people than the Indians. A week after I had departed, a crowd of them attempted to rob a train and its passengers. However, their day, as well as that of the Indians, is quickly disappearing, with civilisation and law and order overcoming the hostility.

145

After travelling for half the night over barren land, without ridges, houses, fields, woods or animals in sight – only vast even plains, it was a blessing to see a camp of white tents and an army of black soldiers who were there to wage war against the red Apaches. These soldiers were anxious to receive any reports that brought the outside world closer to them.

Cacti

Apart from the mountainous drums that can be seen in the far distance, there was nothing specific on these plains to draw one's attention, except these marvellous plants known as cacti or prickly pears. It is said that there are more than three hundred kinds growing in this area. Some are coloured green and are as small as the tiniest of eggs; they are prickly and are covered with minute holes. Others have thick, round leaves similar to spiky thorns whilst others are in different sized tufts, covered with leaves, or rather long, thick, triple-edged 'swords' which are as sharp as needles and as hard as wood. Falling over one of these tufts, some of them several feet in diameter, could be fatal. Out of the stalks of some of them, one sees growths of around fifteen feet, similar to thin, flat, branchless and leafless sticks. Others have no growth on their spines, only multi-bladed tufts growing quite compact on their heads. Others are like some kind of wood with branches that are covered with prickly, thick, twisted leaves. On others, thick prickly leaves cover the stem from base to tip. One kind, maybe one that should be called a 'palm-tree', grows to a height of sixty feet. That is the most spectacular one of all, not only because of its size but because of its colour and formation. Its ridged stalk is three feet in diameter at ground level; it then tapers gradually as it grows to a point. All over the stem, sharp, spiky growths varying in length from one to three inches appear. Some of these coiled, prickly, ridged and gigantic cacti have five or six 'spires' growing outwards and upwards from their spine. A picture of them would be similar to that of the paintings of the Tabernacle's candlestick. The green and yellow colours of these 'spires' complement each other excellently. A flower blossoms on their peaks once a year and they produce a fruit which is much enjoyed by the Indians. This kind is called 'boss cactus'. The woodpecker pecks a hole in it near its top and it is in this hole that the bird nests and hatches its chicks. Apart from the woodpecker, it is said that the rattle-snake, the lizard and the owl are the other live creatures to be found where these plants are in abundance. High, sandy land, at the base of rocks – places where no trees or any other plant can grow – are the prime areas of the cacti species.

Antiquities

Mention has already been made about ancient remains, at the beginning of the journey through New Mexico, but much more can be said. However, it is in Arizona, on the line to California, that one finds the most astonishing vestiges. Tucson (population 5,000) is three hundred and seven miles west of El Paso. It was proclaimed that it was the oldest town in America by the most elderly inhabitants but unfortunately no-one is able to determine between it and Santa Fe these days. This is how Tucson was described by a traveller twenty-five years ago:-

> Tucson is the capital of the territory now with a population of 600, almost half of them Mexicans and the rest a mixture of Apaches, Pimos, Papagoes and throat-cutters. No doubt, not within the walls of any city would you find such a collection of horse-thieves, gamblers, murderers, wasters and all kinds of rascals. One could believe that the place was a hill foremostly and that it had been struck and scattered by judicial lightning and that the muddy, dirty, awful, wretched holes are the remains of the destruction within which the corrupt group chose to breathe. No white wall or green tree was visible. All one could see were relics of sheds, old riddles, old cauldrons and broken vessels, derelict corrals, dead horses, live dogs, drunken Indians, naked children, mules, pigs and all kind of contamination. Never had I seen such a sight within the boundaries of civilization. I was overcome with a loathsome sensation. There was no fonda (public house) of any kind there and after arriving at a place which should have been a plaza (a park in the centre of town) all that remained was complete confusion and perplexity as to where to go next. At last we found an old earthen ruin. We laid our blankets on the earthen floor and cooked our meal on an earthen hearth and when night fell we collected all that we possessed, namely a waggon, mules and all else within the earthen walls before bolting the doors. We decided that the best thing to do was to go away and we departed early in the morning.

The town is much more attractive than that description now. Buildings of the latest fashion have been erected and the inhabitants have higher standards. It has, however, lost its birthright to be the capital of the territory since the borough of Prescott seized that honour.

Ten miles from Tucson is situated the famous old church of San Xavier del Bac – 115 feet long by 75 feet wide. It was built by the Jesuit missionaries in the form of a Cross two hundred years ago and is still quite solid and very beautiful with remarkable ornamentation which makes it a pleasure to look at. The amazing thing is, that such a brilliant and costly building has stood up throughout the ages, right in the midst of poor, half-naked Indians. These people come here to say their morning prayers in the west wing. The south wing is used as a convent where four kindly sisters attend to the sick and educate the Indians.

About twelve miles north of Casa Grande station and south of the Gila River, Casa Grande (Big House) is situated. It is a large structural ruin standing amongst many others, along a distance of several miles and surrounded by a canal derived from the Gila River. This particular house is 63 feet long, 45 feet wide and the ruined walls rise to 40 feet in height and are 5 feet deep. It has many long and narrow rooms, as well as two smaller ones and it used to be a four-storey building. It is reckoned that such houses were built eight hundred years ago. They are in exceptional condition but it is said that even the largest here is tiny compared to some elsewhere. The foundation of one building is 350 feet long and 150 feet wide. Amongst the demolition, pieces of vessels and tools are found. If the present Pimos, Maricobas, Cuchans, Mojaves, Papagoes, Zunis and Moquis are descendants of earlier natives, they have degenerated immensely. They have no knowledge regarding the construction of these buildings and the missionaries did not receive any explanation from the Indians when they were here three hundred years ago either. It is said that further upstream, on the banks of the Gila, there are ruins which are also just as strange. An old canal, sixty miles long by fifty miles wide, has been discovered there, as well as man-made lakes. At the summit of a narrow, steep mountain ridge, there is a large, strong castle. Occasionally, cremation urns containing ash and burnt human bones are found in this area. Hieroglyphs of men, animals, birds, reptiles and so on, have been deeply carved and painted on the rocks.

The Wilderness of Gila

After being on wheels for a long stretch west of Casa Grande, we travelled through rugged, bare and rocky hills, ones showing signs that in times long ago, they had been lit up by blazing explosions erupting from the earth's crust. Patches of the ground still show the colourings and signs of the scorch marks with lava covering the entire lowland. We were now in a horrible, empty desert similar to the Desert of Arabia. Nothing can be seen growing out of this fine sand except scatterings of thin bushes – sages and other crinkly plants. I saw one large lake with its water white and thick by alkali mud. We carry water on the train over a distance of one hundred and fifty miles – for railroad use and as a drink for passengers. The temperature is very hot, as high as 125 degrees in the

148

shade and sometimes higher. There are no buildings from Maricoba to Yuma apart from the ones erected for railroad purposes. These buildings have two roofs, one around two feet above the other to prevent the sun's intense heat from penetrating. After travelling for a long time on the south side of the Gila River, we crossed it by Adonde. Here, only volcanic residue covered the ground and filled the fissures between the stones. The mountain peaks embraced us and the rocks on the northern side appeared like castles transmitting heaviness and seriousness.

After travelling two hundred and forty-seven miles west of Tucson, I came to Fort Yuma, on the banks of the Colorado River, where the Gila joins it one hundred miles north of the Gulf of California. The Gila widens by several miles before it pours itself into the Colorado which is the most romantic river in the world. Sailing takes place on it over an area of five hundred miles. Three hundred miles of the river passes through a deep, straight fissure that varies in depth from 1,000 to 3,000 feet. Yuma is an amazing town consisting of plain, adobe dwellings. The houses have no lofts and the walls are made of sun-baked turfs and bricks, four or five feet in depth, with roofs made of soil, two feet deep. The houses are surrounded by wide verandas propped up by sticks and large poles and all dwellings are enclosed with fences made of earthen materials. This is the most mundane and dismal town I have ever come across. There is no greenery here at all – only rocks, dwellings, cloudy water and people with ashen complexions! The population is made up of Indians, Mexicans, Spaniards and Americans. People sleep on top of houses and are clad with as little clothing as possible. The Indians have one garment which is a pocket handkerchief used for the same purpose as Eve's fig leaf. From this piece of clout, some of the more wealthy and conceited ones have a red ribbon hanging down behind them like a monkey's tail and long enough for it to drag behind on the ground, depicting the style of a high society lady's gown worn in Britain. Roman Catholicism is the religion and it is said that the people, in spite of their natural differences, have fairly good moral values.

This town had an interesting beginning. Shortly after Arizona became a member of the United States, people from California came here, with a short stay intention, to seek valuable minerals. After estimating the materials needed and all the costings, they decided to return home to save enough money to enable them to carry out the necessary work. They came to the Colorado River and discovered that they could not cross it. On the other side was a German who owned a boat but they did not have twenty-five dollars (the asking charge) to pay him. They decided to camp overnight by the river. In the meantime, very early the following morning, one of them had a brainwave and acted upon it early the next day. With a compass, some sticks and small banners, they began to measure the land, divide it into lots and plan imaginary roads. The German, seeing the activities, rowed over to see what was happening. They told him that they intended to construct a city as well as a harbour for merchant shipping and that the area was to become an important trading venue. The German, on hearing this, became very enthusiastic and wanted to buy two lots. These, they sold to him with the condition, that in exchange, they would be transported in his boat across the river as part-payment; thus they crossed the river quite safely. All the Californian adventurers had in mind was trickery and I suppose the Welsh proverb applied here: *os na byddi gryf, bydd gyfrwys* (if you can't be strong, be cunning). Word got around and construction work did begin. By now Yuma is a town of 3,000 inhabitants and on the increase.

The Colorado Desert

After crossing the Colorado River I was in fact in the largest, richest and most famous state in the Union – California; the country of aureate prosperity, incomparable orchards, large fruit, natural crops as well as cultivated ones; a country of evergreen meadows, ageless woods, delightful climate and lovely glades where flowers blossom all year round; a place where winter does not touch and neither snow nor ice can spoil its beauty. A country, it is said, where the blessings of the seas, the skies, the mountains and the valleys are its heritage. Was that the way I found it? No, indeed, far from being so. Over one hundred and fifty miles north-west of Yuma there was hardly anything to see except wilderness; parts of it were very barren with nothing but white sand in some areas. In other parts species of sagebrush appeared along with other feeble plants. This region is called the 'Wilderness of Colorado' because its borders run alongside the Colorado River. This river traverses between two long chains of mountains. After travelling sixty miles beyond Yuma, we started to descend into deep crevices until we had dropped 266 feet below sea level and 300 feet below the surrounding shoreline which was actually 40 feet above the water when this sunken area was a sea in reality. Clear proof is available to show that this was a fact, hundreds or maybe thousands of years ago. Salty water can still be scooped up if one digs deep enough. After the region ceased to be an arm of the Pacific Ocean, it had a period of being just a lake of clear water as the multitude of shells and small, smooth pebbles seen in layers on the slopes confirm. They look so new and prominent as if it was only yesterday the water had receded. The Pacific Ocean lost a large area of its territory here because the desert's sand pushed it out. The lovely lake ceased to exist too because the sand absorbed the streams that supplied it and the river lost its identity. It was amazing to think that I was travelling in a place where ships had cruised hundreds of feet above where I was standing and also where whales had played in the deep, but like Jonah[14] of long ago, I also came up safe and sound!

Around this wonderful valley, there are twenty-five square miles of mud-springs; some are cold ones but most are hot and their content is similar to gruel or porridge, forever boiling and puffing out of the ground. They have varying depths, some 200 feet and some lower. Some are level with the ground while others rise in a conical form to a height of 25 feet. They have a foul smell and sometimes a thundery sound can be heard underground. Sometimes gales create sandstorms in this region and at other times, parts of it are flooded by cloudbursts that occur above higher ground causing rivers to rise to 30 feet as they flow through sandy valleys. It is said that on the left side of San Jacinto's mountains thunderous sounds can be heard. As yet, nobody has been able to shed any light on these disturbances. All of a sudden a peal of thunder can be heard as if ten grenades are fired simultaneously and sometimes this happens three or four times a night. At other times, several days will elapse before they are heard. They wake everyone within hearing distance and the houses shake far more than when an ordinary earthquake occurs. The source of these tremors has not been discovered and the Indians refuse to go near the area. It is reputed that some of them came across the spot by accident when hunting once and that they discovered that the noise came from a dark, gigantic cave. They believed that the old *tah-quish* (evil spirit) was trying to escape from his hot prison in order to breathe fresh air and in so doing was frightened by something from outside. These Indians reckoned that the noise heard was that of a door banging as the spirit retreated. Almost everyone accepts this theory.

The Valleys of the South

After advancing from the seabed and travelling quite a distance, keeping the mountains of San Bernardino to our right and the mountains of San Jacinto to our left, we moved through the San Gorgonio Pass, 2,600 feet above sea level. We were within sight of the San Bernardino valley and there I found something which was akin to California – fruitful vineyards, orchards, apple tree enclosures, golden apple areas and so on. Two crops are produced each year; barley is the main one – 50 measures per acre, then Indian corn, 50-60 measures per acre; also a crop known as alfalfa, one which is perennial once sown; this one is more profitable than any other and five or six crops are grown annually.

Four miles from Colton's station lies the town of San Bernardino (population 6,000). In 1847, this town and its surroundings were occupied by the Latter-day Saints. They were being persecuted in Illinois and their leader ordered several of them to move onwards in order to inhabit this particular glade. Since they were surrounded by mountains and deserts, the leader thought that this place was ideal as a peaceful settlement for all the saints. After 300 of their families had worked hard to irrigate the land, grow crops, plant trees and construct the city by the same plan as the urban district of Salt Lake was built afterwards, the prophet came to the conclusion, because of the acclaim the area was receiving, that they would not experience this trouble-free life for long; that other peoples would be sure to come to disturb them. Therefore, he issued a command to his followers; they were to leave the happy neighbourhood they had created for themselves, pick up their packs and start on a long pilgrimage over the rugged Sierra Mountains and the wilderness of America in order to settle in the wasteland of Salt Lake. Most of them obeyed but some remained where they felt their roots were by now. Where can one find such extraordinary example of exodus and self sacrifice for the sake of religion? The Israelites left Egypt for a land flowing with milk and honey – (Joshua 5,6) but these people left excellent countryside and surroundings and escaped to the wilderness in order to be able to enjoy their religion according to their beliefs. It was surprising that Brigham Young, he being a prophet, did not foresee that a railroad would eventually be constructed and that other settlers would arrive in the city of Salt Lake several years before anyone would ever venture to the valley of San Bernardino. As far as the saints who decided to stay put were concerned, they themselves said, that in spite of their fertile land and every other natural comfort and facility, they were like the captives by the rivers of Babylon, weeping and longing to be with their own people – (Psalm 137,1). They numbered about one hundred and fifty in all, all belonging to the Joseph Order; ones who refused to recognize Brigham as a prophet and loathed the idea of a man having several wives.

After another forty-two miles, I arrived in Los Angeles (population 12,000), two hundred and forty-nine miles north-west of Yuma. This is the largest and most famous town in southern California. It is situated on the south side of the Sierra Santa Monica mountain range; is connected by rail and is about eighteen miles from the town of Santa Monica – on the Pacific Ocean's coast. It was founded by the Papal Missionaries in 1771, therefore as a town in California, it is considered old. The whole setting is rich and paradisean – gardens and rows of orchard trees producing golden apples, lemons, limes, grapes, figs, bananas, peppers, melons, pomegranates, almonds and all other produce available in an equatorial region. Near San Gabriel, only a short distance away, one finds the largest orange orchard in the state, measuring 500 acres. This area does not experience wintry weather such as snow and ice and without a doubt, it is an ideal place to live in. I understand that there are some Welsh people residing in and around Los Angeles but I was so unfortunate when I was in that region, not to have known that there were some cousins of mine there, ones who had been my playmates as a child.

Over Mountains and Wilderness

This is a very strange land! Nothing ordinary or moderate relates to this area; everything is in extreme – extreme wilderness or extreme fruitfulness; eternal winters or eternal summers; snow and ice all year or constant greenery. After travelling hundreds of miles over baking wilderness and parched land, I came to the delightful valleys of San Bernardino and Los Angeles – places where the best of fruits can be gathered. Yet again, I am about to proceed over craggy mountains and one hundred miles of unpleasant wilderness and after going over, through and between mountain ranges, I find myself in a very picturesque place. I have arrived in a most fertile region that cannot be excelled anywhere under the heaven's stars.

On the mountain of San Fernando, we went through a straight tunnel – 7,000 feet in length. After travelling some distance, we came to a long gap, twenty-five miles long, with its engulfing walls rising from 500 to 2,000 feet in height. This area is inhabited by Mexicans and the pass is called Robbers' Roost. Many people were captured by the Mexicans in this nestle of theirs. Some of them were brought to justice and had to pay for their actions. They were beheaded by the 'men of law and order' without hardly any protests. After descending from these mountains we covered a large area of around one hundred miles of fine sand with only a few sages and palm-trees sparsely scattered here and there. These trees, like the cacti, flourish in soil that would destroy any other vegetation. Palm-trees are often referred to in the Scriptures. There are many varieties of them and their benefit to the children of the desert is beyond any reckoning. I also thanked them for interrupting the harsh monotony of the wilderness. Paper is the only product made from them in these parts and there are mills for this purpose nearby.

We ascended from this barren desert to a high mountain, a place located at the peak of the Tehachapi Pass. We had reached the highest point of this railroad and were 3,964 feet above sea level. The next stop was Caliente, twenty-five miles further again. We descended 1,674 feet, went through seventeen tunnels and over many bridges and viaducts; the drop in some places was sensational. The most amazing mechanical feature relating to the train on this route is 'the loop'. It is 3,795 feet long and the higher kerb is 78 feet above the lower one. What is it? Well, it is the way the railroad is made to turn and cross over itself many times, similar to a bow-tie. Along the route there are other turnings known as corkscrews and at the base of the ascent lies Caliente, one hundred and forty-six miles from Los Angeles and three hundred and thirty-six miles from San Francisco.

The Valleys of the Plains

The valley of San Joaquin, along with the regions of Tulare and Kern, are on a high plateau three hundred miles long and on average thirty-five miles wide. This area is situated between the Coast Ranges and the Sierra Mountains and it is one of the best agricultural glades in this famous state. It is irrigated by rainfall but there is a necessity for canals as well; some canals are forty miles long, between 100 and 275 feet wide and about 8 feet deep. Occasionally, artesian wells are constructed; they are deep holes dug down to the depths of the earth until a water vein is reached. The vein, if its source is from higher ground, spurts up its contents with great force. This territory is mostly divided up into ranches. A ranch is much larger than a farm the same way as a farm is larger than a garden. Close to the line I was travelling on, there is a ranch seventy-three miles long by twenty miles wide – a farm where 85,000 cattle and 40,000 sheep are reared. Two crops of barley and wheat are grown annually as well as six crops of alfalfa. There is no need for barns or even the task of thatching ricks or sheaving corn. The rainy season does not start until all the grain has been threshed and stored. Snow and ice do not touch this area and every kind of fruit tree is found here. Some of the ranchers employ their own craftsmen and manual workers for the purpose of assembling their own machinery and furniture.

One of the largest ploughs in the world belongs to one rancher who lives in this area. It is called 'Great Western' and weighs over a ton. It is pulled by 80 oxen and is capable of ploughing a furrow eight miles long, five feet wide and three feet deep in one day. The owner of this plough has another, called 'Samson' and this one is pulled by 40 she-oxen and is used to dig trenches. Water-courses and canals cover one hundred and fifty miles of this ranch; there are two artesian wells here as well and they are 260 and 300 feet deep respectively. Both wells continuously spout two columns of water to a height of twelve feet above ground. They are seven inches in diameter and supply a daily provision of 80,000 gallons. Ordinary farmers are powerless to till this land because they are unable to finance an irrigation system nor can they afford to drain the marshy land. The wealthy landowners are fortunate enough to be able to complement one with the other and when construction of all the canals and the accomplishment of every other necessary progression are completed, the aim is to split the ranches into smaller farms according to the buyers' wishes. In Madera, in this valley, two hundred and ninety-seven miles from Los Angeles and one hundred and eighty-five miles from San Francisco, it is customary these days, for people to leave the train here in order to travel seventy miles east to see the large forest and the Yosemite valley – places which are at the top of the chart pertaining to the natural wonders of the world. In Lathrop we joined the *Central Pacific* line, then we turned towards the west. In Antioch, we proceeded to Suisin Bay which is a continuation of San Pablo Bay which is also an extension of the Pacific Ocean's inland flow. A short distance south of Antioch lies Nortonville, where there is a settlement of Welsh miners. Slightly south again lies the Diablo Mountain. From this mountain's summit one can see: 'all the kingdoms of the world and the glory of them' – (Matthew 4,8). This mountain rises majestically between the valleys of Sacramento and San Joaquin to a height of 3,856 feet. A view of 40,000 square miles covering the main valleys, mountains, rivers, bays and the cities of California (apart from the stretch to the Pacific Ocean) can be seen from this mountain's highest peak. After leaving the before mentioned bay south of us, we travelled for some hours over hilly, rocky land varying in its scenery. We arrived in Oakland (population 35,000) and were taken off the town's wharf and across the Bay of San Francisco by a steamboat. We were, indeed, in the famous city.

San Francisco

In the far west, if such saying is accepted (because the places beyond this area are called far east), there lies a place called the Golden Gate which has been created by the Pacific Ocean covering an area of one mile wide by squeezing itself into this glorious Californian countryside. After succeeding, it spread northwards and eastwards and these areas are called San Pablo and Suisin Bays. They cover sixty miles; another arm flows south under the name of San Francisco Bay. Towards its neck, between the Pacific Ocean and the last mentioned bay's shore, near to the Golden Gate, lies the city of San Francisco, queen of the far west and main port of the Pacific Ocean. The first house was built here in 1835. The city was called Yuba Buena first of all, but since the year 1847, when its inhabitants numbered 459, it has been called San Francisco. In 1848, gold was discovered in the neighbourhood and in 1852 the city's population rose to 34,870. It was almost burnt down six times.

Nowadays, its splendid buildings are usually made of stone and steel. Its present population is 235,000. Between it and Oakland, it will soon be 300,000. San Francisco trades extensively with all the countries of the globe from east to east (since it, itself, is our west). Its population is made up of many nations. The inhabitants, according to their varying occupations, are labouring diligently and 'minding their own business'. The bootblacks carry out their work in a way that the sons of Saint Crispin would be proud of. They make their customers sit on high benches under a shady canopy with their feet on footrests while their boots are polished to such sheen that you can see your face in them. The city's beggars do not hesitate to ask you for money to pay for a hearty meal. One of them refused to let me order a dinner for him in a restaurant because he wanted to appear as a gentleman and request the meal himself. The women of Venus have their own streets and they dress as playgirls. After the lamps are lit, they perform in the 'free theatres' where alcoholic drinks are served. Since there is no charge to enter these buildings, the foolish youngsters assemble there in their thousands and often find themselves on slippery slopes to all kinds of wickedness and perditions.

There is a bright and promising aspect to the city though. There are scores of chapels, churches and charitable societies here. Very virtuous men live here as well; some devoting their whole life to converting the wayward ones. One such man is the Reverend Aaron Williams. He has no money and earns no wage, only: 'give us this day our daily bread' – (Matthew 6,11). He gives of his all, at all times, to missionary work in this big city. He visits the unfortunate, warns the unruly and acts as doorman in the free theatres, abiding his time to advise wild youngsters. Yes, dressed as a cleric, he ventures to the ghettos of the foolhardy folk to see if he can bring shame on them. He is recognized by the bosses of these hellholes as well as the ministers of the ornate pulpits. It was he, who had no cash to spare, once said to me, that if I was ever in need, to approach him; he thought he could be of help to me. Luckily I never had to take up his offer but I was amazed at his trust in the 'Giver of all Goodness', since it was that means he was referring to, no doubt. His life story proves that his optimism was well founded. Today, a Welsh church has been established in the city. Welsh people also worship in a hall that is owned by them. The best of luck to them; may they be very successful.

By the kindness of D. Roberts Esquire, the intricacies of the mint, where the government's money is coined, were shown to me. I saw the miner bringing in the gold-dust in a leather bag, weighing it, putting it in the furnace, purifying it, testing it and weighing it again; moulding it into bars, breaking the bars into round pieces, stamping and putting them on a special board so that it would be known immediately how many coins there were without having to count them. Silver dollars and twenty dollar gold coins were the ones minted that day. This city has spectacular and comfortable hotels, the largest of which is the seven-storey Palace Hotel – 344 feet long, 265 feet wide and 115 feet high. In its foyer, there are several elevators as well as artesian wells spouting 28,000 gallons of water every hour; also other fittings too complex to be described here. There are many streetcars in the city travelling up and down without anything visible operating them. An underground rope is continually controlling them and the vehicles have an arm and a claw passing through an open fissure in the ground. When the claw grasps the rope, the vehicle moves and when it releases its grip it stops instantaneously.

At Seal Rock, near the Golden Gate, about six miles outside the city, there is a very popular promenade and seals are to be seen here in large numbers; some with only their top halves showing in the water whilst others relax on the rocks, calling out: 'Ioi, Hoi, Ioi, Hoi, Ioi,' reminding me of the drovers' call when they were directing their animals. I was surprised to find food and other commodities in the city so inexpensive. There were large fruit of every kind being sold on stalls in the streets, wine as abundant as milk and almost as cheap. Whoever wants to be a fashionable gentleman here, water is the drink for him. Through Oakland, luxurious, long trains run both ways every half hour and they are free of charge. The city's council bargained for this concession when it allowed the railroad to go through the city. San Francisco and Oakland are situated on plains and steep hills. They are shaken by earthquakes at times but no great destruction has been caused by these tremors. Maybe it was in days long ago that the big disturbances were happening.

The Chinese

The Chinese are the people who are given the most attention in California, mostly because of their cheap labour, their mannerisms, attire and customs. They are short, frail looking people usually; however, some are big in stature and quite robust. Their skin is yellowish and they have triangular faces, high cheek-bones, narrow eyes with the outer corners lower than the inner ones. They are not fussy what kind of trousers, boots or hats they wear; sometimes they follow other people's style; at other times they dress in their own traditional fashion with boots similar to little boats. The best garments are always made of satin. As far as tunics are concerned, there is a religious necessity for uniformity. They are made of cotton or satin and only come to just below the waist in men but women wear them full length. The sleeves of these tunics are clerical style. The men shave their heads but leave a tuft of hair, the size of a teacup, on the crown and let it grow to its full length. They then plait three skeins of it into a long, thin tail and leave it hanging over their backs. The women never cut their hair but encircle it round their heads in a very artistic way. Since the men do not have beards and both sexes dress alike, they can be more easily distinguished by their hair than by any other means. A large area of San Francisco is populated only by Chinese and their presence here is so dense that it is unlikely that a mouse could penetrate into their midst and if one did find a mouse here, it would be eaten with relish! Some of their streets are narrow and consist of high buildings with small but numerous rooms. They make use of every nook and crevice though, from the basement to the attic. They feast with chopsticks from the leftovers of some poor, white people. An evening stroll along these streets is an eye-opener. On a corner, every so often, one finds a frail, needy Chinese, standing by his stall with a wan, blue flame that casts enough light to expose the dark and to show that he has something edible to sell. Through the gloom, the stallholders' squeaky, childish, piercing voices could be heard calling out for customers; they sounded as if they were coming from underground. Apart from that, no shouts or cries are heard only the sound of lightfooted people intermingling in the darkness. The smell in that district was quite offensive, making me wonder whether I really was at the gateway to hell. Along the wider streets there is more lighting, as well as shops and theatres with round, multicoloured, satin lanterns hanging on the outside walls. All is as Chinese in appearance as an American city can possibly be. They worship their idols in their joss-houses. In their theatres there are some awful pictures, such as that of spirits rising from bottomless pits making harsh sounds, similar to cats miaowing, apparently about something that happened twenty thousand years ago. After being in them once, there is no desire to return. The Chinese are very useful people in California and strangely enough, because of this, they are hated by many. They are prepared to take on all kinds of work – indoors as well as outdoors; they sometimes take on work normally done by women for half the wages paid to other people, even less than half sometimes. The Irish are their worst enemies because they have outdone them with pick and shovel work. The anti-Chinese party is strong, even in the senate of the country which has been trying to bring legislation against their entry for many years. What grounds they have for this animosity, I do not know. It is said that because of their cheap labour, they are taking 'the bread and butter' from other people's mouths and that they pollute the morality of the community. Pharaonic fears are spread around that they will multiply and become the rulers of the country. To understand the enmity towards them, take the following tables from the country and city of San Francisco for the year 1878 when the Chinese population was 25,450. Admitted to hospital: Americans – 913, Irish – 948, Chinese – 0, others – 1,140. Admitted to almshouses: Americans 138, Irish – 175; Chinese – 1, others – 150. Imprisoned for drunkenness: 6,127 – not a single Chinese. During this year, the Chinese paid the government $550,000 internal revenue taxes (in the city alone); poll taxes (in the state) $180,000; licences (in the state) $41,000; property taxes – $220,000; duties paid on imports – $1,768,000. They exported commodities (part of which were 209,000 barrels of barley) to the value of $3,103,320. These people are experts in vineyard work and they are unequalled when it comes to hard and diligent labour. It is doubtful whether the railroad would have been completed had it not been for the Chinese workers. They endured high temperatures in the arid desert of the south-west. Fair play to the children of the sun I say; they are the main launderers in the west.

The Geysers
About one hundred miles north of San Francisco, strange wells, known as geysers, spout boiling water out of the earth. To go there, I took the steamboat to Donahue, a distance of thirty-four miles; then the train to Gloverdale. I was told that I was travelling through a country producing large quantities of fruit as well as milk. On this line, not far from San Pablo Bay, lies Petaluma, the town where the Reverend Rees Gwesyn Jones, D.D. lives. It was late by the time I reached Gloverdale. I stayed there overnight and since there was no train to take me to the geysers the following day, a distance of sixteen miles uphill, I decided to walk. It was a pleasant day with the road winding alongside a lovely, bubbling stream which flowed between rocky and woody banks, displaying a beautiful panorama. I spent the evening gazing at the natural wonders of the area.

The Geysers: I could see their vapour, similar to that of a steamboat, rising high into the sky long before I was anywhere near them and it is said that occasionally one can hear their sound a mile away. They are to be found in muddy, hot, red and bare fissures on the brows of cliffs. I felt that I was trampling on volcanic ground since my soles were getting very hot. From this particular area of land over two hundred springs erupt, all differing in colours and temperatures; usually they are at boiling point – waters of iron, soda, alum, sulphur and many other kinds. Some are as black as ink, others as white as milk, some make a hissing sound like geese, some sing like a tea-kettle, some thunder like a flour-mill, others roar like a steamboat when its steam rises high into the air. The largest spring is called 'Witch's Cauldron' – about six feet in diameter but its depth has not been discovered as yet. Situated in a rocky cauldron, it spurts its dark, boiling water high into the air. It reminds me of Shakespeare's lines whence it had its name:

> For a charm of powerful trouble, like a hell-broth boil and bubble,
> Double, double, toil and trouble, fire burn and cauldron bubble.

There is no greenery and no amiability whatsoever here. It is a strange and awesome place. It is said that one German after arriving here, turned on his heel and said, 'Let's hurry from this place. I know that hell itself is only half a mile away!'

Other Geysers

At nightfall, I sat down to relax a little on the warm, volcanic ground because I thought that a wild animal would not dare venture to this bare, frightful region. I waited for the moon to appear so that I could start my journey back to Gloverdale in order to catch the five o'clock early morning train. I experienced the most frightful occurrences that night. The forward journey had been pleasant but the return one was another story. I was scared and knew that I was far from any habitation. I had only seen four houses on my way up from Gloverdale. I remembered seeing some sheep grazing though and that gave me hope that the wild animals were not too hungry. The moon seemed more beautiful and affectionate than I had ever noticed before; it only appeared intermittently and since I was walking through a deep valley, sometimes rocks or mountains would block it from my view. The moonlight and the shadows of the cliffs and trees would exchange positions every so often, as if they were amusing each other. Only the murmuring sound of the stream corresponded with the footsteps of the lonely traveller. My thoughts, that night, wandered far and wide on the wings of imagination – sometimes over the continent and over the ocean to my wife and two young children in distant Wales; sometimes towards the stars and beyond them even, to the spiritual sphere. Maybe some who were already in this world were now looking down as I journeyed on this track. Sometimes, my mind would insist on conjuring up events of very long ago – the beginning of time and the wonders of the world and wishing to ask the moon and the cliffs when had they started to greet one another the way they were doing this night and what strange events had they witnessed on this path since they had come to know each other. At other times, it was to the distant future I was thinking, imagining the end and reciting:

Chwi gedyrn binaclau y ddaear, gydoeswch a huan a lloer,
Safasoch effeithiau difäol, a threulfawr hin wresog ac oer;
Ond gwelaf ddiwrnod gyferbyn – a ellwch chwi sefyll pryd hyn?
Y ddaear a ymchwel fel meddwyn, a nerthoedd y Nefoedd a gryn.

(You strong earthly pinnacles, with the sun and the moon you have journeyed,
You have withstood devouring phenomena and contrasting weather conditions;
However, I see a day forthcoming – will you be able to cope then?
When the earth will slump like a drunkard and Heaven's energies will tremble).

What next? Well, I went with Emanuel Swedenborg[15] to spiritual territory and there I endeavoured to see heaven and earth, the sun, the moon, the stars, the mountains, animals and everything else – not in their rough, earthly embodiment but in a subjective, spiritual form; in a fresh and heavenly setting, a thousand times more glorious than how they appeared here. Lost in such meditations I was, when I was woken by the sound of the heavy paws of a creature in the bushes on my left. Here I was on a narrow plain which was sheltered by rocks and tall trees. On my right there was an empty building; I don't think there was another one for miles. I kept quite still when I heard the noise. The animal stopped too. When I started walking again, it also moved through the thick vegetation. I slowed down because I remembered that I had been told that it was safer not to hurry or show signs of fear in the presence of a dangerous beast. What it was, I never found out, but it was kind enough not to follow me and when I thought I was out of danger, I practised the military order: 'Quick time-Forward-March'. That was the end of Swedeborgism and all spiritual geysers that night.

After getting all my clothes wet while crossing a wide river, I arrived in Gloverdale and it was two o'clock in the morning. Every house was quiet except one grogshop where a lot of rowdiness and swearing emerged from it. Farther on, in a dark, shady place where moonlight could not infiltrate, I discovered a group of motionless and quiet men who were encircling two men who were in combat on the ground. After another three hours in the station shivering in my wet clothes and the chilly morning air, the train arrived. When I was boarding, I met a bear-hunter by the name of John Wesley Curadon. He told me that I was lucky not to have been a 'breakfast' for some wild creature who would have relished me without pepper or salt or grace!

Mr Curadon owned a small farm of fifteen thousand acres and he could not imagine how anyone felt contented on farms of one or two hundred acres. He said I was welcome to go to his home and he promised me a horse and a gun so that I could join him in his hunting pursuits. His father, a nephew and himself were the only occupants of his farm. He said that he once knew a Welshman by the name of George Davies who was the most ferocious man and the most skilled fighter that he had ever come across. I promised him, that if circumstances permitted, that I would spend a week or two with him the next time I came to California. By the time I reached San Francisco it was gone noon and I was told that there were lads in the region that I had just walked through, who would have escorted me on my perilous journey had they known that I was out alone. I shall not forget that night in a hurry!

Lost in the Woods

Writing about that night brings to mind another anxious nocturnal experience in the autumn of 1871. Because of my love of solitude and wild nature, as well as the desire to have a rest and breathe fresh air, I decided to spend four months in a desolate and thinly populated region in southern Ohio. Mr John S. Davies, my hotelier, loaned me his roan pony so that I could go to an area which was eight miles away. I attempted to return on another route but lost my way. Night-time was upon me and the road amongst the trees was invisible. I had no choice but to go forward without knowing where I was heading. After a while I came to a deep valley where I saw a light shining through a window. The woman who lived there had not heard of John S. Davies nor of the Welsh families. I realized therefore that I was a long way off track. She advised me to go 'that way' by pointing her finger towards a dark forest. 'That way', it had to be then and it was on 'that way' I found myself for over two hours in utter darkness, without seeing anything but woodland. I had loosened the pony's reins with the hope that the animal would have an inner instinct and more sense than I had. I thought momentarily that I would tie the pony to a tree and sit there until the morning but I remembered that people had heard the sound of a wild cat (one as big as a dog and more fierce than a lion) in those areas on a previous night and besides it was very cold. The thought of lighting a fire crossed my mind too as there was plenty of fire material available – piles of dry leaves covering the ground and sticks in abundance. I thought a fire would keep the big cat away and keep me warm. Then I remembered that Chicago and hundreds of acres in Wisconsin and Michigan had experienced fires that had gone out of control that autumn and it was possible that the same misfortune could happen here if a fire was lit. Eventually I came to a log cabin. I called and an Irishman came to the door. I asked him if I could stay there until the morning, that I would sleep on the floor but he did not have any room for my pony. He did tell me, however, that there was a schoolhouse that I knew of, only four miles away. I now realized that my wise animal, after I had released the reins, had continued to advance towards its home. The schoolhouse was not too far-off and I was overjoyed. After another few miles through the woods, I arrived back in Mr Davies' cosy lodgings.

Another Northerly Journey

After returning from the geysers, I decided to travel another eighty miles on the *North Pacific Coast* line as far as Duncan Mills. This line covers beautiful and varying scenery. Unlike the *Denver and Rio Grande* line, it does not run through jagged rocks and deep fissures. It does have its steep ascents, horseshoe bends, bridges and high viaducts though. It winds through spectacular valleys, symmetrical hills and tall trees – all clad in fresh and welcoming greenery that can only be found in California. Several of the hills have undulating formations, like oyster shells or a Chinese fan and their verdure is incomparable. Since large areas of this state experience warm weather all year round, new shoots can be seen sprouting as soon as the leaves are shed. New growth can be seen replacing the old everywhere – the decaying vegetation just drops off.

There is a kind of prickly, horny frog in California; one that is quite harmless. The two horns which emerge from its head are larger than the other horns on its body. We travelled nearly twenty miles, near to the narrow Bolinas Bay and found ourselves in a land famous for its milk and butter as well as its sawmills. Madrono trees are found in this region. Every year they discard their bark and are of a distinct crimson colour. Oak, cypress and other varieties are found here too but the most spectacular are the redwoods. The interior of these trees are red but on the outside they are of an unbroken, deep green colour. They are absolutely straight and grow to a height of more than 300 feet. About 60 feet above the ground, the branches reach out making one believe that one is in a large, green, dense and shady paradise and enjoying a kind of strange seclusion and tranquility not to be felt anywhere else. Such green earth! Such green roof! Such far-away mysterious spaces one can see between these large branches in every direction. I saw a hollow trunk of one of these beautiful trees; it was large enough to hold a congregation! These trees are comparatively small when compared to some found in this state. Their dimensions are around 30 feet in diameter, 90 feet in circumference and over 400 feet in height. One tree is 37 feet in diameter and 112 feet in circumference. Another felled one is 40 feet in diameter and 120 feet in circumference and men walk along 200 feet of its cavity and come out the other end through a gap in a bough without stooping at all. Through the trunk of one tree, a pathway for horses and trucks was created. One cannot but marvel at the diversity of the Almighty's accomplishments.

Through California

I had intended to go from San Francisco to Oregon and the territory of Washington, but I was told that since the rainy season had started, that there was not much purpose in this plan. I therefore began my homeward journey. I took the *Central Pacific* railroad and glanced for the last time at the bays, the hills, the city and the islands of the Golden Gate. After arriving in Carquinez Strait, which is a mile and a half wide and situated between the bays of Suisun and San Pablo, our train embarked onto a large, 4,000 horsepower steamboat called *Solano*. This vessel's measurements were 424 feet long, 116 feet wide and 18 feet high. It had four railroads on board to enable as much as twenty-four passenger carriages or forty-eight freight-cars to be ferried to the other shore. This is the shortest route from San Francisco to Sacramento (population 22,000). Sacramento is the capital of California and is situated on the banks of the Sacramento River. It has a grand Statehouse in its centre.

After journeying over twenty miles north-east from Sacramento, we started to ascend the Sierra Nevada Mountain Range which is five hundred miles long and between sixty and one hundred miles wide with more than one hundred of its peaks rising to over 13,000 feet above sea level; some of them reach as high as 15,000 feet. Gold, silver and other minerals from these mountains (as the history of California testifies) have been a magnet for people from all corners of the globe. After climbing for about thirty miles, we found ourselves on the famous Cape Horn. In Grand Canyon, Colorado, we were in a deep fissure gazing upwards for about 2,000 feet at the straight rocks but from Cape Horn, I was looking down 2,500 feet – a place where I could imagine myself jumping to the bottom without touching anything.

Some people have come some distances to see these sights but after arriving here, they find that they cannot stomach the thought of looking down. We were spiralling upwards at a radius of 120 feet per mile and we could see, not only the horrific drop, but also the toothed rocks, the wild cascades and the snow-capped peaks far and wide. We were ascending through the American Canyon, between two walls of rocks 2,000 feet high. We had left the warm, green and fruitful valley of Sacramento hours ago and the higher we went, a cold and horrid winter was closing in on us. The rocks and the rugged hills which surrounded us were covered with snow. Farther up again we found ourselves travelling through narrow, dark buildings, called 'snow-sheds'. Their purpose was to keep the road clear from snowdrifts and since some drifts can be as high as 30 feet, the sheds are much needed. They were made from wooden boards and since they could be set alight easily, a purpose-built steamengine pulling ten water containers is always on track in the vicinity – ready to put out a fire at very short notice. After continuing to climb and passing through several snowhouses, we were on top of the Sierra Nevada Range. What marvellous scenery there is from this point! Rocks beyond rocks, cliffs beyond cliffs and peaks beyond peaks – all reaching higher and higher, farther and farther in all directions. The rivers, waterfalls, lakes and thin trees were all covered with snow and icicles. The whole terrain appeared very rough and the temperature was low. Near a place called 'Summit', we were on the highest point of this railroad, 7,017 feet above sea level and one hundred and ninety-three miles from San Francisco. We were travelling through a combination of a tunnel and snowhouses, in all – twenty-eight miles long. There were a few openings at certain points though, where we could peep at the scene outside.

As we were descending, we came to the town of Truckee, near which lies two well-known lakes and many tourists flock to see them. One is called Lake Tahoe (Big Waters) which is twenty two miles long by ten miles wide. The other, Lake Donner, three miles long by one mile wide, is a delightful lake but unfortunately it has a sad history. A Mr Donner, his wife and animals perished on its shore when they were cut off by snowdrifts as they journeyed through California during the winter of 1864.

Through Nevada

About two hundred and twenty miles north-east of San Francisco, we crossed the terminating point of the line that runs from California to Nevada. We also dropped several thousand feet leaving the snow-capped peaks of the Sierras for a warmer climate. In Reno, twenty miles from the terminus, we branched out from the main railroad, in order to travel on the picturesque route to Carson and Virginia City, where possibly one finds the most prosperous mineral mines in the world. Many Welshmen work here; amongst them, Senator J.P. Jones, a man considered to be one of the three or four wealthiest people in the world. Above Virginia City, Davidson Mountain appears quite majestic and people can be seen rambling on it whilst admiring the views. Below the city, at a depth of 2,000 feet, miners are digging out treasures from the earth's core.

Soon after leaving Reno, we started our way through Nevada. Here and there, we could see steam rising from boiling wells. Apparently, this is nature's method of letting the earth's intense internal heat escape, thus preventing an explosion. Sporadically, one can see near to a place called Mirage, a large lake of clear water which is fed by sparkling rivers and surrounded by evergreen trees. However, as one approaches this spot, the lake disappears and all that one discovers is bare scorched wilderness. Many a thirsty traveller has been tricked by this illusion.

Farther on, our railroad leads us to a real lake, Lake Humboldt, thirty-five miles long by ten miles wide. Ten miles south again lies Lake Carson – twenty-three miles long by ten miles wide. Lake Humboldt cascades to Lake Carson in the summer but in the winter or during the rainy season both are just one big mere, eighty miles long. It is the Humboldt River, after running its course of three hundred and fifty miles, that flows into Lake Humboldt at its northern point and it is the Carson River, after running its course of one hundred and seventy-five miles that flows into Lake Carson at its most southern point. They create what is called the 'Humboldt and Carson Sink' from which no water flows out. What happens to the water then? Some say that it disappears into the sand; others say that it evaporates in the sun's rays; others will say that it travels by way of underground rivers to the west and since there are strong-flowing rivers emanating from the western side of the Sierras, it is deemed that this explanation could be true. There are several lakes with similar indications on these plains too. Residues of ash cover the ground, indicating that earthquakes occurred here at some time. Also, it must have been a location for the sea or a large lake once, because there are shells, skeletons of fish and other aquatic items to be seen here. Where did this sea or lake disappear to? No doubt, to the same place that today's rivers and lakes flow into. I read in the newspapers that Lake Ruby had suddenly disappeared since my last time here.

We journeyed further along the Humboldt valley with mountains sheltering us on each side. We went through several minor stations,

Indians

nevertheless quite important ones, since large quantities of minerals are sent to the markets via them. In this valley too, one finds large ranches. One rancher rears 80,000 animals with 28,000 acres of the ranch fenced in. We passed Battle Mountain, where thirty-five years ago, there was a bloody and determined battle between the white settlers and the Shoshone Indians. Although the Indians fought ferociously, they were defeated and their force was diminished in a way that could never be regained afterwards. Few frail and dirty tramps remain – children of the desert, holding their hands up against everyone and vise versa. They steal if need be and beg if necessary. Some of them approach the stations to beg from the travellers and with the curiosity that they generate, myself included, they are given food and other requirements. It is a pity to see their papooses (babies). They are tied to a board or a kind of cradle that has a canopy supported by rods one end, in order to shade their little heads from the sun. Thus, they were carried on their mothers' backs or in their arms without being able to move head or limb. Indeed, the little ones did appear impatient; they are trained to suffer from infancy.

On we went past the Valley of the Hot Springs, where we saw steam rising from the red earth; past a colony of pelicans and a little farther on we came across a lonely grave which had been closed in and a Cross erected on it which had the inscription 'The Maiden's Grave' on one side and 'Lucinda Duncan' on the other side. Lucinda Duncan was the name of this virtuous young lady who died when she was eighteen. She became ill while she and the rest of her family waited for floods to recede when they were on their way to California. Far from any habitation, the family could do no other than bury their dear girl in that place and put a headboard over the grave. Several years had gone by before workmen came to lay the railroad. When they eventually came across the grave, they erected a wall around it as a protection and in the year 1871 a beautiful Cross was placed there by the railroad's Inspector.

After passing a station called Carlin, we went through a gap in the rocks called Five Mile Canyon. Quite a way higher again, we came to Humboldt Springs – twenty wells in a small valley, 5,400 feet above sea level, They appeared like small lakes about seven feet in diameter and almost circular. Nobody has been able to plumb down to their bottom but it is thought that they are the remains of underground explosions. Their waters pass invisibly through the sand to the Humboldt River which then flows to the Humboldt marshland, three hundred miles below, where they disappear as secretive as the way they emanated.

Utah

After departing from Tacoma's station, I crossed the line to Utah and all this region was just an ugly, empty wilderness. It is called the 'Wilderness of America' and I do not believe it could support any living animal. It is obvious from the oceanic residues found here that it was a seabed or a large lake at one time. The present Salt Lake is probably a sequel of the former one and by all indications was situated at the lower end of it. It is said that the waters of Salt Lake receded a great deal some time after the lake was first discovered but that in latter years the water level had risen again by 12 feet. After travelling about eighty miles in Utah, I noticed these words written in bold letters on an upright plank: TEN MILES OF TRACK IN ONE DAY and the same sign again ten miles further. It appears that it was here that the achievement of laying the most track in one day was accomplished. Nearby, the *Union Pacific* and *Central Pacific* lines connect to create one long railroad from east to west. May 10th, 1869 was a memorable day since thousands of people assembled from every corner of America and from other trustworthy nations to witness the construction of the last section of the railroad and to see the last nail being hammered in. The adventurous owners had been mocked by many for daring to construct a railroad over the Rocky Mountains and the Sierra Nevada Range – the land of snow and ice, great wilderness, uninhabited desert and hundreds of acres occupied by dangerous barbarians. The enterprise had been considered as absolute foolhardiness. However, the victorious day had dawned on the courageous men. A train full of visitors from the eastern cities arrived on the *Union Pacific* and on the *Central Pacific*, trippers from San Francisco and other western cities turned up. Then the last tie – a handrail, beautifully carved and adorned with decorative silver plates, arrived from California; also a gold nail from the same state and a silver nail from Nevada. In very high spirits the railroads' most senior officials stepped forward in order to hammer these nails into place. Firstly though, an interval of respectful silence prevailed, when Dr Todd from Massachusetts pronounced that the blessing of Almighty God be bestowed on the railroads and the associated workmanship. Then, with a silver hammer, which had a wire attached to its handle to create a bellowing and far reaching sound when triggered, Leland Stanford, president of the *Central Pacific* tapped the last nail in at 12 noon and with this last knock the trigger was released to announce the news to all of the country's cities. No doubt that completion of this line of railroad is amongst the most successful achievements of our lifetime. It covers an area of about two thousand miles from the Missouri River to the shores of the Pacific Ocean. The two steamengines were driven to touch each other and thus east and west shook hands.

We soon came to more fertile land than that of the desert. After arriving in Ogden (population 6,000), I found myself amongst the saints and in the centre of their country. Ogden has a Mormon Tabernacle and an apostle in the person of F.D. Richards Esquire, a man of Welsh blood. In my next book: *HANES TALEITHIAU UNEDIG AMERICA A'R CYMRY YNDDYNT* (THE HISTORY OF THE UNITED STATES OF AMERICA AND THE WELSH LIVING IN THEM) I shall write a summary about the most famous Welsh people in America, of every profession and occupation.

Salt Lake City

The Mormons are strange people and their neighbourhood as well as their city are both strange. To go to Salt Lake City, I left the main line in Ogden and took another line to go thirty-seven miles south. En route, on my right, I could see Salt Lake in one long stretch. On my left I could see the gigantic Wasatch Mountains, ones which encircle the valley in half-moon shape. As we approached the holy city, we saw a very high peak, known by some as Prophecy Mountain – 1,200 feet above the valley and above a bubbling, boiling spring. It has been named thus because that's where the renowned prophet, Brigham Young[16], used to strive to get close to the Lord. Salt Lake City (population 21,000) stands at the foot of one area of the mountain. This city has been the Zion and Jerusalem of the Latter-day Saints in recent times. It has been planned impressively. Its facade is excellent and the roads are parallel with each other with rapid streams having been created along the sidewalks to irrigate the gardens and leafy trees, to cleanse the pavements and quench the thirst of the citizens. It has many beautiful buildings – many of them mansions. The most formidable of all, in my view, is the Tabernacle. One cannot say that it is beautiful but it is large and distinguished. It is oval in shape but the basement is 250 feet long, 150 feet wide and 65 feet high. On the outer side, there are 46 square columns which, when compounded with the doors and windows, create a wall upon which rests the massive arched roof. This building is similar to half an eggshell resting on a long tobacco box. Including its big gallery, it can seat approximately 8,000 people. The platforms and the organ (the largest in America apart from one other) are placed at one end.

Near to the Tabernacle, the construction of the Temple has been taking place for many years; it measures 186 feet in length and 99 feet in width. This is obviously not as large as the Tabernacle but it will be much higher and more spectacular. It is intended to be one of the wonders of this era and a glory on earth. I saw Brigham Young's old dwelling house – a long low building with many doors and windows. It was the side of the house which faced the road and its roof consisted of several skylights as is custom in some old buildings in this country. I also saw his new mansion which is a three-storey building with elaborate decor and a tower emerging above it. Another large building in the centre of the city is 'Zion's Co-operative Mercantile Institution'. Until the Temple is completed, this will be the grandest building in the city. It is a shop selling all kinds of merchandise and there are branches of this Institution in many Mormon villages providing a good supply of commodities to the people who dwell in this territory.

Sometimes the sign above these retail shops is abbreviated to Z.C.M.I. with a picture of an eye as a logo and the wording 'Holiness to the Lord' inscribed on it. It is expected that all Mormon followers should trade and purchase goods at these outlets. This is the materialistic face of this church. The gentiles are multiplying in the city and in the country. There is a Catholic Church in Salt Lake City as well as two or three Protestant Chapels and their trading and political powers are increasing also. Therefore the redemption from malice that Brigham Young tried to practise when he ordered his people to leave the fertile San Bernardino valley is backfiring here. Many feel that if he had not advised his people to seek minerals – gold, silver and other sources which create wealth – that they would be happy with their world now and that Utah would be a front-line state as far as the Union was concerned. Instead of that, other people control the wealth of the region whilst the saints labour on land that is not very fertile. Between everything and the fact that church taxes are imposed on them, the saints are quite disadvantaged. Polygamy is the main difference between this denomination and other people since many find the practice obscene. This sect is persecuted for this reason and some of them, because of poverty, have to live with only one wife and some without one at all!

In Utah there is a colony of Welsh people called 'Wales' where the wives have refused to allow their husbands to practise polygamy. When one man tried his luck by taking on another wife some years ago, all of the neighbourhood's wives got together and placed this woman on a wooden horse and after carrying her to a distant meadow, left her to find her way home the best she could. From then on, the men gave up this loathsome practice.

Three Days in Salt Lake City
The first place I stayed in was a guesthouse, owned by a gentile. Although it was grand and appeared decent, it was only in this house that I ever encountered anyone trying to rob me. I woke up suddenly about two o'clock in the morning; there was a light in my room and a big Irishman with a ruddy face was approaching my bed. When he saw me, he quickly extinguished his candle and left the room. The next house I stayed in was owned by Anthony Thomas Esquire, Secretary of the Territory – a young, talented and amiable Welshman. He is one of the gentiles and he told me the history of this territory and the plight of our nation here. I visited the elder, George Bywater, one of the church regulars and one who is well thought of by the saints and all the gentiles. I found him to be a wise and friendly man, wanting to convey spiritual goodness to me with all his heart. His conversation was sound and serious. He gave me a copy of the Mormon Book. He urged me to go and see the elder, Mr John S. Davies, a printer and a Welsh literary man; he said that this man would be able to educate and inform me further. John S. Davies was advanced in years by now but as a young man he had been employed by Brutus as a printer. 'What did Brutus think of John S. Davies?' I asked Mr Bywater. He answered that Brutus had said that it was a tragedy that one of the brightest Welshmen was succumbing to such a vile practice as Mormonism. 'What did Brutus say about you?' I asked John S. Davies when I saw him. He replied that Brutus had told his

father, whom he blamed for allowing him to socialise with the saints, that his son had come to him as a devil but was leaving as a saint. I discovered that Mr Davies was living in a grand house. I had an idea that he was a cunning man and that he considered me to be a spy who had come to expose the bareness of the country. I felt that he was keeping information from me and no doubt he had grounds to feel that way, since many scribblers had visited these people with only one purpose in mind, namely, lying glibly about the sect. I told Mr Davies that Mr Bywater had commended him to me. Mr Davies then gave me several songsheets, composed by him. The songs implied that Mr Davies' beer was better than that of anyone else. One song was called 'Davies' Cronk Beer'. He also gave me several copies of a book, the size of *Rhodd Mam* (The Catechism) entitled 'Bee Hive Songster' – a collection of original songs, composed by 'Ieuan' who was Mr Davies himself. By appointment, I visited Mr Davies again. I found that there was a dentist there this time; he had come to extract one of Mr Davies' teeth. A doctor was also present; he was there to take care of Mrs Davies. The doctor carried an electrical box for the purpose of relieving illnesses and I was told that this medic, through his knowledge of electron energy, could cure me completely of my stomach disorder. When he saw me staring at the box full of wires, he said, whilst looking straight into my eyes, that he could see that I was quite inquisitive and if I was prepared to accompany him to his home, he would explain to me the workings of the machine. He also said that my stomach complaint called for a transmission of spiritual energy and since he was not skilled in that methodology, he suggested that his wife, who was thus gifted, should see to my needs. He was clever in diagnosing my ailment but I was told that his wife would be the one to identify my nature and circumstances – all without any payment. I had read that spirituality and mesmerism were important elements in the Mormon faith but I had not gone out of my way to seek this practice nor had I tried to influence its opponents to vilify it. It was an opportunity for me to see for myself and in the same spirit as a moth trails a candle (an insect which literally plays with fire), I promised to go to his house that evening in spite of the possibility that I would be hypnotized. I was greeted politely. He was a tall, thin man; his wife was tall and stout. He asked her to 'read' me. She replied that she was afraid that my anima was of a kind, that her spirit would not be able to control. She said that she had not always been very successful with learned gentlemen. After this 'compliment', she began to drift into the spirit world. After a minute's silence she said that I was gifted with a strong disposition and she reckoned that if I was a spiritualist I would be a very skilled 'medium'. Gradually, my circumstances became more transparent to her and she began to understand my background and situation, including my family back home and other phenomena. It was more of a game of chance really. Anyone could have likewise assumed truths and untruths. She continued to complain that she was unable to gain full control of my spirit and that there were other spirits obstructing her from achieving the proper objective. By now, another lady had entered the room – apparently the most able 'medium' in the city. However, my time was up and I left without feeling any wiser or dafter after the experience. The doctor and his wife mentioned that they were not Mormons but that they did admire the sect.

In the Saints' Congregation on the Sabbath
I was fortunate enough to be in the city on an important Sabbath. An election had taken place in the territory to elect a representative to the Congress in Washingon. George Q. Cannon, the leader of the twelve apostles, had the most votes but his opponent, a gentile, claimed that he should be the one elected because Q. Cannon should be disqualified because of his polygamy. There was controversy throughout England regarding Charles Bradlaugh[17] at this time too because he was refusing to swear an oath on the Bible in the House of Commons. Q. Cannon was going to the 'battlefield' in Washington on the Monday following the Sabbath that I had the privilege of listening to him – the occasion when he addressed his large congregation. I must say the congregation's seating arrangement was not very systematic but I suppose a service in rural Wales could be compared to it. Many children attended the service and I now understand why people say that children are Utah's largest crop! Over on the platforms, row upon row, in front of a large organ and in a half-circle arrangement, sat the bishops, elders and deacons.

First of all they sang, then a young man prayed in a very thoughtful and comprehensive way. Afterwards, bread was cut up by 'seven men of honest report' – (The Acts 6,3) and then placed in dishes so that the congregation could partake of it. Everyone was included, even the children, who stopped chipping at their sticks and placed their knives to one side whilst they received the Communion. Following that part of the service, an address was delivered by an elder. His utterance, indeed, made me think that he was an illiterate Englishman or Welshman. He pronounced 'hand' as 'and' and 'and' as 'hand'. He proclaimed that he had 'seen the light' in Liverpool forty years earlier and that he was one of the missionaries who had gone over to England the previous April; that he had visited London and South Wales where he had met some old

173

friends. He had found both countries in spiritual darkness but he thanked God that his mission had not been in vain. He felt that he had been successful in the sense that he had been able to imprint some morality on the minds of some people and had inspired them to return to Zion. I talked to him after the service and found out that he was English but had been brought up by a Welsh couple who could not speak any English.

After the bread was shared out, the seven deacons poured water (not wine) into cups and it was distributed amongst the congregation. Then G.Q. Cannon, the renowned preacher, came forth; he was an elderly man, shorter than average but quite sturdy. His face reflected the appearance of an intelligent man. He was bald on top but had a thick crop of grey hair covering the lower part of his head. He had a pleasant voice and delightful grimaces. No doubt he was a very able orator. His text was from the Book of Mormons, page 301.

> O remember, remember, my son Helaman, how strict are the commandments of God. And he said: If ye will keep my commandments ye shall prosper in the land – but if ye keep not his commandments ye shall be cut off from his presence.

His sermon was based on the hostility of the gentiles towards the church and the plans that had taken place from time to time to destroy it; about the miraculous defence and holy guidance that had become them; the way they had been guided through the great wilderness; how the religion had been planted in that region and how it had been cultivated and nurtured. He said that all eventualities had been foreseen by the famous prophet, Joseph Smith, and he urged the people to obey the Lord's commandments and to be extra careful not to fall prey to foolhardy devilry, especially adultery – the sin which the saints committed most often apparently; even Joseph Smith himself had been guilty. However, the ones that had testified and had seen the angel with golden blades, after committing this sin, seceded from the church and became its enemy. These wrongdoers stuck to their faith though and the preacher believed that God's divine wisdom had prevailed in such cases. No-one could therefore proclaim, that it was just the faithful churchgoers who were able to testify about the establishment of the church. That was the essence of his sermon. He was not concerned about the future. He was happy to go to Washington and was not bothered by what the future had in store for him. He was sure the church would flourish if it kept the Lord's commandments. After the last hymn was sung and the organist stopped playing the harmonium, we left.

The Remainder of the Journey in Utah

I left the famous city for Ogden, where I joined the *Union Pacific* railroad. In the vicinity of Uinta, the station next to Ogden, there had been in the year 1862, what was known as 'The Massacre of Morrises'. A certain gentleman, by the name of Joseph Morris, had claimed that he was the true prophet and not Brigham Young. He had 90 able men as followers – all ready to wage war; he also had 300 women and children supporters who were of the Joseph Order doctrine which was linked to the church of the Latter-day Saints whose belief was that polygamy was obscene. They were attacked by 750 of Brigham Young's Mormon followers as well as volunteers and five artilleries. These people were led by Robert T. Burrton. After three days of skirmishing, the Morrises surrendered and Burrton grabbed all their possessions, in the name of the church! He was so callous that he shot Morris after which a little old lady approached him and said: 'Oh you bloodthirsty people. Is it going to be another Mountain Meadow massacre here?' Burrton replied: 'I do not allow women to talk to me this way.' He then shot her.

Soon, we began to climb the Rocky Mountains, through Weber Canyon, a narrow gap of forty miles. We ascended through steep and craggy rocks along a wild, rash stream which was bubbling over like a boiling cauldron when undertaking its turnings. Up we went however, through Devil's Gate and alongside Devil's Slide, which is the crest of a low rock that slopes over a steep verdancy. We came to the 'Thousand Miles Tree', a lone, small tree, a thousand miles from Omaha. On its lowest bough there was a plank hanging with the inscription '1000 miles' on it. Soon, after coming through the Weber Gap, we found ourselves travelling through another picturesque pass, called Echo Canyon, then on past an unusual rock, named Steamboat Rock because of its shape.

We were admiring the scenery when one of the other travellers, a Mormon missionary who was on his way to England in order to enlighten that dark country, asked a man who was reading a book: 'Are you reading the Mormon book?' 'Yes,' replied the reader, who was a gentile, 'I am reading a book I received as a gift in Salt Lake City.'

Mormon –   What is your opinion of it?

Gentile –   I have not read enough of it to come to any conclusion regarding its merit but I realize that it contains good guidance.

Mormon –   I am glad that you like it. Read it without any prejudice; it will be of benefit to you.

Gentile –   The following quotation satisfies me but it is puzzling:

Behold, the Lamaists, your brothers – ones that you detest because of their impurity and the curse that was imposed upon them – are more righteous than you. They do not forget the Lord's commandments; the ones that were handed to our fathers, namely, that they should have only one wife and no concubines and that there should not be any adultery amongst them. They are now obeying these commandments; therefore, because they are obedient, the Lord does not dispose of them but is merciful towards them and one day they will be blessed people.

Gentile – The passage, as it stands, pleases me but the fact that you build a church on the guidance of this book confuses me when you practise polygamy.

Mormon – You speak quite sensibly. That sin used to be considered as disobedience of the Lord's commandments. When He condemned polygamy, it was a sin. Now, however He has given his consent. Polygamy is permissible.

He then read the revelation Brigham Young received from God regarding this way of life.

Mormon – Apart from the revelation that Brigham Young acquired, the Scriptures also take this view. Consider Abraham, Jacob and David and many others.

Gentile – Are all the wives of one man equal in your midst, or are there some who have higher status than others? Have you any concubines in your faith?

Mormon – No, indeed, all the wives are considered equal.

Gentile – How is it that you are following the example of the patriarchs then? Abraham, Jacob and David had concubines and since they had several wives and they were righteous, how were the people of Nephi, the ones referred to in the passage that I have just read, more unjust than the Lamaists by having several wives?

Before replying to these questions, the Mormon Missionary spent a good half-hour explaining how God gives certain instructions at one period and other ones at other times. He was very eloquent if not constant in his reasoning. He drew attention to himself and everyone who was within hearing distance listened to him because he had aroused curiosity.

When he finished speaking the gentile said to him: 'You better hear my situation. I have a wife and young children at home. What would happen if I joined your faith and my wife refused to do so? Where would my duty lie then?'

Mormon –   When you read, if indeed you did, 'Pilgrim's Progress' about a Christian leaving his wife and children to go it alone . . .

Gentile –   This kind of religion is absurd in my view – the fact that a man can forsake his good wife, possibly the only one that he could ever love and leave her and the children in the most awful plight.

Mormon –   It is the religion of Jesus Christ. 'And every one that hath forsaken houses, or brethren, or sisters, or father, or mother, or wife, or children, or lands, for my name's sake, shall receive an hundredfold and shall inherit everlasting life' – (Matthew 19,29).

Gentile –   According to this quotation, it is very unfortunate for a man to have a wife at all; more so when he has more than one to despise!

Mormon –   Oh no, if the wives are also followers of Christ and worship him, then there is no reason to despise them.

Gentile –   What are we supposed to understand by following Christ and worshipping him?

Mormon –   Believe in him, follow his example and keep his commandments.

Gentile –   I am sure that my wife believes in Christ and observes his commandments more than most. I understand that Christ did not have a wife. Bachelors are therefore the ones who are righteous in this instance. I am sinful and you are very sinful. (Laughter). Do you now think that it is Christ's will for me to leave my good wife when I have made a solemn promise to be with her until death?

Mormon –   Until death! I would not give thanks to a marriage until death. Such an idea is not worthy to be called a marriage. We wed our wives spiritually and that spiritual union continues eternally.

Gentile –   Bugger it! If the union is eternal, I prefer to stick to the one I've got: When you get a good thing, keep it, keep it.

Everyone who was listening roared with laughter at this comment and thus the discussion ended.

Through Wyoming

Between the stations of Castle Rock and Wasatch, we crossed the line from Utah to Wyoming and a little further, we passed a place that used to be a very flourishing town known as Bear River City. The most dramatic event in the history of this town was the one when the ruffians (louts, gamblers thieves, murderers and so forth) undertook a very resolute but unsuccessful resistance against law and order. They were hounded the same way as they had been thrust from other regions. By now, we had ascended again to the land of permanent snow and ice and passed through several icehouses, similar to the ones on the Sierra Range. After being on wheels for quite a while, we came to the banks of the Green River. This river's waters have a greenish tint and its rocks resemble castles. Looking up at the mountains, we saw a plank with the wording: CONTINENTAL DIVIDE written on it. This is where the backbone of the large continent of America is located – 7,100 feet above sea level. There are some peaks which are much higher and this railroad runs up to higher locations too. However, this is where the dividing line runs. It did not appear that we were on high ground; it was like being on a large, rough, pot-holed, bumpy, rocky, frosty plain with snowcapped peaks emerging on both sides before they disappeared into the clouds. Way over in the distant north, we could see the dark striation of the Black Hills. After more travelling, we came to very pleasant places – to the Laramie prairies, where in times long ago, one could find hundreds, thousands even, of wild buffaloes roaming the land with Red Indians hunting them. There was much grandeur associated with these animals, especially when they travelled in multitudes, thus causing the ground to quiver all around. They are now on the point of being exterminated. In a little while, they will no longer exist and the same goes for the Indians. Many species of animals are disappearing from the American continent with others taking their place. The large plains of Laramie are in the possession of pale-faced people now and instead of buffalo trails, large ranches are found where cattle, sheep and horses are reared. The town of Laramie, which is situated on this line, is flourishing. It was in Laramie, for the first time in any place on earth, that a panel of twelve women jurors was sworn in, in a court of law. The case before the jurors concerned one of the ruffians of the West. A divine guidance was asked for before returning the verdict. While the women were sitting on the jury, their maids were in their homes singing:

Nice little baby, don't get in a fury
Cause mamma is gone to sit on the jury.

From the West to this point, it was the Chinese people who worked on the railroad, a factor by all accounts, why no mice are present or houses serving alcoholic drinks in towns. The pub landlords and the Irish are against the influx of Chinese people into the country.

Farther on again and we are in Sherman, the highest point on this line to California. It is situated 8,242 feet above sea level, one thousand three hundred and sixty-five miles from San Francisco and five hundred and forty-nine miles from Omaha. After arriving in Cheyenne (population 4,000) we found ourselves in the largest and most important town on this line between Ogden and Omaha. From this point, there is a railroad which runs south to the large state of California with its prosperous gold mines. State trains are used here to convey people to the famous mines of the Black Hills in the north.

While I waited outside a public house in this place, I was invited by the landlord to go to his chapel to listen to his sermon. I accepted the invitation and was led to a spacious room in his house. On the walls there were various photographs of the Mormon church's prophets and apostles. The preacher read, preached and prayed to a congregation of six people. He was wise enough to keep the service short. His text came from Genesis 2,7. He tried to enlighten us by saying that it was the Lord who installed life in us when we were created and that He was continually supporting us. If He failed to provide for us, we would cease to exist like butter melting in front of a fire. After the service ended, he told us that he used to sell alcoholic drinks in that room and that he could not look his customers in the eye then. However, he had converted the room into a chapel and it was a custom with him now to invite people from the street to join him and his family in prayer meetings and other services. The room had been used as a chapel for twelve years by this time and he went on to say that he could now look at his congregation with a happy heart and without shame. He said he belonged to the Joseph branch of the Latter-day Saints' church and that he loathed the Brigham division with its polygamy aspect. He had been present in the massacre of the Morrises.

Through Many States
After travelling through the last of the snowhouses, I glanced for the last time at Pike's Peak – one hundred and seventy-five miles south of us. We arrived in Nebraska and I began to feel that I had arrived on the other side of the far west. After passing some spectacular rocks and going through prairie-dog country, we arrived in a land where there were large farms, each one rearing around 500 animals. The largest of them is Iliff

Farm, one hundred and fifty miles long and on average twenty-five miles wide. This farm can graze 48,000 animals. A shopkeeper in the town of Sidney, in this region, owns and farms some land as a pastime occupation and keeps 8,000 cattle and 3,000 sheep.

The Indians were reluctant to approach the train but gradually they became more trustful. In a place not far from Big Spring station, on this line, a group of them once tried to derail a train full of passengers by suddenly driving scores of ponies in front of the engine when it was undertaking a bend. They failed in their attempt; however many of the ponies were killed and the redskins discovered the might of the passengers. After this daring assault, the Indians refer to the train's engine as 'Fire Waggon! – Big Chief! Nasty! No Good'!

In North Plate City I was in a place that I had visited on a previous occasion. Nearby is where the Platte River is crossed. We soon came to a land full of cornfields. When I was here before, the whole area was full of productive maize crops. Several miles north of the town of Columbus there is a Welsh settlement. After leaving Omaha and the Missouri River, I came to the end of the renowned line that leads to the Pacific Ocean. I crossed the Missouri to Iowa and went on to Gomer and Red Oak regions where there is a flourishing Welsh colony. From there, I went through Des Moines, Davenport and Rock Island, where I crossed the Mississippi; then on to Braceville and Braidwood, Illinois. These two towns border each other and are inhabited by many Welsh miners. Then on through Joliet (population 17,000) to Chicago. From here I took a north-west direction to Praire-du-chien, still on the banks of the Mississippi and then to the Welsh settlement of Picatonica, where I spent the Sabbath and had the pleasure of listening to the Gospel being preached in the melodious Welsh language by the Reverend J.R. Daniel. It was by now winter with snow covering the ground. I also stayed in Dodgeville and Madison and hastened on to Milwaukee. Although it was not the most appropriate time of year, my intention was to go north, to the shores of Lake Superior.

Reasons to be Grateful

About midnight, I boarded the *Wisconsin Central* railroad to Ashland, a distance of three hundred and fifty-one miles. The unnatural chill I felt was followed by a high temperature and extreme thirst. I was feverish and had a headache. I started to wonder what would befall me if I became ill for a long time amongst strangers in an unknown town surrounded by Indians and miles of forests. I wished I could meet a Welshman. It was nine o'clock the following night before I reached my destination and I was all aches and pains. I was directed to a respectable and comfortable house. As I was sitting down a tall, nimble and well-dressed man with a piece of almond tree stuck in his buttonhole came in and sat by me; he asked:

'Are you sick?'

'Yes sir.'

'Did you come on that train?'

'Yes sir.'

'Where from?'

'From Milwaukee.'

'Do you live in Milwaukee?'

'No sir, I live in Wales.'

'Oh boy, you are Welsh, shake hands.'

'What part of Wales do you come from?'

'Oh, from near Aberystwyth, in Cardiganshire.'

'I am so glad to meet you, boy,' he continued in slightly broken Welsh. 'I have not met a Welshman for ten years. I am so sorry that you are unwell but take heart, you will have good care in this house. I lodge here and I shall look after you as well as if your wife was attending to you.'

After ordering me to my bed in the best bedroom in the house, he asked: 'Have you ever heard of Twm Chaen Bwlet?'

'No, I can't recall.'

'Never heard of Twm Chaen Bwlet. Twm Chaen Bwlet was the best man in Wales. Have you ever heard of Tom Sayers?'

'Tom Sayers, the fighter, yes, many a time.'

'Well, it was Twm Chaen Bwlet who trained him to fight and Twm is my brother.'

Thus, I found myself in very good hands. He made sure I was tucked up comfortable in bed and until I felt better, he was like a father to me. A doctor came to see me in the morning by instructions of Mr Thomas, the man I am referring to, who was a true Good Samaritan. He told the doctor to take great care of me and that he would pay whatever the fee amounted to. When that doctor left, another medic came to see me, at the request of the owner of the house. When this man left, another doctor arrived; he had been sent by some merciful woman; this woman had also given orders that any payment would be met by her. After the third doctor left, the deputy governor of the state came to see me. He had heard, by some means, that I had a letter from Governor Smith. He also told me to be careful and to let him know if I needed anything. By now, I was overcome by surprise and gratitude and wondered why these people had taken such interest in a complete stranger. The illness that I had contracted was cured in the nick of time and instead of a month resting in bed and maybe a grave in a foreign land, I was able to get up after three days. Mr Thomas kept me occupied by reciting his poems and telling me about his past activities.

Ashland and its Surroundings

Ashland stands in a very picturesque region. It is adorned from behind by green hills, valuable pinewood and other trees in very good condition. In front of it lies Chequamegon Bay, Lake Superior – the main and most beautiful bay of all the Great Lakes. Many rivers flow into this bay near Ashland and the formation of the estuaries are quite spectacular. The water is pure and the rivers are full of fish. In the surrounding countryside there are crystal-clear lakes containing large fish and in the bays there are enchanting islands where many fishermen take up their hobby. Between this scenery and the charming wilderness all around, the area is a magnet to tourists during the summer months. The area is an amalgamation of earth, water, people and animals and an ideal location for people who are keen on fishing and hunting. For those who prefer to admire the wonders of nature, their curiosity can be fulfilled here.

People who are frail and who suffer physical disorders are restored in this locality. They benefit from the fresh breezes and the invigorating influences encompassing the area. Many wealthy people come here to spend entire summers. They camp on islands or lakeshores. Elegant ladies who would not dream of spending a day without their luxuries – their easy chairs and feather beds – when at home, think that they are in heaven when they sleep on the ground all summer with only a canvas between them and the sky. They collect firewood as means of fuel to cook their food. Chequamegon Hotel has a good reputation and is sited in an idyllic spot. The governor, W.E. Smith, said that he had never observed such lovely views as he had seen from this hotel, namely: Chequamegon Bay, the shore and the islands, although he had been to the main areas of attraction in other regions of America, Europe, Asia and Africa.

A little east of Ashland, through the dense forest, lies Odanah, land of the Chippewa Red Indians. Because of the many wars that were waged between this tribe and other hostile people over the years, their numbers have declined. They are, by every aspect and custom, true Indians but quite harmless. This can be said about the Indian tribes living near Lake Superior too. Some of them live to a good age and it is said that you will never see an Indian with grey hair or a tooth missing, despite their longevity. No doubt, social progress, in its present imperfect form, creates wickedness as well as goodness. These Indians grow rice and their main delicacy is castor oil which they use in vast quantities. The government gives them an allocation of this oil and when a survey was made as to why so much of it was requested by them, it was discovered that they used it to roast potatoes.

About eighteen miles north of Ashland, lies its small, beautiful sister – Bayfield, opposite which the Apostle Islands are situated. These islands come in various sizes and shapes; some are bare whilst others are covered with pretty, evergreen pines. The trees and the high, cavernous rocks throw their shadows over the dark, deep waters that flow beneath them. About fifty years ago, in La Pointe on Madelaine Island, which is the largest of the Apostle Islands, the first missionary station was established amongst the Indians by Father Marquette, one of the Jesuits. It is still standing and it appears like an old, very strange town consisting of a small, old church which is stranger still and a small, old and peculiar graveyard where the converts of many ages are sleeping.

Tents on an Island

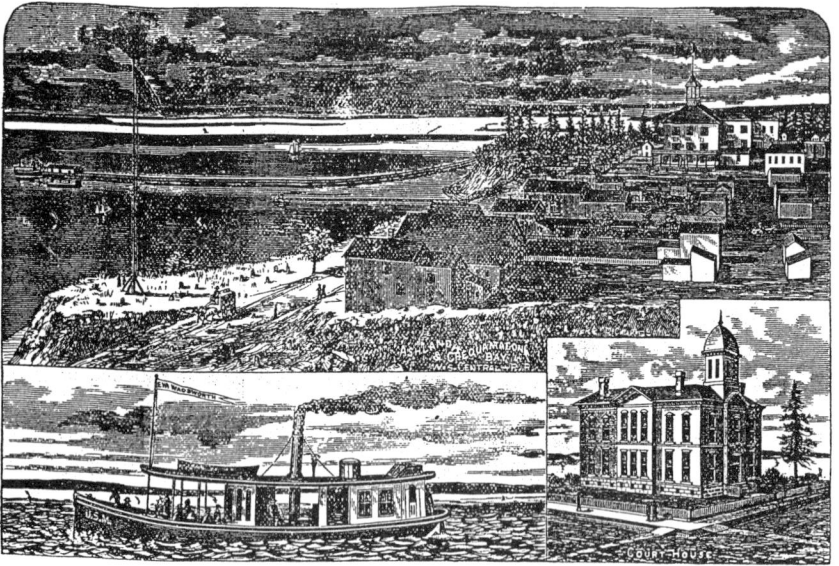

Ashland, Wisconsin

The Chequamegon Hotel

From Ashland to Milwaukee

I was hindered by illness on my way up but I endeavoured to catch sight of the wonders of this route on my return journey. Six miles south of Ashland, we crossed the White River. The long, high bridge that crosses it, is one of the most ingenious workmanship I have ever seen. The Indians call it 'The Bridge of the Massive Spider'. Farther on, I came to a river which is renowned almost worldwide, not because of its size or history but because of its rash formation – its frequent turnings, its gigantic varying cascades and accompanying fabulous scenery. It is called the Bad River. The railroad crosses it seventeen times within a distance of nine miles. The passengers, as excited and boisterous as the river itself, jumped from one side of the carriage to the other in order to see the views. Over a stretch of thirteen miles, as the crow flies, the river drops 2,000 feet and its zigzag route is often composed of wondrous cascades which are squeezed through narrow fissures with such velocity that it would appear that the ageless mountains are pushing them through. The drop can be anything between 80-100 feet in some places. In some spots, the river slides, whilst frothing and roaring over rocks and huge boulders. When we were crossing this river at a narrow gap, we were also going over the Penokee Mountain Range.

All we could now see were never-ending forests. However, it was interesting to see such an abundance of tables, rafters, trellis, poles and other forms of woodwork, all arranged in huge piles near the stations – ready for transportation. The lumberjacks consisted mostly of Swedes, Norwegians and other foreigners. They are strong men with rugged features. They dress in vivid colours wearing red, white and blue caps, blue shirts, scarlet trousers, wide red belts and high boots. They look so impressive amongst the green pinewood.

These forests are classified as favourable areas for immigrants. There is, without a doubt, very fertile land in this area and it is said that cleared forest land is the most productive of all. It was to these forests that the immigrants from Wales used to come but of late, it is considered that the western prairies are easier to cultivate. There are many advantages to erecting a new home in the woods. There is no need to plant trees on the land and there is no big expense when building material is required. Log houses can be erected in no time and they are as clean and warm as any other. There is no shortage of fencing supplies or firewood since logs are the source of fuel in a forest home. There is no need to be anxious about the failure of crops in the early years either. Employment is obtainable by felling and treating wood for use by railroad construction workers or pine-tree companies and decent payment is made for this work. For these reasons and others, it can be concluded that poor people would be wise to purchase cheap land in these forests, organize their workload and pay their way as they progress. They are able to work for employers when they are short of money. If our pioneers were able to forge ahead when there were no conveniences, surely the people settling in these woods today have an advantage over them. There are railroads, villages and many services at their doorstep. After passing places of great interest such as Phillips, Waupaca, Neenah, Lake Elkhart and others, I came to Milwaukee.

Oberlin

From Milwaukee, I took a south-easterly route of one hundred and ninety-five miles through Lafayette (population 15,000) to Indianapolis (population 76,000), the capital of the state of Indiana. I then went on to Cincinnati, one hundred and fifteen miles further and after travelling another one hundred and fifty-three miles, I was moving through Columbus and then on to Newark, where in my brother's house I stayed for a while in order to prepare and collate material for the book: *HANES TALEITHIAU UNEDIG AMERICA A'R CYMRY YNDDYNT*. (THE HISTORY OF THE UNITED STATES OF AMERICA AND THE WELSH LIVING IN THEM). From Newark, I travelled one hundred and twenty-seven miles north to Oberlin (population 4,000) where I spent some time in the Academy once. It was one of the most religious and influential places that I ever attended. I believe that it is only in this Academy that one finds that the intake is not discriminated by gender, nationality or status. Men and women, white and black are all treated equally in the classrooms. Apparently, this is the way of life in Oberlin. Religion is strong here and thus it relays good guidance. Prayer meetings for the young take place every Monday and Thursday evenings when talented graduates as well as youngsters from the town congregate together – descendants of 'Shem, Ham and Japheth' – (Genesis 10,1), ignoring any disharmony that may have been instilled in them previously. 'Endeavouring to keep the unity of the Spirit in the bond of peace' – (Ephesians 4,3). No aggression or breakdown in self-control occurred here and no languor or dawdling amongst the different clans. The building attracted a good congregation and everything was conducted decently and orderly making it obvious that everybody was very happy. Alternating with the emotive prayers and songs of praise, one or two would want to express and share an experience; another would read a psalm; another would unfold a reassuring element. Very often requests for prayers on behalf of individuals or specific causes would be complied with. At three o'clock, daily prayer meetings were held and this was not something that took place at specific times; they occurred all year and every year. This was a place where I discovered complete and perfect Sabbaths. The minister was the revivalist and great orator, Charles G. Finney. He was an elderly, tall man with eyes sparkling with enthusiasm and zeal. He was often misunderstood and therefore misquoted sometimes. Whatever can be made of his beliefs on some subjects, he was without a doubt, a very conscientious and religious man: 'Ye shall know them by their fruits' – (Matthew 7,16). The townspeople of Oberlin are indebted to Finney in many ways. It is his influence that has created such kindness, compassion and goodness amongst them. If every town followed Oberlin's example, it would be paradise on earth. Alcoholic drinks are not sold here and there are no theatres either. A circus made an application once, but Finney prayed with the congregation at the beginning of the morning service, for the townsfolk to obstruct such dissipation. The circus people's waggons were wrecked three miles out of town. The impressive evening service, which was held every Sunday, usually ended by singing the English translation of William Williams Pantycelyn's[18] hymns: O'er the gloomy hills of darkness . . . (*Dros y bryniau tywyll niwlog*); Kingdoms wide that sit in darkness . . . (*Ar ardaloedd maith o d'wyllwch* . . .); May the glorious day approaching . . . (*Gwawria, gwawria* . . .); Fly abroad, thou mighty gospel . . . (*Hed fel mellten, bur efengyl*).

Oberlin was an important underground railroad station. The reader knows, I'm sure, that it was on these underground lines the philanthropists put their doctrine into practice. Some places, Oberlin being an example, were more willing to help the needy to flee from enslavement to the freedom of Canada. If a fugitive came across one of these undercover agents, he could be sure that he would be helped onto an escape route. The refugees' faces were painted white and their curly black hair covered by red wigs. They would be disguised for weeks and escorted from station to station. Care was taken of them all the way. By doing so, the philanthropists endangered themselves, since it was an offence to free these people. Once, twenty of Oberlin's dignitaries were captured in Cleveland for helping fugitives. They spent the Sabbath in prison and neither Oberlin nor Cleveland had experienced such a Sabbath before. First of all, prayers were said in church for the prisoners and afterwards, people assembled around the prison gates and the prisoners preached to them, the same as what happened in Philippi – (The Acts 16,26). They preached until the walls of the prison were vibrating! On the Monday, the case was dismissed and the disappointed prosecutors had to return to Dixie Land (The South). They had caused a terrible transgression; not only had they prosecuted black men but they had also held and imprisoned white, free and respectable men. Such soul destruction was unimaginable. I have travelled and seen many marvellous places and events but I am placing quiet and godly Oberlin high up in my esteem. Religion was a way of life in this place.

Niagara Falls

From Oberlin I went west for two hundred and seventeen miles along Lake Erie, through Cleveland, Ashtabula (population 5,000) and Dunkirk (population 7,000) to Buffalo (population 156,000). Buffalo is an old, famous town on the east side of Lake Erie wherefrom the Niagara River has its source. This river, after running its course of thirty-three miles northwards, pours itself into Lake Ontario. Fifteen miles north of Buffalo the famous Falls are situated. So much has been said about these Falls, that it is hard to think of anything new. Their misty vapour can be seen and their sound heard some way off. I found the surrounding area quite different to what I had anticipated. I did not expect the land to be flat and about a mile or two above the Falls, the wide river is compressed by its banks. It therefore rushes down topsy-turvy with its surface covered by white froth. When it reaches the Falls it is divided by a small island, known as Goat Island. Most of it falls down between the upper side of this island and Canada, in the shape of a horseshoe; this cascade is called Canada Falls or Horseshoe Falls and measures about 149 feet in height and 2,100 feet in width. Another section of the river faces Canada and flows behind the island before it transforms into a long sheet-like declivity. This drop is called American Falls and measures about 162 feet in height and 1,125 feet in width. It is considered that a hundred million tons of water drops down these two Falls every hour. After bubbling and frothing at the base of both Falls, the river flows in a narrow and deep bed of about 800 feet in width and 300 feet in depth.

Standing opposite these Falls watching the wild river gushing and bouncing, ready to take the supreme jump, is a sight that cannot be compared or described. Such volume of water continuously rushing and cascading; misty thick vapour rising from the deep whirlpool; mighty streams being engulfed as if disappearing into a cloud; a shining, multi-coloured rainbow emerging from that cloud; turbulent ebullition underneath and the deafening thundery noise combine to make such a magnificent sight that one cannot really describe it in words. It is easy to use adjectives such as 'big' and 'magnificent' but it is not easy to portray the magnitude and excellence of these Falls. I was lucky weather-wise, the day I was there, because the clouds when covering and uncovering the sun made the greenish shade of the water change from light to dark and they also caused the rainbow to disappear and reappear in different glistening degrees. A beautiful picture of this scene will be shown in my next book.

Hi wisga'r goleuni yn fantell am dani,
Lle dawnsia'r pelydrau fel myrddiwn o sêr;
Llaes addurn ei godrau sydd gwmwl yn codi
O'r dyfnder berwedig, brigwynawl, a thêr,
Am ei gwasg y mae gwregys o enfys lliwiedig,
Dysglaeriach na'r gemau rhagoraf a gaed;
Dan goron ei balchder hi chwardd yn wyrenig,
A'r gorddyfn ferw yn balmant i'w thraed.

O raiadr ferth! mae yn hardd ac yn wridog,
Tra'n gorphwys ei phen yn chwareugar a llon
Ar fynwes fawr arian ei chariad dihalog,
I deimlo gwaedguriad cariadus ei fron.
Ei hymffrost a glywir yn nhwrf ei chwympiadau,
Ei balchder a welir ym mawredd ei nerth,
Tra'n rhedeg heb orphwys, heb flino, hyd risiau
Y dalgraig fawreddog, ddaneddog, a serth.

(The glare of the light is like a cloak around it,
Where the sun's rays dance like a myriad of stars;
It's wide, sparkling base splashes up in a cloud
From the boiling, white-crested and clear depth.
Around its middle there is a colourful rainbow
Glistening more than the brightest of gems;
Under its proud crown, it shakes with laughter,
While its deep, bubbling bedrock acts as a footing.

Oh! what cascading hedge! It is pretty and glowing,
It rests its head playfully and merrily
On the broad, silver bosom of its undefiled lover,
In order to feel its loving pulsating heartbeat.
Its pride is captivated by the noise of the torrent
Its contentment is noticed in the grandeur of its power,
Whilst it continuously gushes unwearingly over the staircase
Of the majestic, craggy and robust rock).

Bad River Waterfalls

Bridge over White River

The European Harbour, Philadelphia

Ardmore Station

City of Berlin

To Philadelphia and its Surroundings

I returned through Buffalo and arrived in the Welsh settlement of Cattaraugus. When a friend was taking me in his vehicle past an abattoir in this area, he told me that they had deacons in that particular slaughter-house and before I could gather my thoughts, another piece of conversation cropped up and I forgot to ask him why they selected deacons in such a place. When I recalled the comment, I could not understand the situation at all. I had observed the procedure of appointing deacons in Wales when I attended Aberffrwd's monthly meeting many years ago. It had been conducted by ministers though and in a chapel. How on earth did a butcher administer this process? I would still be in the dark had it not been for an explanation from a respectable deacon. Apparently, many people in this region kept cattle for the production of cheese and in order to collect all the milk, it used to be a custom to cull the calves when they were three days old and throw them to the dogs. However, a man who happened to be a deacon, came to the area and began to buy calves' skins with the purpose of producing some commodities from them. For that reason, those skins were named 'deacons' skins'. In casual conversations, the phrase had very often been abbreviated with 'skins' being dropped; after a little while 'skins' was completely passed over and the term 'deacons' was adopted. The saying was used in a different context to my line of thought after all.

From this place I proceeded through Corry (population 6,000), Oil City (population 10,000) and Braddy's Bend to Pittsburgh. On this journey I travelled through a region yielding petroleum. The laden carriages proved that this crude oil was plentiful and an important commodity in Pennsylvania. The scenery around the Allegheny River attracts many nature lovers also. From Pittsburgh I went to Harrisburgh, then south to York (population 14,000); from York to West Bangor and then to Elkton, Maryland and Wilmington, Delaware (population 43,000) and eventually to Philadelphia, the city of brotherly love.

It is proper that the city is called thus. Brotherly love was the concept of its existence. Brotherly love purchased the land, planned the city and built it. Everyone who possesses elements of this love and is well versed in the history of the city, is charmed by it. It has enjoyed a great degree of tranquility and achieved such fascination and fame that it is worthy of its name. Two hundred years ago, William Penn, a Welshman and a godly Quaker, after obtaining security regarding the territory from the King of England, bargained very fairly with the Indians and others and gained the trust of these people and their continuous admiration. His aim was to have a country and a city where people could experience freedom to worship God according to their conscience. This doctrine is still in existence in the most important cities of America today.

The streets of Philadelphia run parallel with each other; almost all of them the same distance from each other and are as straight as an arrow. The city is situated on a piece of land that juts out between the Delaware and Schuylkill Rivers and although it is eighty miles from the sea, large ocean liners dock in its harbour. This is the most populated city in the entire country. Its large and beautiful buildings and its various institutions are so numerous that it is impossible for me to describe them. It was in this city, in the year 1774, a 'Declaration and Resolve regarding the Colonists' Rights' was adopted and thereafter, in the year 1776, the 'Declaration of Independence' was announced. From 1790 until 1800, Philadelphia was the government's capital.

Many Welsh people live here and there are more still of Welsh blood. Many references to the first Welsh settlers are discovered in the state. When I came here from Slatington once, I travelled through three stations close to each other and their names were: 'North Wales', 'Gwynedd' and 'Penllyn'. Quite near to the city 'Jenkin' station is situated and on the way outwards, in the same county, one finds 'Bryn Mawr', 'Pencoed' and other Welsh names. It was here that I found farm buildings, barns and cowsheds that could very well belong to Welsh people and in the surrounding area, one finds superb houses painted with varying colours on their walls and they appear to me as if they had been copied from the speckled, black and white dwellings of Montgomeryshire. An example is a picture on the previous page of Ardmore station. Many inhabitants have Welsh names and occasionally one finds Welsh books and scripts in their homes. These people are true Americans by now though. More mention about the first settlers will be made in my next book:- *HANES TALEITHIAU UNEDIG AMERICA A'R CYMRY YNDDYNT*. (THE HISTORY OF THE UNITED STATES OF AMERICA AND THE WELSH LIVING IN THEM).

Towards and on The Ocean Again

By taking the New Jersey branch of the first-rate *Pennsylvania* railroad along the banks of the Delaware, I went eighty miles through Trenton (population 30,000), Elizabeth (population 29,000) and Newark (population 137,000) – very important places in the early days of this territory – before arriving in Jersey City (population 121,000). This city, because of its important harbours and different railroads, is considered the main thoroughfare of the region, It was here that I descended for the last time from the American train. I had become fond of it, having made it my home for a year and a half. It carried me in its lap, safely and comfortably, over all kinds of terrain. Whatever ordeals other people have experienced on it, I myself, can only praise it for its care and faithfulness. Taking a last, sad glance at it, I boarded a boat and crossed the river to New York. There I met the Reverend Theophilus Davies, Mineral Ridge, Ohio. He was there, not to meet his loving wife, well and cheerful as he had hoped; alas, it was to see her with an ashen face, dressed in a shroud in a coffin. She had been travelling with her six children to join her husband who had preceded her a few months earlier. On the day the ship arrived with her mortal remains in the country where her grieving husband was waiting, I trust that her spirit was sailing to the spiritual land where her heavenly Saviour is reigning triumphantly.

By the time I reached New York, I felt that I was only a step away from home and I was so anxious to take that step that, without any hesitation, I boarded the grand *City of Berlin*, not the fastest steamship, nevertheless one of the better ones that cross the Atlantic. Ten years previously I had been accompanied on my voyage by the Venerable William Jones (one of Llanllyfni's three stalwarts) and his daughter, on board the *City of Baltimore*. I had called round to see Mr Jones in his home in Wisconsin this last time. Although, he was elderly and somewhat lonely now, I did find him in fairly good spirit. The most astonishing aspect of my homeward voyage was the fiery presence of the waves. I spent hours after dark, watching the waters being separated by the steamship and listening to the far and near gurgling noises. The waves appeared as if they were in a turbulent, towering rage. Some said that multitudes of live creatures, ones similar to glow-worms were causing these goings-on. Whatever was happening and it may have been the phosphorus condition of the waters, the ocean did appear as if it was on fire. On the tenth day we arrived back in Liverpool.

The Journey Back in Wales
After crossing to Birkenhead, I boarded a train and entered a small compartment with only a partition between me and the first class passengers. I was back again in Great Britain.

After travelling to the countryside, six very respectable men entered on their way to a denominational conference. It was quite obvious that they were of different backgrounds. Three of them appeared as if they held high positions; the fourth was a young man who seemed to be starting on the career ladder; the other two were wise ministers of religion. At least that was what I believed, because they possessed quiet, compassionate attitudes and they had quite an unique aura about them – a kind of modesty, which is sometimes present when people of that calling are in the presence of distinguished people. The first three I mentioned spoke very seriously about what was on the agenda.

It was put forward that proof-reading was a necessity. What is that? one person asked. The reply he had was, that a committee would be set up to check the scripts before they appeared in the newspapers and that a chief editor would supervise every editor in Wales. Discussion went ahead on the item of choosing a suitable title for the English section of the conference. The conversation was enthusiastic and many decisions appeared to be taking place in that compartment, therefore all would be 'ready-made' in the real conference!

When the mentioned people left the train, their place was taken up by sheep dealers and the topic of conversation with these folk related to their occupation, mainly whether it was advantageous to cut sheep's tails. All kinds of tails were thrown on the table until eventually it was asked why men did not have tails the same as animals. When a man, who had not taken part in the conversation as yet, was seen smiling, one of the others said to him:- 'Excuse my boldness but since you appear to be taking an interest in our conversation, can you explain to us why men have been deprived of tails while all animals have them?'

'Because it has been left to man to acquire a tail for himself,' was the reply.

'That is it,' shouted one man. 'A man who cannot procure enough tails of titles or tails of silk, is not worthy of a sheep's tail.'

After these people left, the small compartment was filled by some people who were neither Welsh nor English. Yet, in some kind of Welsh and some kind of English they uttered some obscene remarks without blinking an eyelid. Between their speech, their irresponsible behaviour and the smoke from their tobacco, it was a blessing when they left.

After they departed, I had the compartment to myself all the way to Aberystwyth and I noticed that good old Wales, when compared to the various regions in America, had not lost any of its beauty and amiability – its green slopes; its gentle valleys; its small and lively rivers and waterfalls; its fields and hedges; its bright bushes; its secluded dwellings; its tame animals and the assortment of winged singers. How paradisean, how homely and how lovely they all appeared. A true Welshman can travel the world, yet keep his undefiled affection and admiration towards the country of his birth.

Dros gyfanfor a chyfandir, draw i fro-dir machlyd haul;
Dros frigwynion donau mawrion, gyrwynt geirwon heb eu hail;
Dros noethdiroedd, pell goedwigoedd, anial-leoedd craslwch mân;
Dros fynyddau, cribawg greigiau, oesawl gartre'r eira glân;
Ni chanfyddais i, er hynny, dlysach gwlad na gwlad y Cymry,
'Cymru, gwlad y gân'

Dros gyfanfor a chyfandir, ym mhlith brodyr o bob hil –
Dynion gwynion, cochion, duon a melynion lawer mil;
Ewropeaid, Americaniaid a Mexicaniaid ryfedd ran;
Meibion Asia, plant Ethiopia, gyda gwallt fel nos o wlân;
Ond ni cheir ym mhlith y rheiny bobl megys pobl o Gymru,
'Cymru, gwlad y gân'.

Dros gyfanfor a chyfandir y canfyddir ffrwythau fyrdd;
Dychmygion pob rhyw ddynion, pob rhyw ffwdan, pob rhyw ffyrdd,
Pob rhyw gredo, pob rhyw grefydd, pob gwehelyth heb wahân,
At bob dawn a dyfais dofir daear, awyr, dŵr a thân.
Yn eu plith yn hoew, heini, gwelir camrau meibion Cymru,
'Cymru, gwlad y gân'.

(Over the ocean and the continent, over to the land of the sunset;
Over white crested gigantic waves and through turbulent gales;
Over desert land, through far-away forests and hot wilderness;
Over rocky mountains and the home of the clean snow;
Nevertheless, I never discovered a more beautiful country than Wales.
'Wales, the land of song'.

Thousands of white, red, black and yellow men;
Europeans, Americans and many Mexicans;
The sons of Asia, the children of Ethiopia with dark, woolly hair;
Amongst all of these, I never found anybody comparable to the Welsh people.
'Wales, the land of song'.

Over the ocean and the continent many talents are discovered;
The imagination of all people; every chaos and every means;
Every belief, every religion, every lineage without exception.
Land, sky, water and fire are tamed for every purpose and every invention;
Amongst everybody and everything, one always discovers the footsteps
of people from Wales.
'Wales, the land of song'.

I arrived in Aberystwyth early in the afternoon and was home before night-time. I suddenly realized, after almost a year and a half of absence from my family, that I had accomplished a peregrination of almost thirty-eight thousand miles.

Father of all mercy had preserved me and mine from all adversity so that we are able to be at home together again – each one of us well and happy. Will we thus be able to complete our journey through the complexities of life? Will we, after troubles and hazardous risks and journeys through distant lands, be able to rest untroubled in a home full of happiness and eternal joy?

Mae'n hyfryd meddwl ambell dro, with deithio anial le,
Ar ôl ein holl flinderau dwys, cawn orffwys yn y Ne'.

(It is nice to think at times, whilst travelling through the wilderness
That after all our troubles, we shall be able to rest in Heaven one day).

NOTES

¹ Ham –

In Old Testament, one of the sons of Noah – said to be the ancestor of the Ethiopians and Egyptians (Genesis 6,10).

² Harrisburgh

The modern spelling is Harrisburg.

³ Ebensburgh

The modern spelling is Ebensburg.

⁴ George Fox (1624-91)

W.D. Evans refers to the founder of the Society of Friends (Quakers) as John Fox. His name was George and not John. This minor mistake has been corrected by the translator.

⁵ Nimrod

He is the mighty hunter referred to in the Old Testament. (Genesis 10, 8 and Book 1 of Chronicles 1,10).

⁶ Professor Rhys (1840-1915)

Professor John Rhys hailed from Ponterwyd, Ceredigion and the village school has been named after him – Ysgol John Rhys.

⁷ Grand Canyon and Royal Gorge

The translator has corrected a few geographical inaccuracies that were printed in the Welsh version of this chapter.

⁸ Jehu

He was a King of Israel (circa 841 BC) and was known to be reckless when driving his chariot. (Book 2 of Kings 9, 16).

⁹ Aztec

Native American people (c. AD 1100).

¹⁰ Quetzalcoatl

A god in Aztec mythology.

¹¹ Drooping Tree

This tree was probably a willow.

¹² Hades

The underworld in Greek mythology.

¹³ Mites

Two mites equals a farthing (New Testament – Mark 12, 42).

¹⁴ Jonah

Hebrew Prophet and his missionary journey. (Book of Jonah in the Old Testament).

¹⁵ Emanuel Swedenborg (1688-1772)

Swedish scientist, theologian and mystic.

¹⁶ Brigham Young (1801-77)

Mormon leader who was the founder of Salt Lake City.

¹⁷ Charles Bradlaugh (1833-91)

English politician who was elected M.P. for Northampton in 1880 but was unseated because he refused to take oath on the Bible.

¹⁸ William Williams (1717-1791)

William Williams, Pantycelyn – Welsh hymnographer.

Index to Pictures